D1082892

THE RISE AND DEMISE

of the

HERSHEY JUNIOR COLLEGE

THE RISE AND DEMISE

of the

HERSHEY JUNIOR COLLEGE

AN HISTORICAL - DESCRIPTIVE STUDY OF
THE HERSHEY JUNIOR COLLEGE,
HERSHEY, PENNSYLVANIA
1938-1965

Richard Russell Klotz

PREFACE

The purpose of this historical-descriptive study was to examine and record the particular history of the growth and development of the Hershey Junior College, Hershey, Pennsylvania, from its founding in 1938 to its closing in 1965. Specifically, this study purports: (1) to determine the origin of the Hershey Junior College; (2) to examine the history of the institution in terms of its objectives, problems, and achievements during the period of its existence; (3) to examine the influence of Mr. Milton Snavely Hershey, the Hershey community, the Derry Township Board of School Directors, administrators, faculty, and students on the development of the Junior College; (4) to describe the institutional program under the leadership of the two deans who served the Junior College; and (5) to consider the immediate reasons for the closing of the institution.

Inasmuch as no complete historical study of the institution had been undertaken, all available literature pertaining to its growth and development were investigated. Of particular importance to this study were such primary sources as minutes; reports of evaluating committees; catalogs; student publications; yearbooks; letters; newspaper articles; official institutional records and reports; personal files of the two deans; deeds of trust; and personal interviews.

This study revealed the institution was founded by the industrialist and philanthropist, Milton S. Hershey, as an outgrowth of the depression of the 1930's and his quest for a means by which young people might become profitably occupied. Mr. Hershey created and endowed a foundation through which the College was financed. The institution was administered by the Derry Township Board of School Directors. This study disclosed that the College was unique in the history of higher education in that it was founded as a publicly controlled, privately financed institution which offered two years of tuition-free, college education to residents of Derry Township and, later, to employees and dependents of employees who were employed in the Township.

The study indicated there were several reasons for the closing of the institution. The primary reason, according to the Board of Managers of The M. S. Hershey Foundation, was that the income which was produced from the trust became insufficient to meet the increasing costs of operation. During 1964–65 the College functioned as a branch of the nearby Harrisburg Area Community College, the first public community college to be established in Pennsylvania. The Hershey Junior College ceased to exist as an institution of higher education as of July 1, 1965.

The conclusions of this study include the following: (1) the depression created the conditions which prompted Milton Hershey to see the need for and value in post secondary vocational education and, consequently, to found and to finance the Junior College; (2) the function of the institution underwent some changes, primarily a change in emphasis from terminal to transfer programs and a broadening of the residence eligibility requirements for admission; (3) the major problems with which the students, faculty, and administration had to contend were concerned with facilities, sharing of personnel, and the administrative organization; (4) the two deans of the College, A. G. Breidenstine and V. H. Fenstermacher, had a definite influence on the institution and both were dedicated to the students and the College; (5) the College has an enviable record of accomplishment and it can serve as a model of the integration of teaching and guidance; and (6) in view of the circumstances under which the College was operating during its last few years, its financial status, and the external changes that were taking place in higher education, it was a logical (although unpopular) decision to merge the institution with the Harrisburg Area Community College and, subsequently, have the Hershey Junior College cease to exist.

ACKNOWLEDGEMENTS

This study would not have been possible if it had not been for the assistance and cooperation of many individuals. Grateful acknowledgement is made to Dr. C. O. Williams, Dean of Admissions Emeritus, The Pennsylvania State University, for suggesting that a study of the Hershey Junior College be undertaken as a doctoral thesis. The writer is appreciative of the assistance and support of the members of his doctoral committee: Professors Harry K. Hutton, Arthur M. Wellington, Donald J. Willower, and especially to his major advisor, Robert E. Sweitzer, for his guidance and encouragement.

The writer is indebted to the many members of the alumni, faculty, and staff of the Hershey Junior College and to the officers of the Hershey Interests for their cooperation in this study. The writer is especially indebted to Dr. Aaron G. Breidenstine and the late Dr. Varnum H. Fenstermacher, the two deans of the College, for their valuable assistance. He is also obliged to the staff of the Hershey Community Library for their helpfulness and the use of resources.

The writer is thankful for the permission which was granted by the Derry Township Board of School Directors to undertake this study.

Sincere appreciation is extended to the officers of the Hershey Educational and Cultural Center and the Hershey Library for their willingness to publish this study.

To his wife, Nancy, and children, the writer is grateful for their patience and understanding during the course of this study.

It is hoped that this book will be of interest to those individuals who were associated with the Hershey Junior College, particularly the alumni, faculty, and members of the College's governing bodies.

March, 1973   RICHARD R. KLOTZ
Womelsdorf, Pennsylvania

TABLE OF CONTENTS

LIST OF TABLES

LIST OF FIGURES

CHAPTER I

INTRODUCTION

Background

The past decade has been characterized by an unprecedented increase in both the number and proportion of students pursuing post-secondary school education and the corresponding growth of institutions of higher education of all types, particularly the two-year community college. It is, therefore, an anomaly that a highly respected junior college should cease to exist. This is especially true in view of the fact that the community colleges now in existence in Pennsylvania are outgrowths of the development of the *public* junior college.[1] The passage of the Community College Act of 1963[2] by the General Assembly resulted in the rapid development of community colleges in Pennsylvania. This legislation was enacted only two years before the Hershey Junior College closed its doors.

As Wickersham has aptly observed, "Colleges die like men, some prematurely, some violently, and some of old age. An account of our dead Pennsylvania Colleges has an interest as a moral, if not as a history."[3]

The Hershey Junior College was established in 1938 as a two-year community college in Hershey, Pennsylvania; it closed its doors in 1965. The Junior College would not have been founded and sustained for 27 years had it not been for the altruistic and philanthropic interest of Milton Snavely Hershey (1857–1945). Nevertheless, as an integral part of the Derry Township School District,[4] it was considered the first "public" (publicly governed and privately financed) junior college to be established in the Commonwealth of Pennsylvania.

---

[1] Ralph R. Fields and Associates, "Community Colleges in Pennsylvania," A Report to the State Board of Education, June 30, 1965, p. 4.

[2] Commonwealth of Pennsylvania, Department of Education, Office of Higher Education, Bureau of Community Colleges, *Suggested Procedures For The Establishment of a Community College in Pennsylvania*, Appendix C, Revised January, 1970.

[3] James P. Wickersham, *A History of Education in Pennsylvania* (Lancaster: Inquirer Publishing Company, 1886), p. 424.

[4] The Derry Township School District includes an area of 27.3 square miles in Dauphin County, approximately 15 miles east of Harrisburg, the capitol of Pennsylvania. Located in the Township is the community of Hershey, whose major enterprise is the Hershey Foods, Chocolate and Confectionery Division. The fortunes of the chocolate industry and the development of the community have been closely related since 1903 when both were established by Milton Snavely Hershey. In 1970, the estimated population of Hershey was 10,200; the population of Derry Township was 15,600. "Chocolate Town U.S.A., Progress Through Vision," Official Statement, $2,150,000 Derry Township School Building Authority, School Revenue Bonds—Series of 1970, p. 3.

1

The Hershey Junior College is unique in terms of its founding, financing and governance, educational program, and the conditions which brought about its closing. For these reasons the writer chose to do an historical-descriptive study of the Hershey Junior College.

Origin of the Study

As a college admissions officer, the writer has been concerned with the transfer of college students from two-year to senior institutions and the attendant problems of articulation and adjustment. This study originated in 1966 during the period the writer was responsible for the admission of upper-division students to the Capitol Campus of The Pennsylvania State University, Middletown, Pennsylvania.[5] Due to the proximity of Hershey and the Capitol Campus, a number of applicants had attended the Hershey Junior College. Consequently, the writer became more directly concerned with and interested in the Junior College.

The writer has long known of the favorable reputation of the Hershey Junior College. Dr. C. O. Williams, Dean of Admissions Emeritus, The Pennsylvania State University, has had professional knowledge of the strength of the Junior College and he urged the writer to consider doing a study of the institution. The writer was further encouraged to undertake the study as a result of a discussion of its feasibility with the Superintendent of Schools of the Derry Township School District, Dr. L. Eugene Jacques. The Derry Township Board of Directors officially approved the study.[6]

Need for the Study

Repeatedly, the spokesmen and leaders in higher education point out the need for descriptive and analytical studies of the structure and function of educational institutions. Historians of the twentieth century have emphasized the immediate usefulness of history in dealing with contemporary problems.

John J. Corson cites the lack of such studies:

> The college or university as a form of social organization—as an enterprise dedicated to the achievement of various purposes—has been subjected to little orderly analysis. Analysis of the functioning of business enterprises and governmental units has become commonplace and generally inclusive in charac-

---

[5] The Capitol Campus, an element of The Pennsylvania State University Commonwealth Campus system, is an upper-division and graduate center which opened in October, 1966. Junior- and Senior-level courses are offered leading to the bachelor and master degrees. The Capitol Campus is unique within the University and in Pennsylvania. *The Pennsylvania State University Bulletin*, The Capitol Campus, 1968–1969, pp. 10–15.

[6] Derry Township Public Schools, "Board Minutes," May 16, 1966; and L. Eugene Jacques, Superintendent of Schools, Derry Township School District, Hershey, Pennsylvania, letter to the writer, May 17, 1966.

ter. The college or university as a functioning organism has less frequently been subjected to analysis, and then not often in terms of its total operation. . . .[7]

Burton R. Clark underscores the need for institutional analysis:

> Education is one of the major American institutions whose organized life has remained largely unanalyzed. A sizable body of knowledge exists now about the business firm, the government bureau, the trade union, the hospital, the political party, and special private associations. In comparison, the church and the school have received little systematic study.
>
> . . . .
>
> The junior college has something to tell us about the pressures of modern society on education.[8]

T. R. McConnell also comments on the type of research that needs to be undertaken:

> The research that most needs to be done at this time, in my view, is essentially descriptive and analytical, rather than evaluative or experimental; and research on broader problems, even with relatively crude methods of investigation, is more important now than on narrower issues susceptible to greater methodological control.[9]

Nevitt Sanford has also emphasized "the paucity of empirical studies" of the structure and function of educational institutions.[10]

Arguing for historical studies in general, Leighton H. Johnson reminds his readers in the *Phi Delta Kappan* that:

> In the early years of the twentieth century many valuable and provocative theses in education were historical studies. Today, when few students are encouraged to employ the historical method, there are infrequent examples of outstanding historical work . . . .
>
> . . . .
>
> We need historical studies in American education today. In no other way can we obtain the perspective, the values, the facts, on which our most crucial decisions depend. . . .[11]

Each institution should have a written record of its own growth and development. Prior to this study there was no record of the Hershey Junior College covering the entire period of its existence. It should be of interest to the staff who served and the students who attended the College.

This historical record should be of value to college educators to enable them to better understand the problems of the past and their direct and indirect influences on the present. It should be of particular interest to the

---

[7]John J. Corson, *Governance of Colleges and Universities* (New York: McGraw-Hill Book Company, Inc., 1960), p. 4.

[8]Burton R. Clark, *The Open Door College: A Case Study* (New York: McGraw-Hill Book Company, Inc., 1960), pp. 1, 3.

[9]T. R. McConnell, "Needed Research in College and University Organization and Administration," *The Study of Academic Administration*, Terry F. Lunsford, editor, (Western Interstate Commission for Higher Education, Boulder, Colorado, 1963), p. 115.

[10]Nevitt Sanford, *The American College* (New York: John Wiley & Sons, Inc., 1962), p. 1012.

[11]Leighton H. Johnson, "Education Needs Historical Studies," *Phi Delta Kappan*, 36: 157, 159, January, 1955.

administration and faculty of new institutions, particularly community colleges, in Pennsylvania as well as in other states. The study should make students, professors, administrators, and trustees cognizant of the important roots of an institution and how they are formed as well as how they may be severed.

The study of the educational past is still considered highly important, for increasingly does it appear that the best way to reconstruct and improve social institutions is by a careful study and analysis of educational experiences.[12]

Statement of the Problem

The purpose of this study was to collect, analyze, and record the available data on the establishment, growth, and development of the Hershey Junior College from 1938 to its closing in 1965. The central problem under study was: "What has been the particular history of the growth and development of the Hershey Junior College?"

Specifically, this study purports: (1) to determine the origin of the Hershey Junior College; (2) to examine the history of the Hershey Junior College in terms of its objectives, problems, and achievements during the period of its existence; (3) to examine the influence of Mr. Milton Snavely Hershey, the Hershey community, the Derry Township Board of School Directors, administrators, faculty, and students on the development of the Junior College; (4) to describe the institutional program under the leadership of the two deans who served the Junior College; and (5) to consider the immediate reason or reasons for the closing of the institution.

Limitations of the Study

The scope of this study was limited to the founding, growth and development, influence, and the immediate reasons for the closing of the Hershey Junior College. This study does not include a detailed analysis of the financing of the Junior College. It does, however, attempt to show that Milton S. Hershey provided the primary source of funds for the institution that was public in terms of governance. This limitation was necessitated by the fact that the financial records of Milton S. Hershey and The M. S. Hershey Foundation were not open to the writer.

The purpose of this research was not to compile a detailed historical account of the eventual transition or merger of the Hershey Junior College into the Harrisburg Area Community College. Neither has the writer undertaken a detailed analysis of the college-going pattern of Hershey area students before and after the closing of the Junior College.

---

[12] Edgar W. Knight, "History of Education," *Encyclopedia of Educational Research*, Walter S. Monroe, editor (New York: The Macmillan Company, 1941), p. 580.

4

Lastly, the closing of the Hershey Junior College was an emotionally charged issue among many Hershey residents and those who served or attended the Junior College. Many suppositions regarding the decision to close the institution have been offered. With this in mind, this writer has made a concerted effort to keep his personal biases and preconceptions, and those of the individuals with whom he has consulted in the course of this study, from unduly influencing this historical-descriptive study.[13]

Procedure

Every effort has been made to adhere to the recognized techniques of historiography.[14] The problem was defined and delimited. Data were collected giving due consideration to primary and secondary sources.[15] Whenever possible, primary sources were utilized.

All data were subjected to careful verification.[16] To determine the genuineness of sources, external criticism was employed; to determine the accuracy and value of sources, internal criticism was applied.[17]

The topical-chronological arrangement of data was employed to direct attention to major topics and problems and to make the study more interesting and readable.[18]

When advisable and appropriate, tables, maps, charts, and diagrams were prepared.

Sources of Data

Primary source material was investigated and utilized whenever possible. Secondary sources were consulted when necessary and, primarily, for the purpose of identifying primary sources.

Of particular importance in this study were the "Board Minutes" of the Derry Township School District which are complete and have been carefully compiled. The "Board Minutes," from 1935 through 1966, which were utilized in the study include matters pertaining to the Junior College as well as the elementary and secondary schools of the District. They are housed in the Office of the Superintendent of Schools.

The *Lebanon Daily News* and *The Patriot* and *The Evening News* of Harrisburg covered the events of the Derry Township Schools, including those of the

---

[13] Jacques Barzun and Henry F. Graff, *The Modern Researcher* (New York: Harcourt, Brace, & World, Inc., 1957), pp. 122–23.

[14] Louis Gottschalk, *Understanding History* (New York: Alfred A. Knopf, 1967), pp. 48–52.

[15] Barzun and Graff, *op. cit.*, pp. 98–99.

[16] *Ibid.*, pp. 90–91.

[17] William H. Brickman, *Guide to Research in Educational History* (New York: New York University Bookstore, 1949), pp. 93–95.

[18] Barzun and Graff, *op. cit.*, pp. 233–34.

Hershey Junior College. *Hotel Hershey High-Lights* and the *Hershey News*, weekly journals in which community news was published, were used frequently. These newspapers served as important sources of information.

Of inestimable value were the personal files of Dr. A. G. Breidenstine and Dr. V. H. Fenstermacher, the two deans of the Hershey Junior College. The writer was fortunate to be able to have an interview with Dr. Fenstermacher shortly before his death. Dr. Breidenstine granted several personal interviews; he provided many helpful suggestions as well as encouragement.

Testimony obtained from administrators, faculty, school board members, students, and others who had a direct relationship with the Junior College was utilized in this study.

Other primary sources, readily available, included the following:

- *Hershey Junior College Information Bulletin* (1939-1966)
- Official institutional records and letters on file in the Office of the Superintendent of Schools
- "Administrative Bulletin" (Hershey Junior College)
- "Information Bulletin" (Hershey Junior College)
- Self-studies and evaluation reports of the Middle States Association of Colleges and Secondary Schools
- Periodic issues of *The Literary Artisan* (1939-1958)
- Bimonthly issues of *The Format* (1947-1965)
- *HEJUCO* yearbook (1955-1965)
- Reports of the Pennsylvania Superintendent of Public Instruction
- Biographical literature and books dealing with the life of Milton Snavely Hershey
- Brief histories of the Hershey Chocolate Corporation and the Hershey Community and other news publications
- Hershey Foods Corporation reports to sharcholders
- The M. S. Hershey Foundation "Agreement of Trust" between Milton S. Hershey, Donor, and Hershey Trust Company, Trustee, Hershey, Pennsylvania, December 5, 1935.
- "Selected Hershey Chronology, 1724-1967"

Definition of Terms

The terms used in this study have been defined according to the definitions set forth by the Joint Committee on Data and Definitions in Higher Education sponsored by the American Association of Collegiate Registrars and Admissions Officers.

> *Accredit*: To designate an educational institution as being of acceptable quality in criteria of excellence established by a recognized accrediting agency or association.[19]

---

[19]*Handbook of Data and Definitions in Higher Education*, Committee on Data and Definitions in Higher Education (American Association of Collegiate Registrars and Admissions Officers, 1962), p. 33.

Admission Requirements: Educational, personal, health, place of residence, and other qualifications established as requisites for admission. Requirements reflect the admission policy and implement it.[20]

Community College: A two-year institution of higher education, generally public, offering instruction adapted in content, level, and schedule to the needs of the community in which it is located. Offerings usually include a *transfer curriculum* (credits transferable toward a bachelor's degree), *occupational (or terminal) curriculum, general education*, and *adult education*. So far as possible, courses are offered in morning, afternoon, or evening hours according to the general convenience of the clientele. In addition to organized curriculum, offerings may also include short courses, special lectures, etc., of interest to the community or to groups therein. Most of the students live within the community. Note: The term "community college" generally refers to an independently organized institution (either public or private), or to one, which is organized as part of a local public school system. While there is no hard-and-fast distinction between the terms "community college" and "junior college" (*q.v.*), the former is more community-centered with respect to both curriculum and administration; it is also more likely to derive a larger portion of its funds from local sources (including local taxes), and to be more largely under purely local control.[21]

Course, Terminal: Usual designation of a course, especially a course offered in a junior college, or technical institute, which is practical or technical in content, as opposed to courses designed to meet standards for academic credit courses; credit is usually offered toward an associate degree and may be applicable in whole or in part at some institutions towards a bachelor's.[22]

Curriculum, Transfer (Junior Colleges): A curriculum yielding credits which are normally accepted by other colleges at full (or virtually full) value toward a bachelor's degree.[23]

Cy pres doctrine: The doctrine, applied especially to cases of charitable trusts or donations, which, in place of an impossible or illegal condition, limitation, or object, allows the nearest practicable one to be substituted.[24]

Degree, Associate: Granted upon completion of an educational program of less than four years of college work, generally for the completion of the curriculum of a junior college.[25]

Student, Lower Division: Freshmen and sophomores generally.[26]

Tuition Remission: Sometimes called *Tuition Concession*, or *Tuition Waiver*. An arrangement by which students are permitted to take all or part of their academic work free of charge; educational benefits commonly open to such groups as student assistants, junior faculty, and faculty dependents. Sometimes includes remission of fees in addition to tuition.[27]

[20]*Ibid.*, p. 36.

[21]*Ibid.*, pp. 45–46.

[22]*Ibid.*, p. 50.

[23]*Ibid.*, p. 53.

[24]Jess Stein (ed.), *The Random House Dictionary of the English Language* (New York: Random House, 1967), p. 361; and George Gleason Bogert, *Handbook of the Law of Trusts* (St. Paul, Minnesota: West Publishing Company, 1952), pp. 565–66.

[25]*Handbook of Data and Definitions in Higher Education, op. cit.*, p. 56.

[26]*Ibid.*, p. 114.

[27]*Ibid.*, p. 121.

Review of Related Literature

There have been several studies which have provided valuable background for the undertaking of this study. Burton R. Clark, in *The Open Door College: A Case Study*, has highlighted the factors that determine the character of a junior college by making an intensive case study of the development of the San Jose Junior College in California.

> The San Jose case study is an application to an important type of educational organization of methods of institutional analysis. This sort of analysis represents a broad concern with the character of organizations and particularly with the ways in which dominant patterns of organization take form in interaction with internal and external environments. The intent is to study characteristics of organizations in their own right, the characteristics of "whole organizations" or major components thereof.[28]

In *The Junior College: Progress and Prospect*, Leland L. Medsker critically analyzed the function and characteristics of the junior college in the United States. At the time of the writing of his book, Medsker cited the Hershey Junior College as the only public two-year institution in Pennsylvania, in addition to the branch campuses of The Pennsylvania State University.[29]

James W. Thornton's *The Community Junior College* was particularly helpful in that it reviews the growth and development of the two-year college in the United States, including the philosophic justifications for its founding.[30] *The Community College Movement* by Ralph R. Fields provided a comprehensive assessment of the modern community college through a review of four, two-year institutions.[31] The review of the purposes and programs of the community college by James W. Reynolds provided the writer with further insight into its current and future role in higher education.[32] *The Two-Year College: A Social Synthesis* provided a current assessment of the two-year college.[33] The book was of particular interest because Dr. Clyde E. Blocker, one of the authors, is the first president of the Harrisburg Area Community College, the institution with which the Hershey Junior College merged.

The Magnificent Enterprise: A Chronicle of Vassar College,[34] *History of Cornell*,[35] and *Bennington College: The Development of an Educational*

---

[28]Clark, *op. cit.*, pp. ix-x.

[29]Leland L. Medsker, *The Junior College: Progress and Prospect* (New York: McGraw-Hill Book Company, 1960), pp. 273–79.

[30]James W. Thornton, *The Community Junior College* (New York: John Wiley & Sons, 1966), 300 pp.

[31]Ralph Fields, *The Community College Movement* (New York: McGraw-Hill Book Company, 1962), 360 pp.

[32]James W. Reynolds, "Needed Changes in Purposes and Programs of Community Colleges," *Universal Higher Education*, Earl J. McGrath (ed.), (New York: McGraw-Hill Book Company, 1966), pp. 104-21.

[33]Clyde E. Blocker, Robert H. Plummer, and Richard C. Richardson, *The Two-Year College: A Social Synthesis* (Englewood Cliffs, New Jersey: Prentice-Hall, Inc., 1965), 289 pp.

[34]Dorothy A. Plum and George B. Dowell, *The Magnificent Enterprise: A Chronicle of Vassar College* (Princeton, New Jersey: Princeton University Press, 1961), 131 pp.

[35]Morris Bishop, *A History of Cornell* (Ithaca, New York: Cornell University Press, 1962), 627 pp.

Idea[36] served as helpful guides with respect to the highlighting of important events and the organization of this study.

The writer gained valuable background in the techniques of historiography through the writing of a term paper, "A Historical Study of the Development and Changing Function of Bucknell University, 1842–1963."[37]

The writer identified several doctoral dissertations comparable to this study. Farrell completed a similar study of the Temple Junior College, Texas, in 1964.[38] The historical studies by Hubley[39] and Wisor,[40] although of Pennsylvania institutions of a different type, may also be considered representative.

Rudisill completed a term paper in 1961 on the Hershey Junior College in partial fulfillment of the requirements for a course in the School of Education at the University of Pennsylvania.[41] It was helpful in that it identified several primary sources of information about the College.

Issues of the *Junior College Journal* contain articles which provided valuable background concerning the two-year college, in general.

Barzun and Graff's research manual, *The Modern Researcher*, proved to be both interesting and enlightening to the writer.[42]

Brickman's *Guide to Research in Educational History*[43] and Gottschalk's *Understanding History*[44] were particularly helpful with respect to historical method.

Summary

The purpose of this study was to write an historical-descriptive account of the Hershey Junior College from its founding in 1938 to its closing in 1965. This institution was selected as a thesis topic primarily because: (1) it is unique in the history of two-year educational institutions and (2) because there is no complete record of its growth and development encompassing the entire period of its existence.

The scope of the study was defined and the limitations noted. The recognized techniques of historical research were employed. Data are presented on a topical-chronological basis.

---

[36] Barbara Jones, *Bennington College: The Development of an Educational Idea* (New York: Harper & Brothers Publishers, 1946), 223 pp.

[37] Richard R. Klotz, "A Historical Study of the Development and Changing Function of Bucknell University, 1842–1963" (unpublished term paper, The Pennsylvania State University, July, 1963).

[38] Harry C. Farrell, Jr., "Temple Junior College: Its Founding, Growth, and Development, 1926–64" (unpublished doctoral dissertation, Colorado State College, 1964), 567 pp.

[39] John E. Hubley, *Fountainhead of Good Teachers: A History of the First Ninety Years of Shippensburg State College* (Shippensburg, Pennsylvania: News-Chronicle Publishing Company, 1964), 176 pp.

[40] Harold C. Wisor, "A History of Teacher Education at Lock Haven State College, Lock Haven, Pennsylvania, 1870–1960" (unpublished doctoral dissertation, The Pennsylvania State University, 1966), 325 pp.

[41] Richard H. Rudisill, "Hershey Junior College" (unpublished term paper, University of Pennsylvania, Philadelphia, Pennsylvania, January, 1961).

[42] Barzun and Graff, *op. cit.*, 386 pp.   [43] Brickman, *op. cit.*, 220 pp.

[44] Gottschalk, *op. cit.*, 298 pp.

CHAPTER II

THE HERSHEY STORY

Milton Snavely Hershey

An account of the Hershey Junior College would be incomplete without a review of the early life of Milton Snavely Hershey and the simultaneous growth and development of his chocolate enterprise and the unique community of Hershey, Pennsylvania. Mr. Hershey's philanthropies, including the Junior College, probably would not have come into existence had it not been for the phenomenal success of his chocolate business.

Little that has been written about Milton Snavely Hershey has been documented. Historian Paul A. W. Wallace, who, with Katherine B. Shippen, wrote a biography of Mr. Hershey, explained:

> The Hershey Chocolate Bar is known all over the world, but the man who first produced it is merely a legend, embodiment of the Great American Myth: the poor boy who, by industry and thrift, made a fortune. The core of the legend is sound, but folk tradition has so blemished the surface that even Mr. Hershey's friends are unable to agree about some of the elementary facts of his career.
>
> It was not his habit to write letters. John Snyder and Ezra Hershey did that for him. He kept no diaries and prepared no memoirs. He did, however, leave a vivid impression on the minds of all who were near him.[1]

Milton Hershey's ancestors were members of the Mennonite sect who emigrated to Pennsylvania from the German-speaking section of Switzerland. Mennonites were known for their industriousness, earnestness, frugality, and agricultural skill. They, and other people of German, Swiss, and French Huguenot background, became known as the "Pennsylvania Dutch." Mennonites and the Amish who settled in Pennsylvania were referred to as "plain people" because of their belief in simplicity in living and plain dress.[2] Attracted by the many advantages of the Lebanon Valley, Milton Hershey's great-grandparents, Issac and Anna Hershey, moved from Lancaster to Dauphin County where they built the "Homestead," a field-stone farmhouse, in 1826.[3]

Milton Snavely Hershey was born September 13, 1857, to Henry and Fanny Snavely Hershey in the Homestead near what is now Hershey, Pennsylvania, in

---

[1] Paul A. W. Wallace, "Milton S. Hershey" (Hershey: Milton Hershey School, 1956), p. i. (Mimeographed).

[2] Katherine B. Shippen and Paul A. W. Wallace, *Milton S. Hershey* (New York: Random House, 1959), pp. 19–21.

[3] *Ibid.*, p. 19

Derry Township, approximately 15 miles east of Harrisburg.[4] There was a marked contrast between Milton's parents. His mother was a devout Mennonite, thrifty, and a good housekeeper.[5] His father, Henry Hershey, apparently loved to read and talk and he possessed great energy and an "inquisitive mind." However, he was considered to have a "poor sense of timing," leaping at opportunities but failing to grasp them.[6] Henry was described as tall, bearded, well-dressed, and courteous.[7]

Milton Hershey estimated that his father failed in 17 separate careers.[8] It was noted that Milton's father was often away from home. Furthermore, it is reported that the family changed residence 37 times.[9] As a consequence of the many moves, Milton's childhood was difficult and unsettled. One such move took place in 1860 when Milton was three years old. Upon learning of the discovery of petroleum along Oil Creek in Western Pennsylvania, Henry mortgaged the farm and rushed to the area. The oil speculation venture was not successful and the family, with the help of relatives, returned to the Homestead.[10]

In 1866, the family moved from Dauphin County to a farm near Lancaster where Henry experimented with trees and shrubbery.[11] It is said that the nine-year old Milton did not want to move and the moving day was an unhappy one for him. Allegedly, he told his mother, "When I grow up and get to be rich I will take care of good little boys better than my father does me!"[12]

Both parents wanted Milton to have an education. Henry was particularly ambitious for Milton but Henry's adventuresomeness interfered with Milton's schooling. By 1870, Milton had attended six or seven different schools before he reached age 14 and he never advanced beyond the fourth grade.[13]

Milton's education took a different direction when his father decided his son should be apprenticed to a printer in anticipation of his becoming an editor. At the age of 14, Milton started to learn the trade of printing as a "printer's devil" on a pacifist German newspaper, *Der Waffenlose Waechter* (*The Weaponless Watcher*), in Gap, Pennsylvania.[14]

Milton Hershey was not interested in the printing trade and he soon became a confectioner's apprentice at Joseph Royer's Ice Cream Parlor and Garden in Lancaster.[15] Milton liked the candy and ice cream business and he learned rapidly.

---

[4] *Ibid.*

[5] Joseph R. Snavely, *An Intimate Story of Milton S. Hershey* (Hershey: J. R. Snavely, 1957), p. 4.

[6] Samuel F. Hinkle, *Hershey: Farsighted Confectioner, Famous Chocolate, Fine Community* (Princeton: Princeton University Press, 1964), p. 9.

[7] Shippen and Wallace, *op. cit.*, p. 21.

[8] "His Deeds Are His Monument," *The Evening News* (Harrisburg), August 23, 1963, p. 4.

[9] Hinkle, *op. cit.*, pp. 9–10.   [10] Snavely, *op. cit.*, p. 6.

[11] Shippen and Wallace, *op. cit.*, p. 30.   [12] Snavely, *op. cit.*, p. 7.

[13] Shippen and Wallace, *op. cit.*, pp. 28–33.

[14] Hinkle, *loc. cit.*

[15] Shippen and Wallace, *op. cit.*, pp. 36–37.

On June 1, 1876, at the age of 19, Milton established his own candy business in Philadelphia expecting to profit from the visitors to the Centennial Exposition.[16]   He did meet with some success in the manufacture of caramels and cough drops, partly through the assistance of his mother and his aunt. However, Milton reportedly suffered several setbacks and seven years later, at the age of 26, closed his first business.   Although not a financial success, Milton S. Hershey knew how to make candy.[17]

After a brief stay in Lancaster, Milton went into business in Denver, Chicago, and New Orleans for brief periods. It was in Denver that he learned the secret of making delicious candy with fresh milk.[18]

In October, 1883, Milton opened a small caramel factory in New York City.[19]   The business grew and he prospered for a time but after three years, during which time he suffered several instances of bad luck, Milton Hershey was again forced to return to Lancaster. Due to his "frank, unassuming manner," Hershey was successful in obtaining from the Lancaster National Bank a $250,000 loan which he required to go into business.[20]   Here Hershey achieved success, principally through the sale of chocolate-coated caramels. Branches were opened in Mount Joy and Reading, Pennsylvania, and in New York City and Chicago. The variety of candies he produced soon exceeded a dozen different items.[21]

In October, 1892, Hershey attended the World's Columbian Exposition in Chicago.   There he saw German manufactured chocolate-making machinery which he purchased and had shipped to Lancaster.   M. S. Hershey had decided to make chocolate rather than caramels. By January 1, 1894, the first Hershey almond and milk chocolate bars, cocoa, and baking chocolate were manufactured.[22]

On May 25, 1898, Milton Hershey, at the age of 41, was married to Catherine Sweeny of Jamestown, New York, in St. Patrick's Cathedral in New York City. They set up housekeeping in Lancaster.[23]   It is interesting to note that, during this same year, Milton was able to have his father return to the Homestead which Milton had purchased a year earlier. Henry lived there until his death in 1904.[24]

Underscoring Milton S. Hershey's business success was the sale of his Lancaster Caramel Company to the American Caramel Company on August 10, 1900, for $1 million.[25]   But Hershey retained the chocolate manufacturing machinery and the right to manufacture chocolate.[26]   After the sale of the

[16]Snavely, *op. cit.*, p. 22.   [17]Hinkle, *op. cit.*, p. 11.

[18]Snavely, *op. cit.*, pp. 23–25.

[19]"Selected Hershey Chronology, 1724–1967," (Milton Hershey School, 1967), p. 4.

[20]Shippen and Wallace, *op. cit.*. pp. 71–78.

[21]*Ibid.*, pp. 87–91.

[22]"Selected Hershey Chronology, 1724–1967," *op. cit.*, p. 5.

[23]Snavely, *op. cit.*, pp. 33–34.

[24]"Selected Hershey Chronology, 1724–1967," *loc. cit.*

[25]Shippen and Wallace, *op. cit.*, pp. 98–105.

[26]"Selected Hershey Chronology, 1724–1967," *op. cit.*, p. 6.

business, Milton and his wife, "Kitty," took a trip but it was short-lived. While in Mexico City, Milton decided he wanted to return to the chocolate manufacturing business.[27]

Henry Hershey had earlier advised that "if you want to make money, you must do things in a large way."[28] Presumably, Milton took his father's advice. After considering a number of locations, including Lancaster, Baltimore, and Yonkers and Kingston, New York, he decided to locate his chocolate factory at Derry Church, later renamed "Hershey," near the Homestead where he was born.[29] The Dauphin County site was chosen because the price of the land was favorable, it was good dairy country, and Mr. Hershey assumed "loyal, reliable, intelligent" workers were to be found in his own "Pennsylvania Dutch" country.[30] Although Hershey later denied it, sentimentality for the area may have been an influencing factor. Mr. Samuel F. Hinkle, former Chairman of the Board and President of the Hershey Chocolate Corporation, suggested that the decision to locate the factory in the cornfields of Derry Township was "one of the first deliberate moves in the decentralization of industry."[31]

On January 28, 1903, corps of surveyors arrived in the Derry Church area and on March 2 of that year, in spite of much local skepticism about the project, ground was broken for the construction of the chocolate factory. Milton's father, who died February 18, 1904, did not live to see the completion of the factory in June, 1905.[32] The opening of the factory marked the beginning of a new period of expansion of M. S. Hershey's chocolate business. It also marked the founding, growth, and development of Hershey which was to become a model community.

The Hershey Community

"Chocolate Town, U.S.A." denotes that the growth and development of the chocolate business and the town of Hershey after 1905 are closely interrelated. Although a detailed account of this growth and development is beyond the scope of this study, a brief account is included. This review is necessary because the founding of the Hershey Junior College is a direct outgrowth of M. S. Hershey's successful chocolate business venture in Hershey.

The remarkable growth and development of the industrial town of Hershey may well be one of the earliest instances of "city planning." M. S. Hershey's careful planning is testimony of his foresight and humanitarianism. Even before the chocolate factory opened in 1905, Mr. Hershey was planning and building a community which would provide for the health and safety, recrea-

---

27Snavely, *op. cit.*, pp. 43–44.
28Hinkle, *op. cit.*, p. 13.
29Snavely, *op. cit.*, p. 44.
30Hinkle, *loc. cit*
31*Ibid.*
32"Selected Hershey Chronology, 1724–1967," *op. cit.*, pp. 6–8.

tion, education, and other needs of its residents. Hershey had observed what he felt were shortcomings in other industrial communities and he did not want his community to become another "company town." Mr. Hershey derived as much personal satisfaction from the building of the many fine facilities as he did from producing fine chocolate. Hershey has come to be described as a model town. Indeed, it has been alluded to as a "Kingdom."[33]

It should also be mentioned that some critics charged that Mr. Hershey was paternalistic and that he, in fact, built a "company town," although with a unique character, for business and personal benefits. For example, the *New York Herald Tribune* questioned, editorially, whether or not Hershey's "paternalism" was a good thing.

> Was it not at bottom a despotism, no matter how benevolent and practical? The entire scheme was enlightened, intelligent and permeated with a rare human decency. And yet, when one comes right down to the truth, it was a sort of feudalism.[34]

Several other writers, at the time of Mr. Hershey's death, although giving him due recognition as a philanthropist, also suggested that he may have been guilty of a "benevolent paternalism." Nevertheless, the building of "Chocolate Town, U.S.A." is a remarkable story.

Two days after the factory site had been surveyed, Mr. Hershey applied for a charter to operate a street car line between Hershey and neighboring communities to insure adequate transportation for his employees. The trolley went into operation in 1904.[35]

Early blueprints included sidewalks and streets, water, drainage, electricity, telephone, and lighting systems. Grading and landscaping were also provided.[36] Certain types of buildings were restricted in residential areas. To give Hershey a distinctiveness the avenues were named for countries and ports from which cocoa beans were imported: Trinidad, Java, Caracas, Areba, Granada, Ceylon, and Para.[37] The main intersection in Hershey was and is at Chocolate and Cocoa Avenues.

Public facilities were built in rapid succession. The Cocoa House, completed in 1905, was built to provide suitable quarters for Hershey employees. Later it was converted into a Y.M.C.A. The second floor became the Men's Club in 1913. The first floor housed a bank, post office, and general store. Later the building served as the Women's Club until it was dismantled in 1963.[38]

The Hershey Ballroom was opened in 1905.[39] There such famous bands as Harry James, Rudy Vallee, Vincent Lopez, Fred Waring, Paul Whiteman, and

---

[33] "Two Capitals and a Kingdom," *The Saturday Evening Post* (May 16, 1964), p. 50.

[34] Ken McKenna, "Milton Hershey's Dream Shattered by Violence in Labor Dispute in '37," *New York Herald Tribune*, March 7, 1961, p. 29+.

[35] Shippen and Wallace, *op. cit.*, pp. 125-26.

[36] "The Model Town," *The School Industrialist*, XIV, November, 1945, p. 11.

[37] Shippen and Wallace, *op. cit.*, p. 132.

[38] "Selected Hershey Chronology, 1724-1967," *op. cit.*, pp. 8, 10.

[39] *Ibid.*, p. 7.

many others played. In that same year the Hershey Volunteer Fire Company was organized and the Hershey Trust Company began operation.[40]

By 1906, the name of the community was officially changed from Derry Church to Hershey with the addition of a railroad and a new post office.[41]

In 1907, the now famous Hershey Park opened for its first season.[42] The home of Mr. and Mrs. Hershey, the "Mansion" located on "High Point," was completed in 1908.[43] In that same year the Hershey Chocolate Company was chartered and Mr. Hershey became Chairman of the Board of Directors.[44] During 1919, the Hershey Park Bandshell opened and the Hershey *Press* began printing operations.[45]

Not all of Mr. Hershey's proposals came to fruition. A case in point was his idea of a cooperative store which was looked upon with suspicion by some residents. The "co-op" did not become a reality although a department store was opened in 1910[46] and has continued in business to this day.

Numerous other additions to the community were made under the supervision of M. S. Hershey. They included a zoo, theatre, the Hershey National Bank, five golf courses, swimming pool, dairy, country club, convention hall, community club, hospital, rose garden, stadium, bakery, experimental candy shop, and many others.[47]

Several major construction projects deserve special mention. They include the Hotel Hershey, the Stadium, the Milton Hershey School buildings, the Sports Arena, and the Community Center. The magnificent Community Center Building, dedicated in 1933, was built at a cost of $3 million. When completed in 1935, the Sports Arena was the largest monolithic concrete structure in the United States.[48] These structures remain, to this day, examples of the finest facilities of their kind. It is significant that Mr. Hershey decided that these projects should be undertaken during the depression years of the early 1930's in order that residents of Hershey and surrounding communities would be employed.[49] It may be said that Mr. Hershey instituted his own private "public works" program. Major projects were completed by 1940.

Management of the growing number of Hershey enterprises became increasingly complex. In order to facilitate a more efficient control of the various properties, they were entrusted to a separate corporation in 1927, the

---

[40]*Ibid.*, p. 8.

[41]Shippen and Wallace, *op. cit.*, p. 134.

[42]"Selected Hershey Chronology, 1724–1967," *op. cit.*, p. 9.

[43]Shippen and Wallace, *op. cit.*, pp. 134–35.

[44]"Selected Hershey Chronology, 1724–1967," *loc. cit.*

[45]Snavely, *op. cit.*, p. 127.

[46]Joseph R. Snavely, *Milton S. Hershey—Builder* (Hershey: J. R. Snavely, 1935), pp. 64–70.

[47]"Selected Hershey Chronology, 1724–1967," *op. cit.*, pp. 12–21.

[48]"The Town That Chocolate Built," *The Review*, Vol. 3, No. 9 (Annville: Lebanon Valley College, September, 1969), p. 27.

[49]Katherine B. Shippen and Paul A. W. Wallace, *Milton S. Hershey* (New York: Random House, 1959), pp. 162–70.

Hershey Estates, which today controls hotels, 33 local businesses, and three public utilities.[50] The Hershey Chocolate Corporation also became a separate entity in 1927.[51]

The Chocolate Industry

Had the "chocolate factory in the cornfield" not been extremely successful during Mr. Hershey's lifetime, the growth and development of the community, described above, could not have been accomplished. In 1901, when Mr. Hershey was manufacturing candy in Lancaster, reported chocolate sales totaled $622,000.[52] The new Hershey factory was completed in 1905 and by 1906 gross sales jumped to $1,200,000. At about this time many specialty items were discontinued and production was concentrated on three items: the five cent solid milk chocolate bar, the five cent almond bar, and breakfast cocoa. These products were distributed nationally and sales, reportedly, took a "meteoric rise."[53] Hershey chocolate "Kisses" were first manufactured in 1907.[54]

In 1908, the Hershey Chocolate Company was chartered in Delaware and it was after this incorporation that Mr. Hershey devoted more of his time to the Hershey community, The Hershey Industrial School, and the raw materials, sugar and cocoa beans, used in the manufacture of chocolate. Production increased and gross sales in 1911 totaled $5 million[55] and factory floor space was increased to 18 acres.[56] New products were introduced including Hershey's Chewing Gum in 1915 which was later discontinued in 1924.[57] Total corporate sales for that year exceeded $10 million.[58]

For Milton Hershey, 1915 was an unhappy year because it was on March 25 that his wife died after a long illness.[59] The following year Mr. Hershey went to Cuba; this marked the beginning of a new venture for him and the chocolate business.

It was, reportedly, at the urging of his mother that Mr. Hershey decided to produce sugar, a basic ingredient in the manufacture of chocolate. A site was chosen on the northern coast of Cuba, 28 miles from Havana, and was named Central Hershey. A sugar mill was completed in 1918 and the electric Hershey

---

[50] "Hershey's Troubles: Big Chocolate Maker, Beset by Profit Slide, Gets More Aggressive," *The Wall Street Journal*, February 18, 1970, p. 1.

[51] Richard Wallace Murrie, "The Story Behind A Hershey Bar," (unpublished thesis, Princeton University, Princeton, New Jersey, 1939), p. 95.

[52] "Selected Hershey Chronology, 1724–1967," *op. cit.*, p. 6.

[53] Murrie, *op. cit.*, p. 41.

[54] "Selected Hershey Chronology, 1724–1967," *op. cit.*, p. 9.

[55] Samuel F. Hinkle, *Hershey: Farsighted Confectioner, Famous Chocolate, Fine Community* (Princeton: Princeton University Press, 1964), p. 9.

[56] "Selected Hershey Chronology, 1724–1967," *op. cit.*, p. 10.

[57] *Ibid.*, p. 12.

[58] Murrie, *op. cit.*, p. 10.

[59] Shippen and Wallace, *op. cit.*, p. 144.

Railway was put into operation in 1922. By 1920, the mill produced 31,669,000 pounds of sugar; 213,583,000 pounds by 1952.[60] Eventually Hershey owned 65,000 acres in Cuba and employed 3,500 to 4,500 people in addition to agricultural employees. The Hershey interests in Cuba were sold in 1946.[61]

Except for 1920, when a deficit of nearly $400,000 resulted from the "sugar crisis,"[62] the remainder of the decade was highly prosperous for the Corporation. New products were marketed in the 1920's and 1930's including cocoa syrup, "Mr. Goodbar," "Biscrisp," "Aero" chocolate bar, "Krackel" bar, "Miniatures," the "War Ration Bar," and cocoa butter soap.[63] Later, during World War II, 500,000 bars of "Field Ration D" were produced daily. It was a proud day for M. S. Hershey when he received the "Army-Navy E" flag and award in behalf of the Corporation.[64]

It is noteworthy that, until recently, the very successful distribution and sale of Hershey products was achieved without national consumer advertising. Reportedly, there had been exceptions, such as the time M. S. Hershey ran an ad when Charles Lindbergh flew the Atlantic with two Hershey Bars in his pocket.[65] The Hershey corporation has, however, stressed "point-of-sale" advertising over the years.[66]

M. S. Hershey believed that a unique product would sell itself.[67] He said, "The best advertising is the right kind of goods. People learn about them and buy all that you can make."[68]

M. S. Hershey also adhered to the policy of promotion from within. An unusually keen sense of loyalty existed between Hershey employees and "M. S.," as he was affectionately known. Mr. Hershey has often been cited for his progressive management policy with respect to profit sharing. He gave employees one-fourth of the earnings, thus making them partners in the business.[69] Mr. Hershey's underlying business philosophy may have been reflected through a motto that hung over his desk: "Business Is a Matter of Human Service."[70]

During the lifetime of M. S. Hershey there were but few labor disturbances. An April, 1937 sit-down strike was ended six days after it began when local workers and dairymen forcibly ejected the strikers from the factory.[71]

[60]*Ibid.*, pp. 145–52.

[61] "Selected Hershey Chronology, 1724–1967," *op. cit.*, pp. 13, 23.

[62] Shippen and Wallace, *op. cit.*, pp. 155–60.

[63] "Selected Hershey Chronology, 1724–1967," *op. cit.*, pp. 14–20.

[64] Shippen and Wallace, *op. cit.*, pp. 180–82.

[65] John C. Perham, "Chocolate Kingdom," *Barron's*, April 30, 1965, p. 3.

[66] "Hershey's Sweet Tooth Starts Aching," *Business Week*, February 7, 1970, p. 99.

[67] Snavely, *Milton S. Hershey—Builder, op. cit.*, pp. 198–99.

[68] James C. Young, "Hershey, Unique Philanthropist," *New York Times*, November 18, 1923, p. 4.

[69] *Ibid.*

[70] *Ibid.*

[71] Joseph R. Snavely, *An Intimate Story of Milton S. Hershey* (Hershey: J. R. Snavely, 1957), p. 4.

As previously indicated, the Hershey Chocolate Corporation was incorporated in the state of Delaware in 1927 and, thus, became a public corporation. Common and convertible preferred stock was issued and placed on the New York Stock Exchange. However, the majority of the stock and, therefore, the control remained in the possession of The Hershey Industrial School,[72] which will be considered in the following pages. As was previously mentioned, the Hershey Estates was incorporated the same year. A third corporation, the Hershey Corporation, was established to administer the enterprise in Cuba.[73]

The "Horatio-Alger-like" story of Milton Snavely Hershey ended with his death on October 13, 1945, at the age of 88.[74] But the fascinating story of Mr. Hershey's "Chocolate Town, U.S.A." and his philanthropies continues.

The rural and yet cosmopolitan Hershey community of some 10,000 people, with a 50 percent increase predicted, continues to grow and is considered an ideal place to live. Recent additions to Hershey include street lights shaped like Hershey "Kisses," an all-year community pool, a public-owned educational television station, a new country club and championship golf course, a motor lodge, and a recreation and cultural center. A new senior high school, built at a cost of $3,200,000 opened in 1966.[75] But of all the new facilities to be erected in Hershey in recent years, The Milton S. Hershey Medical Center is the most impressive. It also has had the greatest impact on the community. The Medical Center will be discussed later in this chapter.

Philanthropy

The headlines of Milton Snavely Hershey's obituary in the *New York Times* stated that he (1) founded a chocolate corporation and a model community, (2) donated millions to charity, (3) produced the Army "D" Ration, (4) established the Industrial School for orphans, and (5) accomplished the above after three failures.[76] *Current Biography: Who's News and Why* lists Mr. Hershey as an American philanthropist and industrialist.[77] Attention is here directed to M. S. Hershey and the philanthropies he created.

Those who knew M. S. Hershey contend that his philanthropies were established for altruistic and humanitarian reasons. "This man's deeds truly are his monuments," states Samuel F. Hinkle. Mr. Hershey may be included with other great givers including Sloan, Kresge, Rockefeller, Carnegie, and Girard but Hershey's philanthropies are considered by Wallace to be "more intimate since they were outgrowths of his own personal deprivations."[78]

[72] "Selected Hershey Chronology, 1724–1967," *op. cit.*, p. 15.

[73] Shippen and Wallace, *op. cit.*, pp. 160–61.

[74] Alexander Stoddart (ed.), "M. S. Hershey, One of America's Gracious Giants of Giving, Reaches The End of Life," *Hotel Hershey High-Lights*, Vol. XIII, No. 17, October 20, 1945, pp. 1–2.

[75] "Selected Hershey Chronology, 1724–1967," *op. cit.*, p. 34.

[76] "M. S. Hershey Dead; Chocolate King, 88," *New York Times*, October 14, 1945, p. 44L+.

[77] Anna Rothe (ed.), *Current Biography: Who's News and Why* (New York: The H. W. Wilson Company, 1945), p. 280.

[78] Hinkle, *op. cit.*, p. 18.

M. S. Hershey contributed to many charities including the Red Cross, Public Welfare, and the Boy and Girl Scouts.[79] The Hershey Hospital and many other construction projects, mentioned above, may rightfully be considered among Hershey's many charitable gifts to the community. It may be of interest to note, that although a Republican, he was not known to contribute to any political party.[80]

Although having been raised in the Mennonite faith and having married a Catholic, Mr. Hershey was considered to be a firm nonsectarian who believed in the Ten Commandments and the Golden Rule and put them into practice in his daily personal and business life. Indicative of Hershey's nonsectarianism, he intended to build a large interdenominational church in Hershey. Apparently there was little support for the idea.[81] He did, however, support the churches of the community and on July 4, 1935 presented $20,000 to each of the five churches in Hershey to eliminate their indebtedness.[82] Mr. Hershey is reported to have given a total of $75,000 to each church in the community.[83]

The most significant outgrowth of the successful Hershey chocolate enterprise is Mr. Hershey's educational philanthropy. The institutions which he personally founded and endowed or aided include the Derry Township Public Schools, from kindergarten through high school, The Hershey Industrial School (now the Milton Hershey School), the Cuban Orphan School, and the Hershey Junior College.

It is probably true that underlying psychological needs led Mr. Hershey to decide to give his personal fortune to boys and girls. He further provided that a large portion of all future earnings of the chocolate business should be used for the care and education of young people, particularly orphan boys.

It has been noted that Milton Hershey's childhood was unsettled and probably unhappy. His education was deficient, at best. In fact, Wallace questions Hershey's ability to read.[84] Hershey wrote practically no letters himself, seldom signed his name, avoided using the telephone, and made his remarks brief. He was considered a "practical man."[85] Hershey wanted boys and girls to have educational opportunities he did not enjoy.

Possibly of greater significance was the fact that Mr. and Mrs. Hershey were childless. However, Milton Hershey was a strongly paternal man. Providing education and homes for many is likely to have met a strong need of Mr. Hershey. He had no immediate heirs who could have inherited his great

---

[79] Paul A. W. Wallace, "Milton Hershey's Approach to Education," Hershey Junior College, Commencement Speech, May 28, 1955, pp. 11-12.

[80] "As One Man Knew Him," The Review, Vol. 3, No. 9 (Annville: Lebanon Valley College, September, 1969), p. 39.

[81] J. R. Snavely, The Story of Hershey: The Chocolate Town (Hershey: J. R. Snavely, 1953), p. 34.

[82] "M. S. Hershey's Life's Aims and Achievements," Hotel Hershey High-Lights, Vol. 6, No. 11, September 17, 1938, p. 3.

[83] "As One Man Knew Him," loc. cit.

[84] Wallace, "Milton Hershey's Approach to Education," op. cit., p. 3.

[85] Young, "Hershey, Unique Philanthropist," New York Times, loc. cit.

fortune. Furthermore, Hershey believed, "Money spoils more men than it makes," and "the inheritance of great fortune is a bad thing."[86]

For the above reasons, The Hershey Industrial School for orphan boys was an ideal philanthropy and the favorite one of Mr. and Mrs. Hershey. Milton Hershey's largest, single gift went to the School. He gave his wife credit for the idea of establishing the private institution.[87]

The Hershey Industrial School was founded on November 15, 1909, with the signing of the "Deed of Trust" which established a trust fund and an endowment of 500,000 shares of Hershey Chocolate Corporation common stock.[88] The actual gift was made in 1918 but not announced publicly until 1923.[89] As of 1927, when the Corporation became a public enterprise, the value of the 500,000 of Mr. Hershey's 729,000 shares was placed at $60,000,000 which had grown to $80,000,000 by 1945.[90] The current value of the holding is estimated at $200,000,000, as reported previously.

Hershey revealed his humanitarianism and altruistic reasons for founding the school for orphan boys in a rare interview in 1923. He said:

> I am 66 years old and I do not need much money. My business has been far more successful than I ever expected it to be. . . . As matters have been arranged, the business will go right on, a considerable part of the profits to be used for the Industrial School. . . . I have no heirs, so I decided to make the orphan boys of the United States my heirs. . . . Our boys are our finest possession. With them must rest the realization of all those high hopes held by this generation, growing up before our eyes. . . . The orphan boy has a harder time than anybody else. . . . The biggest influence in a boy's life is what his dad does; and when a boy doesn't happen to have any sort of dad, he is a special mark for destiny. I am afraid that most of our orphan boys have a bad time of it and that many never get the right start. They tell me that youngsters who go to prison never had a chance. Well, I am going to give some of them a chance in my way.[91]

Mr. Hershey did not intend that The Hershey Industrial School should be an experimental or laboratory school. It was founded as a home for orphan boys who would be provided a "common school education" which would be "supplemented by instruction in the useful crafts." The original emphasis was on manual training, hence, the name "The Hershey Industrial School."[92] The name was legally changed to "Milton Hershey School" on December 24, 1951.[93]

As provided in the "Deed of Trust," The Milton Hershey School bears a close relationship to the Corporation. The School is the principal beneficiary

[86]*Ibid.*
[87]Shippen and Wallace, *op. cit.*, pp. 137-44.
[88]Milton Hershey School, "Deed of Trust," November 15, 1909.
[89]"Selected Hershey Chronology, 1724-1967," *op. cit.*, p. 13.
[90]Paul Gallico, "$80,000,000 Worth of Orphans," *The American Weekly*, December 23, 1945, p. 12.
[91]Young, "Hershey, Unique Philanthropist," *New York Times, loc. cit.*
[92]Hinkle, *op. cit.*, p. 15.
[93]"Selected Hershey Chronology, 1724-1967," *op. cit.*, p. 25.

of all Hershey activities. It owns the controlling stock in the Corporation and receives the dividends. The endowment is administered by the Hershey Trust Company whose Directors are comprised of the various Hershey enterprises officials. Ultimate control of the Corporation, then, rests with the Hershey Trust Company. The Directors of the Trust Company are also the Board of Managers of the Milton Hershey School and trustees of the Fund.[94]

Critics charge The Hershey Industrial School (Milton Hershey School) was founded to avoid paying corporate income tax. The School owns the controlling stock but the Corporation pays the same taxes other corporations engaged in manufacturing must pay. The trusteeship does insure perpetuity to the Corporation, but this, it is argued, could have been achieved in other ways. It should also be noted that there were no national taxes for individuals or corporations when the School was founded in 1909.[95]

One of the earliest public criticisms of the School and its relationship to the Hershey Chocolate Corporation and the community appeared in *Fortune* in 1934.[96] The *Wall Street Journal* suggested that company officials have "brooded" about the *Fortune* article and, as a result, have viewed journalists with suspicion since it was published.[97] Mr. Hershey himself was reported to be displeased with it.[98] *Fortune* did not question Mr. Hershey's sincerity and good intentions in establishing the School. The article stated bluntly, "the chocolate factory makes the money to pay for everything and the school owns practically everything."[99] *Fortune* estimated that income to the School from its stock and other sources totaled $1,675,000 in 1934, $3,000,000 in 1932.[100] It was calculated that the average expenditures for each of 460 boys enrolled amounted to a total expenditure of $472,647.51. Since a student body of 1,630 would be required to use the total income of $1,675,000 "an embarrassingly large surplus is piling up in the school's coffers," the article charged.[101]

The *Wall Street Journal* article, referred to above, stressed the fact that the Milton Hershey School owns a 66 percent interest in Hershey Foods, a holding worth $200 million at the, then, depressed stock prices. Company executives deny, however, that they are influenced by the School. But the article reflected on "another, quite innocent, link" between the School and the Corporation. Hershey Foods needs a million pounds of milk a day and dairy cattle were maintained by the School.[102]

[94] Hinkle, *op. cit.*, p. 20.

[95] Richard Wallace Murrie, "The Story Behind A Hershey Bar," (unpublished thesis, Princeton University, Princeton, New Jersey, 1939), p. 95.

[96] "Mr. Hershey Gives Away His Fortune," *Fortune*, Vol. IX, No. 1, January, 1934, pp. 72–80.

[97] "Hershey's Troubles: Big Chocolate Maker, Beset by Profit Slide, Gets More Aggressive," *The Wall Street Journal*, February 18, 1970, p. 95.

[98] Snavely, *An Intimate Story of Milton S. Hershey, op. cit.*, pp. 377-79.

[99] "Mr. Hershey Gives Away His Fortune," *op. cit.*, p. 72.

[100] *Ibid.*, p. 75.

[101] *Ibid.*, p. 76.

[102] "Hershey's Troubles: Big Chocolate Maker, Beset by Profit Slide, Gets More Aggressive," *loc. cit.*

In commenting on the financial structure of the Milton Hershey School and its relationship to the Hershey Foods Corporation, the writer of the *Wall Street Journal* article noted:

> The orphans have no cause for worry. The school got $8.6 million in dividends on its Hershey Foods stock last year. It is so well heeled that it gave $50 million to Pennsylvania State University in 1963 to build The Milton S. Hershey Medical School and hospital here, and it currently is putting the finishing touches on a huge auditorium and reception hall for the orphanage estimated to cost $15 million.[103]

Fortune presented several criticisms of professional philanthropists. The following major arguments were made:

(1) Perpetuities are open to serious objection.
(2) The supply of orphans was dwindling.
(3) The normal home environment is best for a normal boy.
(4) Orphanage care to be effective must be expensive.

However, the article suggested that if it is granted that an orphanage is a desirable institution, The Hershey Industrial School was less open to criticism.[104]

The wrath of Mr. Hershey and the Hershey officials was probably aroused most by the following:

> On windless summer days the town of Hershey is permeated by what the Pennsylvania Dutch farmers of the neighborhood call "da chockle shtink" — the sweetish, cloying smell of milk chocolate in the making. The moral atmosphere of the town is pervaded by a similar aroma — the sweet and oppressive odor of charity.... To give too much outright saps a community's self-reliance and injures its pride. Not only has Mr. Hershey made his gifts without inviting cooperation from the town, but he has also kept the control entirely in his own hands. His school owns everything and his men, not the community's, manage everything.... It all comes down to the manner of man M. S. Hershey happens to be. On the one hand, he is interested, sincere, warmhearted, with a genuine desire to do good to his neighbors. On the other, he has the strong will, the ego, and the intellectual limitations of many another self-made man....[105]

The *Fortune* article concluded by speculating whether Mr. Hershey would change the terms of the "Deed of Trust" which established the School, particularly the perpetuity provision. During his lifetime, the article pointed out, it would be a simple matter to change the terms. But after his death changes could only be made through the doctrine of *cy pres* and since there would always be orphans, it would probably be impossible to rely upon *cy pres*.[106]

---

103 *Ibid.*
104 "Mr. Hershey Gives Away His Fortune," *op. cit.*, pp. 76–78.
105 *Ibid.*, p. 80.
106 "Mr. Hershey Gives Away His Fortune," *op. cit.*, p. 80.

The perpetuity provision was not changed by Mr. Hershey but it is interesting to note that the filing and subsequent approval of a *cy pres* petition by the Dauphin County Orphans' Court made it possible to transfer $50,000,000 in accumulated income from the Milton Hershey School Trust to The M. S. Hershey Foundation.[107] Signed on August 23, 1963, the decree made it possible to establish The Milton S. Hershey Medical Center of The Pennsylvania State University.[108] At that time, the principal of the Hershey Trust Company, trustee for the School, totaled $298,000,000. In addition, the accumulation of reinvested, unspent income was worth $96,000,000 or a grand total of nearly $400,000,000.[109]

The Milton S. Hershey Medical Center of The Pennsylvania State University was a joint undertaking between The M. S. Hershey Foundation and the University. The founding and construction of the Medical Center was made possible through the creation of The M. S. Hershey Foundation by Milton S. Hershey in 1935. The M. S. Hershey Foundation, "Agreement of Trust" provided for the "vocational, cultural or professional education of any resident of Derry Township, Pennsylvania."[110] A $50 million grant by the Hershey Trust Company made it possible to build and endow the medical college.[111] An explanation of how the College of Medicine of The Milton S. Hershey Medical College of The Pennsylvania State University was born is included in the Medical Center *Bulletin.*

> The bulk of Mr. Hershey's estate was placed in the Milton Hershey School trust. Income from the trust continued to exceed the requirements of the Milton Hershey School despite increased enrollments and constant improvements in the quality of accommodations and educational program. The Board of Directors of the Hershey Trust Company, Trustee of the Foundation, considered it in the intent of the founder to commit the accumulated income to a critical public need that clearly lay within the trust's charitable purposes. After considerable exploration and study, the Board concluded that a medical school in Derry Township with the promise of providing new educational opportunities while alleviating human suffering seemed most consonant with Mr. Hershey's will.

> Accordingly, the Board of the Hershey Trust Company prepared a detailed memorandum in 1963 proposing an award of a portion of the accumulated income held for the Milton Hershey School to The M. S. Hershey Foundation for the purpose of establishing a medical school. Concurrently, discussions were held with the President and Board of Trustees of The Pennsylvania

---

[107] Joseph S. Gumpher, Treasurer of the Hershey Trust Company, Secretary of The M. S. Hershey Foundation, personal interview, July 28, 1967.

[108] "Hershey Provides $50 Million For Midstate Medical College," *Evening News* (Harrisburg), August 23, 1963, p. 1+.

[109] James Welsh, "Milton Hershey's Trust Fund—A Case of Too Much Money," *The Sunday Patriot News* (Harrisburg), August 25, 1963, p. 1+.

[110] *Agreement of Trust*, The M. S. Hershey Foundation, Hershey, Pennsylvania (December 5, 1935).

[111] "Hershey Provides $50 Million For Midstate Medical College," *loc. cit.*

State University. On August 23, 1963, the President Judge of the Orphans' Court of Dauphin County signed a decree transferring $50 million from the Milton Hershey School Trust to The M. S. Hershey Foundation for the planning, construction, equipping, and operation of a medical school, teaching hospital, and related graduate and research programs.

On August 27, 1964, the Foundation and the University signed an affiliation agreement which created the College of Medicine and The Milton S. Hershey Medical Center of The Pennsylvania State University.[112]

The Milton S. Hershey Medical Center is described as "the most recent extension of the sentiment, courage, vision, humanity, and philanthropy of one man.[113]

Ground was broken for the Medical Center on February 26, 1966.[114] The main building, the Medical Sciences Building and Teaching Hospital, is a 750-foot long, nine-story, crescent-shaped structure with three wings at the rear. It includes 2,300 rooms and occupies more than 20 acres of floor space.[115] The Center opened on September 25, 1967, with a class of 37 men and 3 women.[116] The medical school is planned for a total of 256 medical students.[117]

Milton Hershey's acts of benevolence were not limited to the Hershey community. Reference has already been made to the development of a sugar refinery in Cuba. Here, too, he was interested in the welfare of the people, particularly the young. Medical and dental service, recreational facilities, and a school were provided in Central Hershey. In Central Rosario, Mr. Hershey built the Cuban Orphan School on a plan similar to The Hershey Industrial School.[118] The Cuban Orphan School opened February 26, 1925; it was discontinued April 12, 1935.[119]

The Cuban people were grateful to Mr. Hershey and in 1933 he was given the highest honor that Cuba could bestow. He was awarded the Grand Cross of the National Order of Carlos Manuel de Cespedes by President Machado at the Presidential Palace in Havana.[120]

Milton Hershey's interest in and philanthropy to education included the public schools of the community of Hershey. His first significant accomplishment was the consolidation of 15 one-room schools in and around Hershey. At a cost of $250,000 to Mr. Hershey, the M. S. Hershey Consolidated Public School of Derry Township was dedicated on October 13, 1914.[121]

---

[112]*College of Medicine, The Milton S. Hershey Medical Center* (College of Medicine, The Pennsylvania State University, Vol. III, No. 1, August 1968), p. 6.

[113]*Ibid.*, p. 5.

[114]"Selected Hershey Chronology, 1724–1967," *op. cit.*, p. 31.

[115]*College of Medicine, The Milton S. Hershey Medical Center, op. cit.*, p. 36.

[116]"Selected Hershey Chronology, 1724–1967," *op. cit.*, p. 32.

[117]*College of Medicine, The Milton S. Hershey Medical Center, op. cit.*, p. 38.

[118]Katherine B. Shippen and Paul A. W. Wallace, *Milton S. Hershey* (New York: Random House, 1959), pp. 152-53.

[119]"Selected Hershey Chronology, 1724–1967," *op. cit.*, p. 14.

[120]Shippen and Wallace, *op. cit.*, p. 154.

[121]"M. S. Hershey: Chronological Review," *Hotel Hershey High-Lights*, Vol. XI, No. 4, July 14, 1943, p. 3.

In 1925, a junior-senior high school building was added to the public schools. This gift from Mr. Hershey represented, approximately, $750,000.[122] Definitely "progressive" for the time, Hershey built a vocational school building at a cost of $250,000 in 1930.[123] At about this same time, the School received a gymnasium, theatre, playground, football field, and a baseball diamond.

Other benefits accrued to the Derry Township Public Schools through the foresight and generosity of M. S. Hershey. For example, he presented real estate worth $100,000 from which the Schools received the income.[124] Mr. Hershey also paid the operating expenses of the vocational school and the kindergartens. The educational facilities and programs available to the students attending the Derry Township public schools in 1934 would have required a 25 mill tax when, in fact, the school tax was only 15 mills.[125]

The last important addition to the public schools by Mr. Hershey was the establishment of the Hershey Junior College in 1938. The following chapters are devoted to that institution.

Although Mr. Hershey had given his fortune to The Hershey Industrial School, he had accumulated an additional $900,000 by the time of his death on October 13, 1945.[126] In his will of September 29, 1944, he stipulated that the bulk of his personal estate at his death should go to the public schools in Derry Township. Mr. Hershey's holdings in the Hershey Trust Company, estimated at $40,000 in capital stock, was willed to The Hershey Industrial School. His will read as follows:

> I give and bequeath to the Hershey Industrial School all the shares of the capital stock of The Hershey Trust Company which I may have, hold, or possess, and my Executors, hereinafter named, shall assign, transfer and deliver to the Hershey Trust Company, Trustee named in the deed founding the said School, said shares of stock, the same to be held in the manner and for the uses, trusts and purposes set forth in the deed founding said school. . . .[127]

The remainder of the estate, after taxes and costs, also went to the Hershey Trust Company to be invested, and the income was to be paid

> in semi-annual installments to the School District of Derry Township, Dauphin County, Pennsylvania, for the use of said School District, particularly for the purpose of assisting said Township to relieve the tax burden for the upkeep and maintenance of the public schools in said District.[128]

---

[122] *Ibid.*

[123] Joseph R. Snavely, *Milton S. Hershey—Builder* (Hershey: J. R. Snavely, 1935), p. 114.

[124] "M. S. Hershey: Chronological Review," *loc. cit.*

[125] Snavely, *Milton S. Hershey—Builder, op. cit.*, p. 115.

[126] "Hershey Estate Goes To Schools," *The Evening News* (Harrisburg), October 17, 1945, p.1.

[127] "Last Will and Testament of Milton S. Hershey," September 29, 1944.

[128] *Ibid.*

At that time the Township Schools were receiving an estimated $55,000 annually from the Hershey interests in addition to real estate taxes. The Hershey Chocolate Company gave $25,000 yearly to help maintain the vocational school and the Hershey Foundation bore all of the $30,000 per year cost to maintain the Junior College.[129] At the time of Mr. Hershey's death the Township school tax rate was 16 mills. It was reported that he did not want the tax to exceed that rate.[130]

Upon the death of Milton S. Hershey, the editor of *Hotel Hershey High-Lights*, Alexander Stoddart, commented that Mr. Hershey "may not be remembered as a captain of industry, but he will be remembered for his philanthropy—the gift of his fortune at this writing of $84,000,000 to the orphan boys of America. They are his monument. . . ."[131]

Dr. H. H. Hostetter, Mr. Hershey's physician and friend, termed him a "philosopher, inventer, chemist, industrialist, diplomat, philanthropist and educator, although he didn't get past the fourth grade in school."[132]

Most of the 1,850 newspapers in circulation in the country in 1945 reported Mr. Hershey's death, with many of their editors commenting editorially. It is a tribute to Milton S. Hershey that nearly every editor praised his humanitarianism and his philanthropy. The following excerpts are indicative:

> There may be great men like Girard that are better known for their philanthropy toward orphans, but we doubt if any of them really did as much as Hershey . . . for the welfare of orphans.[133]

> If ever there was a gospel of human kindness and courage, written in the American vernacular, it is the career of Milton Hershey.[134]

> It is good to remember that while there may have been "pirates in those days," most American success stories have been built on simple elements of hard work, courage and an honest product—elements that incidentally are still available to thousands of young men who are looking about for a fling at the future.[135]

> Hershey will certainly be remembered for an interest in human welfare which led him to devote as much time and ingenuity to the accomplishment of his humanitarian goals as he did to the success of his business.[136]

> Paternalism is a risky thing in which to indulge and more often than not turns out badly. The reason, we think, is that all too frequently it is born of

---

[129] "Hershey Estate Goes To Schools," *loc. cit.*

[130] "Hershey Bequest Is Termed 'Fine Thing' by Board," *The Evening News* (Harrisburg), October 17, 1945, p. 1.

[131] Alexander Stoddart (ed.) "M. S. Hershey, One Of America's Gracious Giants of Giving, Reaches The End of Life," *Hotel Hershey High-Lights*, Vol. XIII, No. 17, October 20, 1945, p. 1.

[132] "Kiwanians Hear Talk by Doctor On M. S. Hershey," *Lebanon Daily News*, July 28, 1967, p. 9.

[133] "Model 'Useful Citizen,' " *Sentinel* (Carlisle, Pennsylvania), cited in *Hotel Hershey High-Lights*, Vol. XIII, No. 19, November 3, 1945, p. 1.

[134] "Human Kindness and Courage," *Atlanta Journal*, cited in *Hotel Hershey High-Lights, ibid.*, p. 2.

[135] "It Still Can Happen," *News* (Tuscaloosa, Alabama), cited in *Hotel Hershey High-Lights, ibid.*, p. 2.

[136] "Distinguished For Benefactions," *Telegram* (Herkimer, New York), cited in *Hotel Hershey High-Lights, ibid.*

selfishness: the sponsor has an ulterior motive. An outstanding exception is Milton S. Hershey, . . . he founded a model town and owned everything in it. The dominant feature was an industrial school for orphan boys which he endowed with many millions and where now nearly a thousand boys are being instructed. Mr. Hershey apparently had no thought in this enterprise except the welfare of those whose lives it touched. . . . Mr. Hershey's experiment has been a great success, but the chances are we shall never see another like it.[137]

Few men have ever made so much money and given so much away intelligently. His living monument is the community of Hershey, Pennsylvania. . . .[138]

The millions which the "Chocolate King" earned were invested in the betterment of the people and the community he founded and loved. The entire Nation, and Pennsylvania in particular, benefited from his devotion to humanity, his interest in education and his beneficence.[139]

The life of Milton S. Hershey and the growth and development of the chocolate industry and the community of Hershey have been reviewed. With the exception of the Hershey Junior College, Mr. Hershey's philanthropies have been considered. This review should provide an adequate background for the detailed study of the Hershey Junior College.

[137]"The Hershey Example," *Herald* (Titusville, Pennsylvania) cited in *Hotel Hershey High-Lights*, Vol. XIII, No. 21, November 17, 1945, p. 2.

[138]Charles B. Driscoll (syndicated column "New York Day By Day") cited in *Hotel Hershey High-Lights*, Vol. XIII, No. 25, December 15, 1945.

[139]"Devotion To Humanity," *News* (McKeesport, Pennsylvania), cited in *Hotel Hershey High-Lights*, Vol. XIII, No. 27, December 29, 1945.

Figure 1. Milton Snavely Hershey
1857–1945

CHAPTER III

THE HERSHEY JUNIOR COLLEGE IS FOUNDED

The Junior College Movement

The growth and development of two-year institutions in the United States spans a relatively short period. Thornton divides the junior college movement into three periods: (1) the evolution of the junior college, 1850–1920, (2) the expansion of the occupational programs, 1920–1945, and (3) the community college concept, 1945 to the present.[1]

Students of the junior college movement, like Thornton, differ on the founding of the first two-year institution. Bogue cites Lasell Junior College, Auburndale, Massachusetts, as the "first successful and persistent" junior college. It offered two years of standard collegiate instruction as early as 1852.[2] Lewis Institute, Chicago, Illinois, established in 1896, is cited as the first private junior college. It later became a four-year college after which it merged with Armour Institute to become the Illinois Institute of Technology.[3] The first public junior college established in connection with a high school was that at Goshen, Indiana, later discontinued; the first public junior college, organized in 1902, was Joliet Junior College in Illinois.[4]

Ralph R. Fields suggests that Benjamin Franklin attempted to inaugurate plans and provisions for public two-year colleges in Pennsylvania more than 200 years ago.

> ... Benjamin Franklin encountered difficulties in his attempt to establish an "English" branch in his Academy, devoted to the vernacular, modern languages, and occupational courses. Franklin argued that the Latin branch failed to prepare, or even to admit, students who need such education for practical reasons. Perhaps Franklin's experience was prophetic of the long period of frustration that has been endured by the proponents of community education in Pennsylvania.[5]

---

[1] James W. Thornton, Jr., *The Community Junior College* (New York: John Wiley & Sons, Inc., 1966), pp. 46–50.

[2] Jessie P. Bogue, *The Development of Junior Colleges* (Washington: American Association of Junior Colleges, 1957), p. 2.

[3] Saul Sack, *History of Higher Education in Pennsylvania*, Vol. II (Harrisburg: Commonwealth of Pennsylvania, The Pennsylvania Historical and Museum Commission, 1963), pp. 594-95, citing Phebe Ward, "Development of the Junior College Movement," cited by Jessie P. Bogue (ed.), *American Junior Colleges* (Washington, D.C., 1952), p. 9.

[4] Walter Crosby Eells, "The Junior College Movement," *The Literary Artisan*, Vol. I, No. 4, May, 1940, p. 3. *The Literary Artisan* was a magazine published by the Hershey Junior College.

[5] Ralph R. Fields & Associates, *Community Colleges in Pennsylvania: A Report to the State Board of Education*, June 30, 1965, pp. vii–viii.

Saul Sack traces the junior college movement in Pennsylvania to the early academies and secondary schools of the 19th century. They proclaimed as one of their objectives "the preparation of students for entrance to the sophomore and junior classes of college."[6] Sack claims that "the history of at least one institution born in the 19th century in Pennsylvania indicates that priority in the junior college movement has been misplaced." "The distinction," he states, "belongs to another institution which antedates the Lewis Institute by almost 40 years." The Missionary Institute of the Evangelical Lutheran Church, now Susquehanna University, began life as a junior college with the conscious purpose of so remaining. Its founders, in 1858, declared:

> This institute, according to its present design, embraces two departments—A Classical, and a Theological. The Classical department is designed to afford to Students the necessary facilities for acquiring a respectable business education and also to prepare themselves for the Junior and Senior Classes of College. . . .[7]

The first published outline of the curriculum in the "Collegiate Department" was two years in length, embracing the studies of the freshman and sophomore years.[8]

Sack emphasizes that:

> Junior colleges in Pennsylvania in the 20th century, with but one exception, arose either as extensions of existing secondary schools, or as off-campus centers of the colleges and universities. Among the earliest in the former category was that established by the Sisters of Charity at their Saint Joseph Academy, Greensburg. . . . By 1915 the name "Seton Junior College" was adopted, and a regular two-year college program was published.[9]

> Junior colleges or undergraduate centers offering the first two years of college work were established by a few of the colleges and universities of the State largely because of requests from local communities desiring higher educational facilities. The University of Pittsburgh was the first to erect a center at Johnstown in cooperation with the school district of the city of Johnstown, in 1927.[10]

Centers similar to the one established at Johnstown, followed at Uniontown and Erie in 1928.[11]

Bucknell University founded the Bucknell Junior College at Wilkes-Barre in 1933.[12]

Pennsylvania State College, by far the most prolific of the three institutions, established centers at Uniontown, Hazleton, Pottsville, DuBois, Altoona, Erie, and Rydal between 1934 and 1950.[13]

---

[6] Sack, *op. cit.*, p. 595.
[7] *Ibid.*, citing Missionary Institute, "Minutes of Managers," I, August 31, 1858, p. 39 ff.
[8] *Ibid.*, citing Missionary Institute, *Catalogue* (1859–1860), pp. 14–15.
[9] *Ibid.*, p. 597, citing Seton Junior College, *Prospectus* (1915–1916), in Library, Seton Hill College, Greensburg, Pennsylvania.
[10] *Ibid.*, p. 599, citing "Reports of the Superintendent of Public Instruction."
[11] *Ibid.*, citing Starrett, *University of Pittsburgh*, p. 453.
[12] *Ibid.*, citing Bucknell University, "Minutes of Trustees," IV, May 22, 1933.
[13] *Ibid.*

30

Sack, in his *History of Higher Education in Pennsylvania*, provides a background of the junior college curriculum in the State:

> The early conception of the function of the junior college in Pennsylvania coincided rather closely with the definition formulated by the American Association of Junior Colleges in 1922. This was reflected particularly in the nature of the curriculum offerings. Since the junior college was considered primarily as an institution preparing for advanced standing in a senior college, the courses of study were geared to this purpose and corresponded to the freshman and sophomore years of the four-year college. Even in those instances where curriculums other than the liberal arts were introduced, they were nevertheless oriented in the direction of the student's eventually earning his degree.
>
> Terminal education, as a distinct function of the junior college, did not make its appearance in Pennsylvania until 1930. . . . Terminal courses, particularly of a vocational nature, were added, so that by the mid-point of the 20th century, curriculum ranged from offerings in the liberal arts and sciences to technical disciplines requiring specific vocational skills.[14]

Describing the existence of junior colleges in Pennsylvania in 1963, Sack states:

> The history of the junior college movement in Pennsylvania reveals a pattern of contraction rather than expansion. The number of such institutions which once enjoyed life has been continually diminishing. This trend, particularly with respect to the privately controlled junior college, has not been offset by a corresponding increase in the number of undergraduate centers established by the Pennsylvania State University. In fact, the chief characteristic of the junior college in Pennsylvania before the close of the first quarter of the 20th century was that it was a prelude, a preliminary first step, to the achieving of degree-granting status.
>
> It has been noted previously that Pennsylvania's junior colleges, with but one exception, emerged either as extensions of existing secondary schools or as off-campus undergraduate centers of a few colleges and universities. At least one of these sources is drying up. The private secondary schools in the State, finding it increasingly more difficult to compete with the free public high schools, have diminished in number rather than multiplied. Presumably the vacuum might be filled by the local school districts. But thus far we have seen that only one of these, the Board of Education of Derry Township, Hershey, Pennsylvania, has succeeded, with the aid of a benefactor, in establishing a junior college.[15]

The exception to which Sack referred was the Hershey Junior College, founded in 1938. He described it as "Pennsylvania's only municipally-controlled junior college" which "derived its existence from the beneficience of Mr. Milton S. Hershey, of Hershey, Pennsylvania."[16]

Based on the foregoing brief review of the junior college movement in the United States and in Pennsylvania, it is clear that the Hershey Junior College deserves a place in the history of the growth and development of the junior

---

[14] *Ibid.*, pp. 599–600.
[15] *Ibid.*, pp. 600–602.
[16] *Ibid.*, p. 599.

TABLE I

NUMBER OF TWO-YEAR COLLEGES IN PENNSYLVANIA
AND THE UNITED STATES
1938 and 1964[a]

	Public	Private	Total
Pennsylvania			
1938	5	15	20
1964	15	20	35
United States			
1938	250	306	556
1964	452	267	719

[a]Letters of April 7, 1967 and July 6, 1970, from Jack C.
Gernhart, Administrative Assistant to the Executive Director,
American Association of Junior Colleges, Washington, D.C.,
citing Junior College Directory, 1939 and 1965, Washington:
American Association of Junior Colleges.

college. The College was the first public junior college to be established in Pennsylvania and in the eastern United States.[17] It stands as a benchmark in the history of higher education of the Commonwealth.[18]

The M. S. Hershey Foundation Meets Need for a Junior College

According to Dr. A. G. Breidenstine, first Dean of the Hershey Junior College, Milton S. Hershey was concerned about the young people of Hershey who were unemployed and, generally, not putting their time to good use during the 1930–1937 period. Mr. Hershey had been successful in creating employment for adults in the chocolate factory and other Hershey enterprises but he was dissatisfied with the idleness he saw among recent high school graduates of the community. About 1934, Hershey mentioned his concern to Dr. J. I. Baugher, then Superintendent of the Derry Township Public Schools. Dr. Baugher explained that some communities had established junior colleges to help alleviate the problem of idleness which was largely brought about by the Great Depression.[19] Mr. Hershey asked for an explanation of the purpose of a "junior college" and, according to Dr. Breidenstine, the idea of the Hershey Junior College was born.[20] Mr. Hershey recognized that the junior

---

[17]A. G. Breidenstine, "An Idea Becomes A Reality," Commencement Address, Hershey Junior College, May 24, 1954, p. 1.

[18]According to the *Junior College Directory*, 20 two-year colleges were in existence in Pennsylvania and 556 in the United States in 1938. Table 1 provides a comparison of the number of public and private two-year colleges in existence in Pennsylvania and the United States for the years the Hershey Junior College opened and closed.

[19]Brubacher and Rudy comment on the influence of the depression: "Because during this period adults, let alone youth, could only hope to find a job by accident, hordes of the latter descended upon the college, preferring to spend their time there rather than in idleness." John S. Brubacher and Willis Rudy, *Higher Education in Transition* (New York: Harper & Row, Publishers, Inc., 1968), p. 263.

[20]Statement by A. G. Breidenstine, personal interview, July 19, 1967.

college provided still another means by which to improve and elevate the standard of education and the general moral and social tone in Derry Township.

There had been rumors about the possible founding of a junior college in Hershey as early as three years prior to its actual opening.[21] It is probable that Milton S. Hershey had decided to establish a junior college, or an institution with a similar purpose, when he created The M. S. Hershey Foundation by signing an *Agreement of Trust* on December 5, 1935. The Trust was established with 5,000 shares of common stock of the Hershey Chocolate Corporation with the purpose of creating and endowing in perpetuity a Foundation for educational purposes.[22] (R. W. Murrie reported the value of the endowment was $400,000.)[23] The Hershey Junior College was not specifically mentioned in the *Agreement of Trust* but it was through the provisions of this Foundation that the Hershey Junior College was established.[24]

Specifically, the "several uses, intents and purposes" of the Trust are:

(a) For the establishment and maintenance in whole or in part of one or more educational institutions in Derry Township, Pennsylvania; and/or

(b) The support of the public schools of Derry Township, Pennsylvania, and the improvement and elevation of the standard of education therein; and/or

(c) The vocational, cultural or professional education of any resident of Derry Township, Pennsylvania.

The Agreement between Milton S. Hershey and the Hershey Trust Company, Trustee, created a Board of Managers to manage and direct the Foundation.[25] Thus, with the creation of the Foundation, the establishment of a new institution of higher education in Hershey was made possible.

It has been established that the Milton Hershey School was Mr. and Mrs. Hershey's favorite charity and the one to which he left the bulk of his fortune. A junior college located in Hershey would provide orphan school graduates the opportunity for post-secondary education, free of charge. They would also continue to live in the Milton Hershey School homes.

There were, then, practical as well as benevolent reasons for the founding of the Junior College. In addition to the reasons cited above, there was an influx of immigrants from Sicily and Germany who came to Hershey to work in the chocolate factory. It was important that they learn English and the American political system and way of life. The flourishing chocolate industry and other enterprises created jobs for accountants, salesmen, secretaries, machine operators, etc. A junior college, offering a day and evening program, would be

---

[21] Dr. A. G. Breidenstine, "An Idea Becomes A Reality," *loc. cit.*

[22] *Agreement of Trust*, The M. S. Hershey Foundation, Hershey, Pennsylvania, December 5, 1935.

[23] Richard Wallace Murrie, "The Story Behind a Hershey Bar," (unpublished thesis, Princeton University, Princeton, New Jersey, 1939), p. 80.

[24] It has been noted in Chapter II that The Milton S. Hershey Medical Center of The Pennsylvania State University was established under this same Foundation.

[25] *Agreement of Trust, loc. cit.*

mutually beneficial to the individuals and the Hershey Chocolate interests. A free junior college education for Derry Township residents would also prove to be a fringe benefit and serve to attract workers to Hershey.

In speaking for Mr. Hershey and interpreting the Junior College to the residents of Derry Township, Dr. J. I. Baugher emphasized both the practical and benevolent reasons for the establishment of the institution by Mr. Hershey. His paternalistic attitude may also have been revealed through Dr. Baugher's remarks:

> Mr. Hershey, in keeping with the needs of the time, feels that it becomes the duty of communities to provide profitable employment for our young people, that if industry has no work for them until they become 18, 19, or 20 years of age, then education of a realistic and practical nature must fill the gap. For young people are, after all, the most prized asset of any generation. In keeping with these ideas, Mr. Hershey has established the Hershey Junior College for the immediate benefit of young people.[26]

Planning, Purpose, and Early Program

A study of the concept of the "junior college" as a type of institution, and the feasibility and need for such a college in Hershey, was undertaken during the two years prior to its opening. The Board of Managers had discussed the merits of utilizing the income from the Foundation to maintain the public schools already in existence, or establishing a junior college which would offer two-year courses to graduates of the high schools in Derry Township. In 1936, the Managers of the Foundation instructed George E. Copenhaver, then Superintendent of The Hershey Industrial School, and William H. Earnest, a member of the Board of Managers of the Industrial School, to conduct a survey of certain junior colleges. They studied the plan of operation and the academic program at Williamsport, Dickinson, and Scranton-Keystone Junior Colleges, two-year institutions located in central Pennsylvania which offered programs similar to the type contemplated for the Hershey Junior College.[27]

Early in 1937, Dr. J. I. Baugher interviewed the academic and commercial students and addressed the student body of Derry Township Public High School to determine how many students would attend the proposed junior college. Thirty-one indicated such an interest.[28]

It is interesting to note that the Board of Managers of The Hershey Industrial School considered the implementation of the idea of the Hershey Junior College. The April 4, 1935, "Board Records" indicate that definite consideration was given to the possible establishment of a junior college as an integral

---

[26] "Hershey Junior College To Aid Immediate Needs of Young People, Opens This Fall," *Hotel Hershey High-Lights*, Vol. V, No. 48, June 4, 1938, pp. 1–2.

[27] Richard H. Rudisill, "Hershey Junior College," (unpublished term paper, University of Pennsylvania, Philadelphia, Pennsylvania, January, 1961), p. 18, citing Letter, M. S. Hershey to Commissioner of Internal Revenue, April 12, 1937.

[28] *Ibid.*

part of The Hershey Industrial School. The minutes also reveal the Board's conception of the purpose and function of the junior college and that careful planning and study preceded the opening of the Hershey Junior College in 1938. The report was prepared by the Superintendent of The Hershey Industrial School:

There is a plan of establishing a Junior College in Hershey to be a division of The Hershey Industrial School and some study has been made on the organization and administration of that project.

There exists a widespread interest in junior colleges. They have definitely found their way into American education. The presence of the junior college in a community offers an opportunity for those in their teens (as well as some adults) to give themselves a thorough try-out, without great economic disadvantage and without leaving home after high school graduation.

The great expansion in the size of the student bodies in the colleges and universities of this country are gorging them and greatly testing the possibility of successful instruction and the large student mortality in the freshmen and sophomore years of these great institutions has been mortifying and humiliating to thousands of our youth.

The junior college offers the opportunity for students to find out more about their own interests and capacities and helps them through the preparatory stages if they know that they want to become lawyers, teachers, doctors, business people, research workers, commercial or trade people and so on.

It provides for those who have neither the capacity for full college course, or lack financial resources, the chance to round out their education by two years of college grade given in smaller classes with more personal supervision.

The junior college also relieves the colleges and universities of the elementary work of the first two years so they may carry out their greater work with the less fit weeded out.

The facilities of a junior college are practically those of a good high school with some extension of libraries and laboratory equipment and with a higher trained teacher staff.

To justify a junior college there should be an average daily attendance of at least four hundred students in the high school district and the junior college, after the second year, should have not less than seventy-five students.

The Hershey Junior College would have about eighty students during the first year and approximately one hundred sixty-five after that.

The academic courses offered must be such as are offered in standard colleges during the Freshmen and Sophomore years and in the commercial and trade fields they must comply at least with accredited business colleges and trade institutes.

Naturally we should consider whether there now exists in this community a marked social or educational need, not met by other institutions, which would be satisfied through the operation of a junior college, and has this question been submitted to and advocated by educators of sufficient standing and familiarity with college problems to merit consideration on these grounds.

There were called in for consultation, representatives from our State Department of Public Instruction, from the University of Pennsylvania, State College and a representative from one of the best junior colleges in this state, and all highly endorsed and advocated the proposition of founding a junior college here.

One of the basic functions of a junior college is a preparatory course giving the standard social and educational needs of Freshmen and Sophomore years.

Terminal courses should also be a part of the program. These courses apply to the commercial and trade divisions so that the student may at the end of two years, or earlier, have rounded out his education and be qualified to take his vocational activities in a competent and well prepared manner. In other words, terminal courses provide a completion school for those who cannot go farther. Some will be foremen, some managers, but each should be trained for his special abilities when opportunity becomes favorable. These courses would provide also for those who can go elsewhere to prepare for the highest levels. Many lines of engineering and commercial occupations require semi-professional training only. Seventy-two percent of the engineering projects in Pennsylvania are performed by semi-professional men.[29]

The minutes of the Derry Township Public School Board further document the planning and study which was undertaken prior to the opening of the Hershey Junior College. In October, 1936, Dr. Baugher requested and was granted permission to visit colleges in the vicinity, at no expense to the District.[30] The first specific reference to the Junior College is found in the minutes of the January 11, 1937 Board meeting. Dr. Baugher requested and was granted permission to attend a meeting of the Association of American Colleges in Washington, D.C. He pointed out that it "would especially give me help on planning for the Junior College and adult education."[31] In a letter dated May 18, 1937, to the Managers of The M. S. Hershey Foundation, Baugher requested $800 for travelling and investigation in connection with the study of courses and equipment required for the proposed Junior College.[32]

Mr. M. S. Hershey attended the Board meeting of May 16, 1938. The minutes reveal that the Junior College's founding and financing were virtually guaranteed. Basic policy with respect to admission, enrollment, location, curriculum, and faculty was also established:

Dr. Baugher gave a report on requirements for a Junior College, and Mr. M. S. Hershey guaranteed to pay all expenses for operating a Junior College for at least two years but limited the attendance to graduates from the Hershey High School and The Hershey Industrial School. However, all students shall be required to pay a fee of $25 which includes the cost of books and use of all facilities of the Community Club.

A general college course, a commercial course, and an industrial course would be offered in the Junior College.

There would be no less than about 50 or 60 applicants for entrance.

We would need six teachers and about $25,000 per year to operate such a college.[33]

---

[29] Rudisill, *op. cit.*, pp. 19-20, citing The Hershey Industrial School, "Board Minutes," April 4, 1935, n.p.

[30] Derry Township Public School, "Board Minutes," October 12, 1936.

[31] Derry Township Public School, "Board Minutes," January 11, 1937.

[32] Derry Township Public School, "Board Minutes," May 18, 1937.

[33] Derry Township Public School, "Board Minutes," May 16, 1938.

One week later, at a special meeting of the Board, Dr. Baugher reported that "Mr. M. S. Hershey is anxious to get the Junior College started this fall. . . ." It was decided that a letter was to be written by Dr. Baugher and the secretary of the Board to Mr. Hershey "accepting his generous offer to sponsor a Junior College."[34]

Another special meeting was held on May 28, which Mr. Hershey attended. It was at this meeting that the preliminary plans for the College were considered approved. The minutes state:

> After some discussion concerning the opening of a Junior College Mr. Herr made a motion that Dr. Baugher, after making a study of the courses needed, arrange a curriculum and present it to the board for approval, also that Dr. Baugher be authorized to release to the press the Junior College plans.[35]

The motion passed unanimously and at the regular June 17 meeting the Secretary read a copy of the letter to Mr. Hershey "accepting his Junior College offer."[36]

Public announcement of the opening of the Hershey Junior College was made in the weekly *Hotel Hershey High-Lights* of June 4, 1938:

> The Derry Township Board of Education announced this week that the Hershey Junior College will open this Fall, the expenses of which will be paid by M. S. Hershey, founder of this community, who changed a cornfield into an industrial town and has so beautified it that the State of Pennsylvania has called it "The Model Town."
>
> Hershey Junior College will be co-educational. Those who are eligible for entrance are the boys and girls who have graduated from the Hershey Public Schools and the orphan boys who have graduated from the Hershey Industrial School to which Mr. Hershey has devoted his fortune.[37]

Dr. Baugher advised the School Board of the need to have a "Dean"[38] of the College before the remainder of the teaching faculty could be employed and the details of the curriculum decided upon. It was felt that the person who was to assume the position should have had experience with and know "the philosophy and background of the junior college movement."[39] The Dean also had to be committed to Mr. Hershey's concept of the proposed junior college which was to offer up to two years of education to residents of Derry Township at no cost. Hershey envisaged the institution would emphasize courses of a practical nature leading to employment.[40]

---

[34] Derry Township Public School, "Board Minutes," May 23, 1938.

[35] Derry Township Public School, "Board Minutes," May 28, 1938.

[36] Derry Township Public School, "Board Minutes," June 17, 1938.

[37] "Hershey Junior College To Aid Immediate Needs of Young People . . . ," *loc. cit.*

[38] There was no president of the Hershey Junior College. "Data Presented for Consideration of the Commission on Institutions of Higher Education" in 1943, states:
> The rules and statutes are exactly similar to those recorded in the *School Laws of Pennsylvania* relating to the School Directors, the principal, and the supervisory officers. In the Junior College, the Dean serves in the capacity of the principal and the Superintendent of the Schools as the chief executive officer.

In effect, the "Dean" functioned as the chief administrative officer of the College.

[39] Derry Township Public School, "Board Minutes," June 3, 1938.

[40] Statement by A. G. Breidenstine, personal interview, February 8, 1967.

Dr. A. G. Breidenstine was elected Dean at the July 29, 1938 meeting of the Board. At that same meeting it was reported by Dr. Baugher that four men had accepted Junior College teaching positions. Dr. Breidenstine assumed his position as Dean on August 2, 1938.[41]

Much remained to be accomplished before the College opened the following month. Dr. Breidenstine reported that many students and parents were skeptical about its opening which was announced August 1, 1938:

> They had to be shown and early registrations were practically nil. Some timid souls from among the educators actually talked about opening a college without students. For these and other reasons, large posters were hung prominently all over Hershey and registration hours were announced for the opening date as extending from 8:00 A.M. to 8:00 P.M. This extended period was considered necessary to capture the factory workers from all of the shifts and, at the same time, give due warning to those who were still undecided about enrolling.[42]

The Hershey Junior College was not established to compete with other colleges, but rather:

> to extend secondary education of a terminal nature, while at the same time, in separate classes of instruction, offering the possibility of transfer courses to worthy students desiring a degree in a senior college.[43]

Dr. H. H. Hostetter, M. S. Hershey's personal physician, reported that Mr. Hershey personally consulted with five area college presidents regarding the establishment of a junior college. He emphasized that the proposed institution was not to compete with their colleges but that the Hershey Junior College would, in fact, serve as a "feeder" school.[44] Nevertheless, at least two neighboring senior colleges, Elizabethtown and Lebanon Valley, opposed the establishment of the Hershey Junior College, probably because they feared the loss of students from the Hershey area. However, experience has shown that these private, liberal arts colleges have, in fact, profited as a result of many Hershey Junior College graduates transferring to these institutions.[45]

It should be emphasized that in 1938 there was no legal basis for the establishment of the Hershey Junior College as a public, two-year institution in the Commonwealth of Pennsylvania. The College was not issued a charter.[46] The operation of a junior college with tax money by a school district would, then, have constituted a violation of the school code. However, this did not pose a problem because the Hershey Junior College was financed through private endowment and, therefore, conformed to the legal requirements of the Commonwealth. The College was truly public in that it was controlled through

---

41 Derry Township Public School, "Board Minutes," August 8, 1938.

42 A. G. Breidenstine, "An Idea Becomes A Reality," *op. cit.*, pp. 2-3.

43 "Brief Submitted in Support of Application to State Council," October 12, 1939.

44 Statement by H. H. Hostetter, personal interview, July 18, 1967. H. H. Hostetter, M.D., served as Mr. Hershey's personal physician and confidant for 21 years. Dr. Hostetter kept a diary on their conversations from 1918 until Mr. Hershey's death in 1945.

45 A. G. Breidenstine, personal interview, February 8, 1967.

46 *Ibid.*

the Board of Directors of the Derry Township Public School District and it offered free, post-high school education to residents of Derry Township.[47] However, public tax monies were not used to finance the institution. In view of the above, the Junior College may be described more accurately as "quasi-public." As such, it was able to be the beneficiary of grants, gifts, and bequests.

It has already been noted that M. S. Hershey personally financed the College during its first few years of existence and that he provided for the endowment of the College through the *Agreement of Trust* which created The M. S. Hershey Foundation. The Foundation virtually provided all operating funds.[48]

To show its appreciation to Mr. Hershey for his generous support of education in Derry Township, the Derry Township Public School Board passed a resolution in 1942. The resolution included the following with respect to the Junior College:

> . . . Mr. Milton S. Hershey by his gifts, throughout the years has been the sole support of the Hershey Junior College . . ."[49]

Reporting on the M. S. Hershey Fund in 1945, the *Evening News* (Harrisburg) stated that:

> . . . the Hershey Foundation bears all of the $30,000 a year cost to maintain the Junior College, which was created at Mr. Hershey's suggestion, and is supervised by the township board. The school is to be perpetuated, the directors have assured.[50]

The complicated and interlocking funds, foundations, trusts, etc., already noted in Chapter II, make it extremely difficult to gain a clear understanding of the financing of the Junior College. The 1952 visiting committee of the Middle States Association of Colleges and Secondary Schools found this to be true. The report states:

> As there are no separate records or accounts kept for the junior college (all are combined with the general accounts of the Hershey Estates), the committee did not consider it to be its function to examine in detail the bookkeeping records.[51]

Furthermore, the Hershey Junior College did not operate within a budget as is the usual practice, although the Dean and the Superintendent of Schools did prepare a budget. Certain College expenditures fell within the separate budgets of The M.S. Hershey Foundation, the Derry Township School Board, or the Junior College. Income from the Hershey Foundation was paid by

---

[47]O. H. Aurand *et al., A Study of the Schools of Derry Township, Dauphin County, Pennsylvania, 1951–1952*, p. 128.

[48]"Brief Submitted in Support of Application to State Council," October 12, 1939, p. 3.

[49]Derry Township Public School, "Board Minutes," December 7, 1942.

[50]"Hershey Estates Goes To Schools," *The Evening News* (Harrisburg) October 17, 1945, p. 1.

[51]"Report of the 1952 Visiting Committee, Hershey Junior College, Hershey, Pennsylvania," prepared for The Commission on Institutions of Higher Education of The Middle States Association of Colleges and Secondary Schools, April 15, 1952, p. 9.

check directly to the School District. The Treasurer of the school board served also as the Junior College treasurer.[52]

The College had no endowment. There was no tuition income because no tuition was charged. Annual income from the Hershey Foundation totaled approximately $30,000 in the early years and increased to nearly $200,000 by the time the College closed in 1965.[53]

The foregoing review of the planning for the Hershey Junior College necessarily included a description of the basic purpose of the College and its proposed program. Further consideration is here given to the purpose and curriculum of the institution as envisaged before it opened. (Initially, there were no formally stated objectives of the Junior College.)

According to Dr. H. H. Hostetter, Mr. Hershey founded the Hershey Junior College for three principal reasons:

1. To afford young people and adults of the district an opportunity to attend college who for financial reasons might otherwise not be able to do so.

2. To make it possible for youth to attend the Junior College, who, due to various unfortunate circumstances had not achieved according to their capabilities in high school.

3. To make available and encourage his employees and their dependents to take advantage of post-secondary education.[54]

The minutes of The Hershey Industrial School, referred to previously, include the following statement of purpose:

The purpose of this junior college is to provide advanced instruction to persons who have graduated from nearby high schools, particularly the Hershey Industrial School and the Derry Township High School. Courses will also be offered to adults in the community who care to take advanced training in their field of employment.[55]

Special attention was to be paid to "local and individual needs" of pupils enrolled and the College was to be primarily "terminal in nature."[56] The purpose of the College was also exemplified in its functional approach by offering courses of instruction based upon "life needs of students and the demands of the society in which they live."[57]

Five purposes of the Hershey Junior College are stated in the 1938–1939 *Bulletin*, the first published. The purposes are compatible with Mr. Hershey's conception of the College. The same purposes were submitted with an appli-

[52] "Data Presented For Consideration Of The Commission on Institutions of Higher Education of The Middle States Association of Colleges and Secondary Schools," March 25, 1943, pp. 37–38.

[53] A. G. Breidenstine, personal interview, July 19, 1967.

[54] Dr. H. H. Hostetter, personal interview, July 18, 1967.

[55] Rudisill, *op. cit.*, p. 21, citing The Hershey Industrial School, "Board Records," April 4, 1935, n.p.

[56] Derry Township Public School, "Board Minutes," June 3, 1938.

[57] "The Junior College," (special publication for American Education Week) November 10–14, 1947.

cation to the State Council on Education seeking State recognition.[58]   The purposes of the Hershey Junior College were:

1. To provide a two-year program of instruction which will be a logical and progressive sequence of the curriculum of the secondary school.

2. To conserve the enthusiasm of youth by integrating formal education, career planning, placements, and follow-up in the vocations.

3. To promote the development of personality (1) through wholesome social experiences, (2) by prolonging parental influences, (3) by dispelling provincial outlooks, and (4) by cooperating and participating with the various educational agencies and influences of the community.

4. To offer the advantage of adult education on the college level to the citizens of our community in accordance with their needs, interests, and desires.

5. To foster habits of self-criticism and adjustment in a growing democratic community.[59]

The formal admission requirement, as stated in the first *Bulletin* of the Junior College, was in accord with Mr. Hershey's intent. The admission statement is a further elaboration of the purpose of the College:

The College is designed to supply the educational needs of the graduates of the Hershey High School, the residents of Derry Township who have been graduated from a standard four-year high school, and the graduates of the Hershey Industrial High School who are recommended for admission by the authorities of the Hershey Industrial School. All controversial problems of residence are subject to the approval of the Committee on Admissions. Hence all who desire to further their educational pursuits and can meet the residence requirements above stated may file application for admission to the College. Application for admission should be sent to the Dean. All entrants are subject to placement in the division of the College best suited for them both as to interests and ability.[60]

The proposed curriculum fulfilled the stated purpose of the College. According to the "Proposed Plan" three courses of study or programs were to be offered: (1) General, (2) Business, and (3) Industrial.[61]

The public announcement of the opening of the Junior College described the three "types of courses" as follows:

1. A general or academic course for students who wish to take only two years of college work or for students who wish to transfer later to other colleges.

2. Business administration and secretarial course for students who wish to take secretarial work or others who desire to take business science for the higher educational institutions.

3. Industrial course for students who have taken Vocational courses and desire to take up courses that lead to engineering or to continue the trades that they have studied. The first of the industrial courses will take the student

---

[58] "Brief Submitted in Support of Application to State Council," *op. cit.*, pp. 24–25.
[59] *Hershey Junior College Bulletin, 1938–1939*, Vol. I, No. 1, May, 1939, p. 7.
[60] *Hershey Junior College Bulletin, 1938–1939*, p. 8.
[61] Derry Township Public School, "Board Minutes," *loc. cit.*

in engineering to institutions of higher education. The second course aims to turn out machinists, printers, electricians, plumbers, carpenters, and draftsmen.[62]

Another article appeared in the September 10, 1938 issue of *Hotel Hershey High-Lights*, four days before classes began. It summarized the course offerings of the Junior College, emphasizing the vocational and practical aspects of the program:

> Courses will be given as usually offered in the first two years of a regular academic course, engineering course, as well as courses leading to an advanced course in business administration and finance. Special attention will also be given to advanced work in secretarial science.

> Arrangements will also be made for students who are interested in the industries of the community to continue part of their observation and participation in special industries while they are pursuing their related course of a theoretical nature in the Junior College. This is especially applicable to vocational students who do not desire to continue training after completing the work in the Hershey Junior College.[63]

The only cost to the Junior College students was for books and supplies, an expense which ranged from $25 to $40.[64]

Students enrolled in the General and Technical Divisions were required to complete a minimum of 64 credit hours and 64 honor points for graduation. The completion of 68 hours and points was required in the Lower Division. The Hershey Junior College diploma was to be awarded to its graduates.[65]

The Junior College was to utilize the facilities of the beautiful and spacious Hershey Community Building, centrally located in the heart of the Hershey business district. Classes were to be held on the second floor; the theatre, swimming pool, the Hershey Public Library, and other facilities within the Community Building could easily be shared. Approximately 7,000 volumes were included in the Public Library's collection when the College opened.[66]

As previously indicated, there was a serious question whether the beginning enrollment would justify opening the College. Dr. Baugher had reported to the Board of Directors that "approximately fifty or sixty students would be expected to enroll."[67]

The "Proposed Plan" called for a very able faculty.

> The teachers must be of outstanding personality and training. There will be a very real temptation to yield to the pleadings of high school teachers for positions. A number of teachers should have the doctorate degree.[68]

[62]"Hershey Junior College To Aid Immediate Needs of Young People, . . . ," *loc. cit.*

[63]"Hershey Junior College Opens on Wednesday," *Hotel Hershey High-Lights*, Vol. VI, No. 10, September 10, 1938, p. 2.

[64]*Ibid.*, p. 5.

[65]To be eligible for graduation, students were required to earn as many honor points as credit hours in the required work of the curriculum. A grade of A represented three honor points for each credit hour; a B, two honor points; a C, one honor point; a D, no honor points; and an E, minus one honor point. *Hershey Junior College Bulletin, 1938-1939*, p. 15

[66]"Brief Submitted in Support of Application to State Council," *op. cit.*, p. 20.

[67]Derry Township Public School, "Board Minutes," May 16, 1938.

[68]Derry Township Public School, "Board Minutes," June 3, 1938.

According to the plan, nine full-time faculty members would be required. They would include teachers of the following subjects: commerce and finance, mathematics and science, English and foreign language, social studies and history, secretarial science, physical education, and industrial subjects. The librarian of the Public Library could also serve the College. The Dean of the College would teach a subject as well as serve as head teacher, general advisor, and registrar.[69]

Many individuals played an important part in the founding of the Hershey Junior College. Those who were officially concerned with the examination of the original data which led to the establishment of the College were duly recognized in an issue of *The Literary Artisan* as follows:

Founder
Milton Snavely Hershey

Board of Managers
M. S. Hershey, *President*
S. C. Stecher, *Secretary*

Ezra F. Hershey	Wm. F. R. Murrie
P. A. Staples	P. N. Hershey

Wm. H. Earnest

Board of Education

Edward Stover, *President*		Clayton G. Gingrich, *Secretary*
Morris Baum, *Vice-President*		H. N. Herr, *Treasurer*
W. D. Stettler	A. T. Heilman	Frank Nisley

Advisors
J. I. Baugher, Superintendent of Derry Township Public Schools
George E. Copenhaver, Superintendent of The Hershey Industrial School
Professional advisors from the Department of Public Instruction[70]

Thus, through the benevolence and foresight of Milton S. Hershey, the first publicly-controlled, privately-financed "depression college" was to serve as a model in what was already acknowledged to be a model community. The Hershey Junior College was ready to officially open its doors to its first students.

---

[69]*Ibid.*

[70]"Junior College Movement," *The Literary Artisan*, Vol. II, No. 1, (Hershey: Hershey Junior College, May, 1950), p. 3.

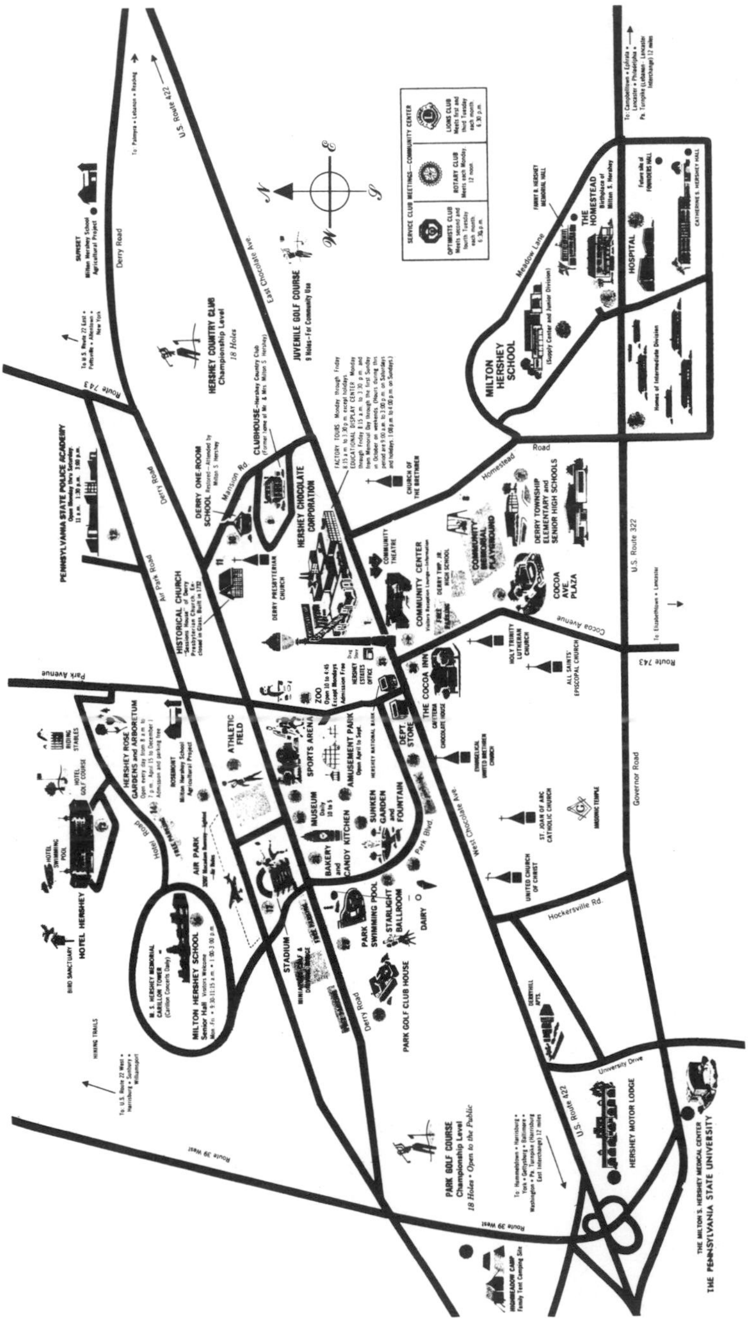

Figure 2. Map of Hershey, Pennsylvania

44

CHAPTER IV

THE INSTITUTIONAL PROGRAM
1938-1947

The first Dean of the Hershey Junior College faced a formidable task in administering the neophyte institution. In little more than a month prior to the opening of the College a student body had to be recruited and registered, the remainder of the faculty hired, a curriculum planned, rules and regulations established, equipment and supplies ordered, and many other details completed. Attention is here drawn to the man to whom this unusual challenge appealed. The remainder of this Chapter is devoted to the institutional program during his tenure.

A. G. Breidenstine, First Dean

Aaron G. Breidenstine was born near Schaefferstown, Lebanon County, Pennsylvania. He attended an elementary one-room school and the Schaefferstown High School and the Elizabethtown Academy. Upon completion of his secondary school education, Breidenstine enrolled at Elizabethtown College from which he earned the Bachelor of Science degree in 1927. He received the Master of Education and Doctor of Education degrees from Temple University in 1934 and 1936, both in education and psychology. Elizabethtown College conferred an honorary Doctor of Literature degree on Dr. Breidenstine in 1966.

Breidenstine began his professional career as an elementary teacher in Prescott, Lebanon County, in 1924. During the ten-year period from 1927-1937 he served as teacher and principal at the East Lampeter High School in Lancaster County. Upon completion of his doctorate in 1936, he became a member of the faculty of his *alma mater*, Elizabethtown College, where he taught education and psychology.

Dr. Breidenstine was elected the first Dean of the Hershey Junior College in 1938 where he served in that capacity until 1947. He resigned his position there to become Dean of Franklin and Marshall College in Lancaster, Pennsylvania, where he remained until 1955 when he became Dean of Academic Affairs at Millersville State College, Millersville, Pennsylvania. In 1967, after ten years' service at Millersville, Breidenstine was appointed Deputy Superintendent of the Department of Public Instruction of the Commonwealth of Pennsylvania. He served as Acting Superintendent for nearly three months during his tenure with the Department. Dr. Breidenstine retired in 1968.

Figure 3. Dr. A. G. Breidenstine, Dean
Hershey Junior College
1938-1947

Continuing his career in education, Breidenstine became Administrative Coordinator for the Brethren Colleges Abroad program on September 1, 1970, and he currently serves in that capacity. Centers are located in Strasbourg, France and Marburg, Germany.

Dr. Breidenstine has received a number of citations and recognitions. He has received the Citation for Achievement in Higher Education from Elizabethtown College; Service to Mankind Award, Wheatland Sertoma Club; Local and Eastern Citizen of the Year (1966), Millersville Lions Club; and he is listed in *Who's Who in America*. Included among the many civic, religious, and professional organizations in which Dr. Breidenstine has been active are the following:

Chairman, Board of Trustees, Elizabethtown College
Director, Bethany Theological Seminary, Chicago, Illinois
Associate, Board of Trustees, Messiah College
Chairman, Eastern District Christian Education Commission,
    Church of the Brethren
Member, Lancaster Rotary Club
Member, Cliosophic Society, Lancaster
Denominational Moderator, Church of the Brethren (1969–1970)
National Education Association (life member)
Phi Delta Kappa Honorary Education Fraternity
Member, Alpha Phi Omega (national service fraternity),
    Millersville State College
Member, Lambda Chi Alpha, Franklin and Marshall College, 1955
Member, Phi Sigma Pi Fraternity (national education fraternity),
    Millersville State College[1]

---

[1] A. G. Breidenstine, Personal Data Sheet, March 15, 1970.

Included among Breidenstine's interests and hobbies has been the collection of old Pennsylvania German books on topics from horse medicine to religion to poetry. He has also been interested and active in vocal musical groups.[2]

It was while Dr. Breidenstine was employed at Elizabethtown College that Dr. A. C. Baugher, President of Elizabethtown and a brother to Dr. J. I. Baugher, suggested that he apply for the deanship at the proposed Hershey Junior College. Several discussions ensued with J. I. Baugher and, as previously mentioned, Breidenstine met with the School Board and was elected Dean on July 29, 1938.[3]

In commenting on his experience as Dean of the Hershey Junior College, Breidenstine stated that it was challenging and interesting and one that he would never forget. He was particularly proud of the first year because it was then that students helped to develop and establish such things as the College seal, cheers, songs, publications, activities, etc. Breidenstine also remarked that because the Department of Public Instruction had no bureau of junior-community colleges, no assistance was available to him or the Hershey Junior College, the first of its kind in Pennsylvania.

Dean Breidenstine's duties and responsibilities were not accurately reflected in his title. He functioned as president, academic dean, dean of students, director of public relations; registrar; director of admissions; director of testing, guidance and placement; business manager; and professor of psychology and German.[4] "A Partial Analysis of the Hershey Junior College Dean's Position" lists 26 responsibilities under the headings of teaching, administration, public relations, and student personnel services.[5]

Breidenstine's writings reflect his personal philosophy of education and his aspirations for the Hershey Junior College. At the close of the second year of the College, Breidenstine stated that if the Hershey Junior College can be characterized by any one generalization, "it is the pioneer spirit." He continued:

> Students, instructors, and patrons in a large measure have shared generously in this attitude. It is to be hoped that as future years reveal their history the same spirit will prevail. No one who has experienced the thrill of new horizons will be content to stand still while new worlds of thought remain unconquered. Should we gain all possible accreditments and undreamed of enrollments and lose the spirit of pioneers, we are doomed. To be sure, we may be permitted to continue an organization, but that is not enough. We must be a vital organism in our community.
>
> Coupled with the pioneer spirit is the attitude of tolerance. . . .[6]

---

[2] Arlene Putt, "Our Dean," *The Literary Artisan*, Vol. VI, No. 1 (Hershey: Hershey Junior College), December, 1944, p. 11.

[3] A. G. Breidenstine, personal interview, February 8, 1967.

[4] *Ibid.*

[5] "A Partial Analysis of the Hershey Junior College Dean's Position," A. G. Breidenstine's personal file.

[6] Dr. A. G. Breidenstine, "What We Hope For in a Junior College," *The Literary Artisan*, Vol. I, No. 4, May, 1940, p. 4.

In talking about the stages of development of a college, Breidenstine suggested they can be compared, generally, with "the periods characterized as infancy, adolescence, and maturity in the life of an individual."

> The immediate task before the College, however, is one of singular importance. The strength of a youth must be directed. Frequent evaluation is necessary to usher him into full maturity. Just so the College must now, more than ever, avoid relaxation and a sense of "having arrived." This of all times is the time for alertness to local needs, a re-examination of our policies and internal objectives. In the analogy of life periods, institutions differ from man in the period of maturity. In spite of anything man has done, he always progresses normally from maturity to old age. Few retain the vigor of maturity past the proverbial three score and ten. Institutions, however, need never attain old age. With the possibilities of constant rejuvenation through alertness to human interests, needs, and desires, many institutions today serve mankind with the vigor of maturity. Is it not a challenge to all concerned to work unitedly for the never-ending maturity of the Hershey Junior College?[7]

Breidenstine was deeply committed to the need for and value of testing and guidance. He believed that "colleges, like people, are characterized by their individual differences." He stated:

> ... every student deserves a tailored program of courses. To have the student started properly on a difficult task is so important that most future considerations depend directly upon it. The program must be so planned and adjusted that vocational choice, intellectual capacity, previous preparation, and individual idiosyncrasies be weighed and provided for so far as is humanly possible. This does not imply, however, that the student's wishes must always be granted. Quite frequently freshman students, and sophomores also, are influenced by various distractions which directly shift them from achieving their life objectives. Those in charge of rostering courses must always consider the best interests of the student, and this frequently means that spurious immediate goals must be torn down. If the student has previously experienced pleasant interviews with his counsellor, there is not the likelihood that great difficulties will arise in the rostering of courses.[8]

In expressing his belief in the need for close follow-up studies of graduates, Breidenstine wrote:

> The junior college's responsibility to its former students does not end with the graduation exercises. The student's responsibility to his alma mater does not end at graduation either. Follow-up studies are valuable in two ways. The junior college needs frank opinions of its graduates concerning the value of the college education so that it can keep courses, techniques, and administrative practices in tune with the demands of the public that is being served. Graduates frequently need further help and direction so that they can become adjusted to the demands made upon them in their new environment. Students in college can also benefit greatly by the records of the experiences of former graduates. All in all, follow-up work is probably the greatest single challenge to modern personnel officers in the junior college field. Much remains undone in the realm of follow-up services and only the united efforts of graduates,

[7]Dr. A. G. Breidenstine, "In The Life of a College," speech written January 6, 1939.
[8]Dr. A. G. Breidenstine, "Toward A New Pattern: Personnel Services in a Junior College," *The Literary Artisan*, Vol. II, No. 4, May, 1941, p. 15.

students, and personnel officers through years of experience can finally develop the necessary techniques and practices.[9]

Breidenstine's writings and interviews with the writer reflect his realistic philosophy of education and of the future of the Junior College. For example, at the close of the first academic year he wrote of the successes that the College and, particularly, the students enjoyed. But he emphasized:

> For the future, as in the present, the success of Hershey Junior College will depend upon the degree to which she attains the objectives set for her. . . .
> . . . .
> It is hoped, finally, that the spirit of the beginning may characterize the future so that the clear vision of objectives may never give way to a rigid crystallization of administrative machinery.[10]

The announcement of Dr. Breidenstine's resignation from the Hershey Junior College, as of June 15, 1947, included the following statement which commended the College and Breidenstine for his leadership as the first Dean.

> Dr. Breidenstine conducted an experiment in public education which was unique in the Eastern section of the country. Citizens of Derry Township were offered two years of accredited college courses, tuition free, either in regular day college classes or in part-time evening college classes. This extension of public education into the first two years of college work was coupled by Dr. Breidenstine with a radically new concept of student conselling, guidance, and placement and a fresh approach to integrated curricula.
>
> The experiment was so successful that Hershey Junior College was soon accredited by every evaluating association, was chosen as the "Junior college with a unique program" by the *School Executives* Magazine [sic] and was placed among the list of the 114 best American public junior colleges in *Look* magazine. Dean Breidenstine succeeded also in making transfer arrangements with more than 50 senior colleges and professional schools; since the founding of Hershey Junior College in 1938, a quarter of all its students who later transferred to senior institutions went on to graduate with honors. Recognized as a pioneer in the field of public junior colleges, Hershey Junior College was making plans for new experiments at the close of the war.[11]

"Our Dean," an article written by a Junior College student, portrayed Breidenstine as a genuine human being. It also disclosed the high esteem the student body held for their Dean.

> . . . Behind this modest appearance is a genuine person. The Dean is an administrator of no mean ability. Being remarkably even-tempered and well-balanced, he is able to get people to work and to like it. He not only professes Christianity, but he lives it, a fact that is evident in his everyday dealings with students. To all he is friendly and sincere; to students he is always helpful with their ever-present problems. His students regard him as someone to be admired and respected, for they have found his advice sound and his psychology practical. They like him because he speaks their language and because he is equal to any situation that they may impose upon him.[12]

---

[9]*Ibid.*, p. 16.

[10]Dr. A. G. Breidenstine, "The Role of A Junior College," *The Literary Artisan*, Vol. I, No. 1, November, 1939, p. 12.

[11]News Release, Hershey, Pennsylvania, May, 1947, from the files of A. G. Breidenstine.

[12]Arlene Putt, *op. cit.*, p. 10.

Writing in the College paper on Breidenstine's resignation (March 13, 1947), the editor commented on Dean Breidenstine as an administrator and as a person.

... Since its inception in 1938, the first venture of its kind in Pennsylvania, the College, under Dr. Breidenstine's guidance, has attained the rich eminence of being rated among the ten leading colleges of the United States.

... But the singular ability of which we students are constantly aware is that rare gift of personal interest in each student.

. . . .

From the bottom of our aggregate hearts we wish him, in his new position as Dean of Students at Franklin and Marshall College, all the friendly wisdom and genial goodness that he has imparted to us.[13]

A letter addressed to Raymond H. Koch, then Superintendent, and signed by eight members of the Junior College faculty, expressed their great respect and admiration for Dr. Breidenstine and his accomplishments. It read:

The faculty of Hershey Junior College has learned of the resignation of Dr. A. G. Breidensinte as dean of the college; the news has been a profound shock to each of us.

In nine years since the founding of the college, Dean Breidenstine has, almost singlehandedly, built an educational institution that has been credited by every evaluating association and has received academic honors that are the envy of older and larger colleges. Among educational circles it is a byword that Hershey Junior College has pointed the way in the Junior College Movement.

Dean Breidenstine has inspired an almost unheard of confidence among his faculty members and student bodies. Students and faculty alike have understood that something wonderful and unusual was happening in their school. Not one of them in the past nine years would hesitate to say that it is Dean Breidenstine who is synonymous with Hershey Junior College.

It is the continuance of this high academic standing and school morale that concerns the faculty. The selection of Dean Breidenstine's successor will be a crucial decision for the future of the college. The Board of Directors are certainly aware of the significance of the selection.

. . . .

It is our earnest desire to assist in choosing someone capable of filling Dean Breidenstine's position.[14]

H. K. Lane	Charles A. DeHaven
Robert B. Patrick	Luella Frank
V. Haag	Elwood S. Hackman
Harry F. Bolich	H. J. Frysinger

Dr. Breidenstine cherished his memories of Hershey Junior College and remained sincerely interested in it throughout its existence and afterward. Breidenstine returned to the Junior College on many occasions as a featured speaker.

The students who attended the Junior College after Breidenstine's tenure recognized the contributions he made to the institution. This is evidenced in

---

[13] "The Format," Vol. I, No. 1, March, 1947, p. 2. "The Format" was the Hershey Junior College newspaper.

[14] Derry Township Public Schools, "Board Minutes," March 13, 1947.

the fact that the first printed yearbook, *HEJUCO*, was dedicated to Dr. Breidenstine in 1955. In concluding his comments to the Class of 1955, Breidenstine wrote:

> Thus the College began, became an infant, then an adolescent, and finally a mature institution. Its reputation, because of illustrious alumni members, complete accreditation, and a promising future is well known in educational documents and listings.
>
> Hershey Junior College has grown in many ways since I left the dean's office in June, 1947. I shall forever be proud to have had a nine-year term as its dean. To be honored by the class of 1955 however, is a distinction of which I have never even dared to dream. Even though undeserved, this honor is appreciated with feelings which cannot be recorded in words.[15]

The Hershey Junior College—The First Year, 1938-1939

It has already been explained that there were those who were dubious about the actual opening of the Junior College. Registrations were below expectations. For this reason, Dr. Breidenstine made a special effort to encourage students to enroll. The registration hours were extended and the opening day was set back by one day. To call attention to the registration times, 40 (24 X 18-inch) posters and 140 (4 X 6-inch) cards were printed for display and distribution. The cards contained the following message:

> . . . You are invited to appear at the preliminary registration for entrance to the Hershey Junior College.
>
> . . . The registration will take place on Thursday and Friday August 18 and 19, 1938, from 9:00 A.M. to 1:00 P.M., and 4:00 P.M. to 8:00 P.M., on the second floor of the Hershey Community Building.
>
> . . . You may come whenever it is convenient for you, on either day, within the time limits mentioned.
>
> . . . Everyone planning to enter the Junior College is requested to appear for personal conference and assignment of courses.
>
> Dr. A. G. Breidenstine,
Dean, Hershey Junior College[16]

Registration announcements were printed by the *Hotel Hershey High-Lights*, compliments of the editor, Alexander Stoddart.[17]

The first Hershey Junior College classes met on Wednesday, September 14, 1938, at 1:00 P.M. in the Hershey Community Building.[18] That night at 8:00 P.M. the "Opening Program" was held in the Little Theatre. The charter freshman class attended the convocation. The County Superintendents of Dauphin and Lebanon Counties, the Director of the Community Center, the Superintendent of The Hershey Industrial School, and Mr. Milton S. Hershey were honored platform guests. The Board of Directors and the Junior College

---

[15] A. G. Breidenstine, "An Idea Becomes Reality," *HEJUCO*, Vol. I, Hershey Junior College, 1955, p. 3. *HEJUCO* was the Hershey Junior College Yearbook.

[16] Registration announcement, from the personal files of A. G. Breidenstine.

[17] Registration information, *ibid.*

[18] A. G. Breidenstine, personal interview, February 8, 1967.

faculty were also in attendance. Dr. Breidenstine presided over the program and explained the offerings of the Junior College. Dr. J. I. Baugher, Superintendent of the Derry Township Public Schools, reviewed the founding of the institution, then hours old. The main address of the evening was delivered by Dr. Lester K. Ade, Superintendent of Public Instruction of the Commonwealth of Pennsylvania.[19]

Three days after the opening of the Junior College, the *Hotel Hershey High-Lights* reported that 162 freshmen had enrolled, 80 percent of whom were attending full-time.[20] Apparently there were late registrations because the agenda of the School Board meeting of the following week records the enrollment at 172.[21] Dr. Baugher later reported to the Board that 83 full-time and 105 part-time students had enrolled.[22] However, the official enrollment as of September 30 was set at 131, 66 full-time and 65 part-time students.[23]

Of the initial 83 day students who enrolled in the first class, 65 were graduates of the Hershey High School and 27 had graduated from The Hershey Industrial School. Sixty-two, 40 and 22 respectively, completed the 1937-1938 academic year. Of the 21 students who were withdrawn from the College, 12 did so to accept employment, eight for poor scholarship, and one for some other unreported reason. In the evening program, 60 of an original 97 completed the year.[24]

The educational background and teaching experience of the first-year faculty was strong, especially when the relatively short time available to recruit the faculty is considered. Listed in the *1938-1939 Bulletin* are 22 members of the faculty, including the Secretary to the Dean. Of this number, seven devoted full-time to the Junior College. The remainder of the faculty were shared by the public schools of the Township or the Community Building which was managed by the Hershey Estates. One professor was regularly employed at Lebanon Valley College.

Of the 13 members of the faculty who taught one or more classes, part or full-time,[25] four had earned the doctorate, four the master's, and five the bachelor's degree.[26]

The first faculty of the Hershey Junior College is shown below:

Jacob I. Baugher, Superintendent of Schools
A.B., Elizabethtown College; A.M., Columbia University;
PhD., Columbia University

19 Opening Program, Hershey Junior College, September 14, 1938.
20 "Hershey Junior College Opens With 162 Students," *Hotel Hershey High-Lights*, Vol. VI, No. 11, September 17, 1938, p. 1.
21 Derry Township Public Schools, "Board Minutes," September 19, 1938.
22 Derry Township Public Schools, "Board Minutes," October 17, 1938.
23 "Student Enrollment and Staff Members—September 30, Annually," personal files of V. H. Fenstermacher.
24 "Factual Report of Hershey Junior College in Its First Year," personal files of A. G. Breidenstine.
25 Derry Township Public Schools, "Board Minutes," October 17, 1938.
26 *Hershey Junior College Bulletin, 1938-1939*, p. 5.

Aaron G. Breidenstine, Dean, Professor of Psychology, Director of Guidance
B.S. Elizabethtown College; M.Ed., Temple University
Ed.D., Temple University

Charles Russell Atherton, Professor of Mathematics
B. S. Civil Engineering, University of Maine; M.S., Columbia University;
Ed.D., Columbia University

Lorna M. Bode, Assistant in Commercial Science
B.S., Catawba College

Alpheus D. Brittain, Director of Physical Education and Health Science
B.S., University of Illinois; A.M., Columbia University

Carl T. Britton, Director of Hershey Community Building
B.S. in Education, Akron University; M.S. in Education, Akron University

Angus H. Douple, Supervisor of Art
B.S., Kutztown State Teachers College

Iris Fridy, Director of Women's Recreational Education
B.S. in Health and Physical Education, West Chester State Teachers College

Louise E. Hoffman, Assistant Librarian
B.S. in Education, Kutztown State Teachers College

William M. Kishpaugh, Professor of Business Administration
B.S., University of Maryland; M.B.A., New York University

Harry K. Lane, Professor of Sciences
B.S., Franklin and Marshall College; Cornell University

August F. Meyer, Director of Men's Recreational Education
B.E., Akron University

Frederick D. Miller, Coach of Athletics
A.B., Colgate University

William B. Miller, Assistant Professor of Technical Education
M.S. in Vocational Education, University of Pennsylvania

Richard G. Neubert, Director of Music Education
B.S. in Music, New York University

Elias H. Phillips, Professor of Languages
A.B., Franklin and Marshall College; A.M., University of North Carolina

Ellen Scholten, Librarian
B.S. in Library Science, Syracuse University

Clyde S. Stine, Assistant Professor of History
A.B., Cornell University, M.A., Cornell University;
Ph.D., Cornell University

Robert T. Stone, Director of Vocational Education
B.S., Pennsylvania State College

Daniel Nash Tippin, Professor of Secretarial Science
A.B., Ursinus College, M.S., University of Pennsylvania

Richard Yingling, Assistant Director of Men's Recreational Education

Orpha M. Fausnacht, Secretary to the Dean[27]

---

[27] *Hershey Junior College Bulletin, 1938-1939, op. cit.*. pp. 5-6.

Four Junior College committees were established the first year. Admissions, Convocation, and Instruction were faculty committees and the Student Committee was composed of five students.[28]

Courses offered the first semester of the first year in nine academic disciplines included drawing, economics and business, English, general arts (arts and music), history, integration (orientation), language (French, German, and Latin), mathematics, and science (biology, chemistry, science survey, and physical education). Twenty-eight different courses were offered, nine in the late afternoon and evening program.[29] There were 551 total course registrations in the day offerings and 111 in the evening offerings. The course titled "Integration," taught by Dr. Baugher, had the highest day registration (52) and "Secretarial Training" had the highest evening registration.[30] (The curriculum of Hershey Junior College will be considered in more detail in a following section of this Chapter.)

The regular curriculum of the Junior College was supplemented by several adjunct programs, even during the first year. For example, various lectures and demonstrations by individuals representing business, industry, and the professions were presented to the students. Dean Breidenstine reported that these programs resulted, in part, from important contacts which were made with industry as well as with the following senior institutions: Lebanon Valley, Elizabethtown, Millersville State, The Pennsylvania State University, Temple, Simmons, Drexel, Gettysburg, and Albright.[31]

The importance which Dr. Breidenstine placed on guidance, testing, and follow-up has already been cited. In October, 1938, the 1938 edition of the Thurstone Psychological Test was administered to the day division of the student body. (Quantative, linguistic, and combined scores were reported.) Excerpts from Breidenstine's report to Dr. Baugher are revealing. He found that the day student body of the Hershey Junior College fell below the national norm at every point in the distribution. Exceptionally brilliant students were noticeably missing in the Junior College student body. Commenting on the above, Breidenstine wrote:

> This would indicate that our instruction, our guidance, and our materials of instruction must be adapted properly for successful progress on the part of the student. We are most fortunate, in this respect, in having instructors who actually teach and in having materials that are vibrant, new, and living. The more practical our classroom instruction the more nearly we meet the needs of students who lack high abstract intelligence.[32]

Test results showed that the Junior College student body fell below the

---

[28]*Ibid.*, p. 6.

[29]"Factual Report of Hershey Junior College In Its First Year," from the personal files of A. G. Breidenstine.

[30]Derry Township Public Schools, "Board Minutes," October 17, 1938.

[31]"Factual Report of Hershey Junior College In Its First Year," *loc. cit.*

[32]"The Student Body of the Hershey Junior College: Report to Dr. J. I. Baugher," November, 1938, p. 2.

national norm at the first, second, and third quartile level. The differences were 12.92, 14.31, and 15.82, respectively.

On the basis of the test information, Breidenstine concluded that the ability of the total student body represented a nearly normal distribution. However, he found that there were marked differences among the students enrolled in the Lower (college transfer) Division and those in the General Division. Lower Division students scored no more than four points lower than the norm group at any point on the scale used. Breidenstine commented on the Lower Division students.

> Recognizing the fact that little selection, as such, was practiced in the choice of these students they make a remarkable showing. When local scores are compared with national scores it becomes evident that in no step of the distribution is the difference greater than four (4) points in favor of the national norms. Considering that the test probably has a P.E. of about as much [*sic*] as we can safely conclude that our Lower Division students are as capable intellectually as the six thousand five hundred and fourteen (6,514) freshmen entering our thirty-six (36) reporting colleges this year.[33]

Students in the General Division, however, fell much farther below the national norms, the differences being 16.02, 22.36, and 27.46 for the three quartile levels. Breidenstine's comment reveals his understanding of the challenge which faced the new institution:

> Such differences clearly indicate that our General Division students deviate most markedly at the higher points in the distribution. This indicates loading at the lower levels of intelligence. Only courageous maneuvering can successfully cope with such a problem at the college level. Skill subjects, habit-building courses, and materials that influence character and personality, rather than abstract materials are needed for this group. An instructional methodology which stimulates, illustrates, practices repetition, and, in other words, does a masterful bit of superb teaching can hold these students and probably do them a great deal of good. Transfer of credits to another institution of higher learning is clearly out of the question for all of these except a few at the upper levels.[34]

Dr. Breidenstine concluded his report emphasizing the value of the testing program:

> The uses of this device are numerous. It is possible, however, that no greater good could come from the test than to use these measures in the evaluation of accomplishment. For years instructors have been longing for some measure which would make possible the grading of accomplishment and all evidence points to the conclusion that, while not perfect, such a device most nearly meets the need. Untold guidance possibilities also suggest themselves.
>
> If possible such a study should be made in the future for incoming classes. The results could then be used for placement purposes. Many students could be guided at the time of registration and with some assurance be accepted into the General or Lower divisions. It must be understood, however, that this is clearly a measure of ability and that high school marks objectively derived show a higher correlation to success in college than any other single measure.[35]

---

[33]*Ibid.*, p. 6. [34]*Ibid.*, pp. 6–7. [35]*Ibid..* pp. 10–11.

At the conclusion of the first year Dean Breidenstine administered the examinations of the Cooperative Test Service of the American Council on Education. The tests were given to all students in all courses except accounting and secretarial science in which case other appropriate tests were administered. The following table shows that the mean score of the Hershey Junior College students was higher in 12 of the 15 subjects administered. (The norms of the Cooperative Test Battery were based on students in teachers colleges and junior colleges.)[36]

TABLE 2

FINAL RESULTS OF FIRST YEAR TESTING IN
HERSHEY JUNIOR COLLEGE[a]

Course	National Mean	Hershey Junior College Mean
Contemporary Affairs	79.0	84.5
English (General)	51.3	51.2
English (Lower Division)	51.3	57.7
French I (Day)	50.9	65.1
German I (Evening)	48.6	58.2
German I (Day)	48.6	46.5
History Survey	56.9	61.3
Latin V	41.7	59.0
Mathematical Analysis	59.5	71.5
Botany (Biology)	77.0	89.7
Zoology (Biology)	104.0	108.6
Chemistry	92.0	95.8
Accounting I	72.8	56.0
Secretarial Science I (Stenography)	95.0	120.0
Secretarial Science II (Typewriting)	178.0	178.1

[a]"Our First Year Achievement Results, Hershey Junior College," A. G. Breidenstine, from his personal files.

It is interesting to note Dr. Breidenstine's explanation of the differences in the German I scores earned by the day students as compared to the evening students. (Dr. Breidenstine taught the German classes.)

> German I as taught to the evening-session group revealed an average score of 9.4 points higher than the National norm. The day-session group, however, was 1.4 points lower than the national norm. Several reasons underlying this difference are: greater maturity of evening group, superior motivation of evening group, and superior intellectual capacity of evening group. The day group started German from scratch and was required, however, to cover regular Freshman College German.[37]

---

[36] Letter to Dean Breidenstine from Cooperative Test Service of the American Council on Education, September 20, 1939.
[37]"Our First Year Achievement Results, Hershey Junior College," A. G. Breidenstine, from his personal files.

Dr. Breidenstine ended the report on achievement during the first year by reporting on 17 students who had not matriculated for the sophomore year. Among the 17, two transferred to other institutions (School of Veterinary Medicine, University of Pennsylvania and Lebanon Valley College), two enrolled in nursing schools, and the others obtained employment, many as secretaries.[38]

Overall, Breidenstine concluded that although the Hershey Junior College student body was "lower in intelligence than college students in general" they had done "strong and effective work." Concerning Junior College students who deserved to transfer to senior institutions, Breidenstine stated they were "as high in intelligence as other college students." Comprehensive test results, as shown above, were reported to be "considerably above average." Finally, in appraising the total first-year instructional program, Dean Breidenstine believed that it provided (a) for the brilliant and studious, (b) for the average and studious, (c) for the mechanically minded, and that it (d) cannot tolerate disinterested and lazy who after counselling fail to respond.[39]

Extracurricular Activities

Several extracurricular activities were included in the first-year program and deserve mention here. The *1938-1939 Bulletin* states that "student activities of the Hershey Junior College include: student participation in government, social functions, organized athletics, weekly convocations, dramatics, publications, and music."[40]

The minutes of the Derry Township School Board reveal that the first extra-curricular activity given definite consideration was basketball. The item, "Basketball plans for Junior College," was placed on the agenda for the September 27, 1938 meeting although there was no report of any discussion of the subject.[41] However, the October 17 minutes indicate that the hiring of Mr. Frederick ("Fritz") D. Miller as the basketball coach was approved. Basketball uniforms were ordered and it was decided that a basketball manager was needed.[42] Mr. A. G. Brittain served as the manager. Basketball is the only sport in which the Hershey Junior College engaged in interscholastic competition throughout the history of the institution except for several years during World War II.

Apparently baseball was never included in the athletic program of the Junior College. It was approved at the March 13 meeting of the School Board but was recinded at the April 11 meeting.[43]

A recreational education program was instituted the opening year, according to the first *Bulletin*. Intramural athletics for men included handball,

---

[38] "Our First Year Achievement Results," *loc. cit.*

[39] "Factual Report of Hershey Junior College In Its First Year," *op. cit.*

[40] *Hershey Junior College Bulletin*, 1938-1939, p. 10.

[41] Derry Township Public Schools, "Board Minutes," September 27, 1938.

[42] Derry Township Public Schools, "Board Minutes," October 17, 1938.

[43] Derry Township Public Schools, "Board Minutes," March 13 and April 11, 1938.

basketball, volleyball, boxing, wrestling, swimming, and others. The recreational education program for women emphasized athletics that had a carry-over value into adult life. Sports included swimming, tennis, badminton, archery, deck-tennis, shuffleboard, and Ping-Pong. Rhythms and dancing "to develop poise and grace" and special corrective measures for "the over-weight and under-weight, and for those with poor posture" were also offered.[44]

The first "Senior Day" was held on February 15, 1939, in the Little Theatre. The program consisted of vocal and instrumental performances and speeches. The printed program indicates that the Junior College's "Alma Mater" had been written the first year and the singing of it marked the close of the formal "Senior Day" program which was followed by dancing and refreshments.[45]

The words to the Hershey Junior College Alma Mater were written by Richard F. Seiverling, a member of the first graduating class. Mr. Richard G. Neubert, Director of Music Education, wrote the music. In the closing month of the Junior College, Seiverling, then Director of Publications of the Department of Public Instruction, wrote:[46]

> Perhaps I feel so strongly about the Alma Mater, since it was my privilege and challenge to write the words for same and Mr. Richard G. Neubert, then vocal music teacher, composed the music.

The words to the Alma Mater of the Hershey Junior College are as follows:

Between the Sand Hills
And Blue Ridge Mountain belt,
Glory and honor
All youthful hearts have felt.
Sing on ye comrades,
Let's make our colors shine,
Long wave the red and white,
Alma Mater mine.

Where knowledge opens
Life's journey and our way,
These halls of learning
Greet all of us each day.
Where truth and freedom
Will live and ever shine,
Yea, shout ye people,
Alma Mater mine.

Thy sons and daughters
Will fill their world with life;
With all your mem'ries
They will combat all strife.
These noble friendships
Forever will be thine,
Sing loyal voices,
Alma Mater mine.

---

[44] *Hershey Junior College Bulletin, 1938-1939*, pp. 26-27.

[45] Senior Day Program, Hershey Junior College, February 15, 1939.

[46] Letter to Mr. W. Allen Hammond, Acting Dean, Hershey Junior College, from Richard F. Seiverling, Director of Publications, Department of Public Instruction, May 20, 1965.

Based on the foregoing account of the first year of operation, it appears the pioneer Hershey Junior College had an auspicious beginning. Finances were guaranteed. Facilities were immediately available and proved to be adequate to meet the demands of the program. An effective Dean and an able faculty were employed. Enrollment exceeded the estimated projection. The purposes of the Junior College fulfilled the intentions of Mr. Hershey, the founder. The curriculum and the extracurriculum met the several needs of the student body. Most important of all, the effectiveness of the total program was evidenced through objective and subjective assessment of student achievement.

The first college year ended June 2, 1939[47] and the Hershey community was pleased with its newest institution.

Facilities

The Community Building, constructed in 1933 to serve as a Community Center for the residents of Hershey, has been described previously. The fact that it included such facilities as the Public Library, Little Theatre, cafeteria, gymnasium, recreation rooms, swimming pool, lounges, and sufficient space for classrooms made it an ideal place in which to house the Junior College. The Hershey Junior College did not have a "campus" in the usual sense of the term.

The director of the Community Center Building, who was considered a member of the Junior College faculty but on the payroll of the Hershey Estates, was responsible for the maintenance of the building. Initially, however, there was close cooperation between the director and the administration of the College.[48]

The Library

The Public Library, located in the northwest corner of the first floor of the Community Building, served also as the Junior College Library. It was open daily from 9:00 A.M. to 9:00 P.M. The seating capacity was 89.

The organizational status and descriptive materials submitted to the Pennsylvania State Council of Education, dated September 12, 1939, reported that the following collections were housed in the Library: 3,850 fiction books, 2,950 non-fiction books, 646 reference works, state documents, 76 periodicals, and "581 volumes which are listed in the syllabi of the college courses."[49] Approximately $1,000 was budgeted by the College for library acquisitions during each of the first two years. The Hershey Estates budgeted more than $700 per year for new titles at the recommendation of the librarian of the Public Library and the director of the Community Center.

---

[47]"Important Dates In History of Hershey Junior College," *The Literary Artisan*, Vol. II, No. 4, May, 1941, p. 9.
[48]"Brief Submitted in Support of Application to State Council," October 12, 1939.
[49]*Ibid.*, p. 20.

(In 1939, the State Council recommended a standard of 4,000 volumes and an expenditure of $500 or more.)[50]

A professional librarian served both the Community Center and the Junior College. She, and later her assistants, were listed as members of the faculty although the Library staff was paid by the Hershey Estates.[51] Because she was not employed full-time by the College, the librarian was not afforded faculty rank. In 1939, the head librarian was assisted by one adult and one student.

The data presented to the Commission on Institutions of Higher Education of the Middle States Association of Colleges and Secondary Schools in 1943 provides a detailed evaluation of the library at that time. The "Shaw list" was the reference used as the standard against which library collections were evaluated. Fifteen percent of the general College Library collection was recorded on the Shaw list. The following percentages of reference books, by subject classification, were included in the library: botany, 11 percent; chemistry, 17 percent; classics, 4 percent; economics, 7 percent; education, 2 percent; English and American literature, 19 percent; fine arts, 2 percent; French, 4 percent; geography, 1 percent; German, 9 percent; health and physical education, 9 percent; history, 20 percent; home economics, 6 percent; mathematics, 8 percent; music, 13 percent; philosophy, 4 percent; physics, 12 percent; political science, 4 percent; psychology, 12 percent; religion, 8 percent; sociology, 7 percent; Spanish, 2 percent; and zoology, 32 percent.[52]

The same "self study" reported that the annual library budget of the College totaled $500 and that the Hershey Estates placed "an unlimited number of books in the library each year." The average expenditure for library books over the four-year period was approximately $800. The expenditure for periodicals for 1940–1941 and 1941–1942 was $96 and $126, respectively.[53]

The total number of new titles accessioned by the Junior College during the five-year period covered was reported as follows: 1938–350; 1939–275; 1940–205; 1941–167; and 1942–115. In addition, the Hershey Estates added 400, 400, 575, 450, and 266 titles in each of those years. As of March, 1943, the Library contained a total of 8,959 volumes. According to the study submitted to the Middle States Association, the College subscribed to 42 magazines and periodicals; the Hershey Estates provided 40 additional publications. Twelve of the titles were bound.

The average number of free loans per student during the 1938–1939 academic year was reported to be nine; average loans to faculty was 256.

[50]*Ibid.*

[51]*Hershey Junior College Bulletin, 1938-1939*, p. 6.

[52]"Data Presented For Consideration Of The Commission On Institutions Of Higher Education of The Middle States Association of Colleges and Secondary Schools," March 25, 1943, p. 25.

[53]*Ibid.*, p. 26.

Books were chosen by the librarian for the public library collection; those for the Junior College were selected by the instructors and heads of departments and approved by the Dean and the Superintendent of Schools.[54]

Other Facilities

Most classrooms and laboratories were located on the second floor of the Community Building, and therefore, it was the hub of the Junior College. The Junior College shared technical and science laboratories with the Hershey High School which was located immediately south of the Community Building. In addition, high school students shared with Junior College students the commercial facilities which were located in the Community Building. This meant, of course, that students had to move from one building to another and, therefore, the scheduling of High School and Junior College classes had to be closely coordinated. The science laboratories were adequately equipped for classes in biology, comparative anatomy, engineering, physics, industrial science, chemistry, and secretarial science. The laboratory equipment, which was the property of the Junior College, easily met the requirements of the State Council.[55]

The main lounge of the Community Building served the Junior College students, the citizens of the community, and visitors. Problems sometimes arose as a result of the overlapping use. (At one time, Mr. Hershey gave some thought to the feasibility of having the Community Building administered by the Junior College.)[56]

The facilities of yet another building were shared by Junior College students. Girls used the Women's Club, located a short distance from the Community Building, for physical education classes and athletics. The men used the gymnasia of the Community Building.[57]

It was expedient to use the Community Building for the Junior College in 1938. Although not designed for educational purposes, the facilities were splendorous and superior to those of many other colleges. During an interview Mr. Hershey granted a few days prior to the opening of the College, he indicated that he did not intend that the Junior College should be permanently housed in the Community Building. In describing the Community Building he said:

> On the second floor we have provided a number of various sized rooms, which may be and are used as meeting places for lodges, musical clubs, and evening school, and will be used temporarily for the Junior College activities. Dormitories occupy the third and fourth floors, and a private hospital is on the fifth floor. We have also a similar club for girls and women called the Women's Club.[58]

---

[54]*Ibid.*, pp. 27-28.

[55]"Brief Submitted in Support of Application to State Council, 1939," *op. cit.*, pp. 20-22.

[56]A. G. Breidenstine, personal interview, August 27, 1967.

[57]*Ibid.*

[58]"M. S. Hershey's Life Aims and Achievements," *Hotel Hershey High-Lights.* Vol. VI, No. 11, September 17, 1938, p. 3.

Mr. Hershey expressed to Dr. Hostetter his desire to build a new high school, vocational school, and junior college facilities. Plans had been drawn. Hostetter reported that on several occasions Mr. Hershey said that "there will be plenty of money to do it." However, Dr. Hostetter explained that unfavorable economic conditions and World War II prevented Mr. Hershey from seeing his plans to fruition.[59]

The "Board Minutes" of January 12, 1939 verify Mr. Hershey's desire to provide the new facility:

> Dr. Baugher reported that Mr. Witmer said Mr. M. S. Hershey is very much interested in a new building for the senior high school, and the junior college, that he had been asked to present tentative functional plans for same; a copy of which is attached hereto.[60]

The plans called for a building for grades 11, 12, 13 and 14 for an immediate capacity of 825, 1500 ultimately. The building would have been modern and functional. Included were such facilities as: auditorium (2,000 capacity), gymnasium, swimming pool, cafeteria (700 capacity), library (for 20,000 volumes), art and music rooms, home economics suite, shops, classrooms, social hall, central administration offices (including one for the Dean and the Registrar), Board room, conference room, commerical department, locker and cloak rooms, and athletic fields (40 acres).[61]

Dr. Breidenstine also substantiated the fact that a new "senior education building" was proposed. During the early 1940's he and Dr. Baugher worked together on the plans for the windowless, airconditioned complex. The modern construction was not immediately approved by the Bureau of School Construction of the Department of Public Instruction. Ultimately it was approved, however.

To get students' reactions to attending classes in a windowless building, Breidenstine moved some classes to the Hershey Chocolate Corporation office building on an experimental basis. The response to the absence of noise and flies and to the climate and temperature-controlled environment was positive, Breidenstine reported. The plans for the senior education building included windows for the dining hall and the gym. Breidenstine explained that the building plan grew out of his research on the "6-4-4" plan which had proved successful in Europe. Breidenstine believed that federal funds through the Smith-Hughes and George-Dean Acts could have been obtained if the building would have been constructed.[62]

The records show that the new building proposal was submitted to and considered by the State Council of Education. It is clear that the Council had some reservations about the "experimental project." The following is the

[59]Dr. H. H. Hostetter, personal interview, August 18, 1967.
[60]Derry Township Public Schools, "Board Minutes," January 12, 1939.
[61]"Tentative Functional Plans for An Upper Secondary School for Hershey," *ibid.*
[62]A. G. Breidenstine, personal interview, August 27, 1967.

May 10, 1940 resolution of the Council on the proposal:

> ... it was voted that the proposed plan of controlled lighting and ventilation in the school building in Derry Township to be erected by Mr. M. S. Hershey be approved as an experimental project, with the proviso that the President be authorized to appoint a special committee to receive, in such manner as may seem appropriate, the points of view of any who may desire to present objections demonstrating why this plan should not be tried as an experiment; said committee to determine whether the matter should be referred back to the Council for further consideration.[63]

Apparently there were objections from the Pittsburgh Plate Glass Company but no representative of the firm appeared before a committee of the Council to present such objections. Therefore, final approval was granted by the Acting Secretary of the State Council of Education.

> ... there would appear to be no reasons why the Board of School Directors of Derry Township should not now proceed to develop the project along the lines of their request in conformity with the approving resolution of the State Council of Education, a copy of which was sent to you under date of May 17.[64]

The "Board Minutes" reveal that the building plans were again presented to the directors. The July 29, 1940 minutes read: "Dr. Baugher explained to the board the blue prints of the new school building which M. S. Hershey proposes to build."[65]

In April, 1943, Dr. Charles C. Tillinghast, Acting Secretary, Middle States Association of Colleges and Secondary Schools, Commission on Institutions of Higher Education, inspected the Hershey Junior College. Concerning the general facilities used by the Junior College, Tillinghast made the following observations:

> The college is housed in the Hershey Community Center, which offers facilities of the first rank for most of the work which is being done. Especially worthwhile is the equipment in physical education, although this equipment is shared both by the high school and by the community itself. This triple use gives rise to some problems of scheduling, but my inspection did not seem to reveal any insuperable difficulty at that point. The laboratory in biology is outstanding. By comparison, the laboratories for physics and chemistry, which are those in the high school building and used both by the college and the high school, seem less desirable.

The Middle States report was particularly critical of the library.

> In the community library, there are some 11,000 or 12,000 volumes, of which only about 1,000, at the most, can be thought of as particularly accessioned for the use of the college. Small library units with both magazines and bound volumes are found in the various recitation rooms and libraries. The librarian,

---

[63] Letter to Dr. J. I. Baugher from C. E. Ackley, Acting Secretary, State Council of Education, Department of Public Instruction, May 17, 1940.

[64] Letter to Dr. J. I. Baugher from C. E. Ackley, June 25, 1940.

[65] Derry Township Public Schools, "Board Minutes," July 1, 1940.

a very recent appointee, seemed none too well informed about these various smaller units and I could not discover that there was any record of the use of these books and magazines in terms of loans.[66]

Under *COMMENTS AND RECOMMENDATIONS* Tillinghast called particular attention to the deficiencies he found in the facilities of the College:

> The small size of the library plus the fact that the library of the college is the public library of the community. [*sic*] Recognizing that the librarian with whom I talked was new, it would seem that the work of the college itself would be greatly strengthened if the librarian or an assistant could be appointed, whose major interest would be in the work of the college itself rather than in the general administration of a community library. It would be highly advantageous if the number of volumes for the college itself could be materially increased.
>
> It is unfortunate that the work in home economics is so curtailed because of lack of space.
>
> The comparison between the biology laboratory and those used for chemistry and physics is to the disadvantage of the two latter and would lead one to express the hope that at some time or in some way laboratories in physics and chemistry equal to the one now used for biology could be provided for the college itself.[67]

There were few changes or additions in Junior College facilities as a result of the Tillinghast report. The "Board Minutes" do show that in 1944 a language room was refurbished to serve as a social room for the junior college girls.[68] In the fall of 1946, another High School facility was shared by Junior College students when they were given permission to use the cafeteria.[69]

In the fall of 1946, the Hershey Junior College submitted data to the Middle States Association, Commission on Institutions of Higher Education, for reevaluation after a three-year period had elapsed. There was little change in the information submitted pertaining to the Library. The percentage of general books on the Shaw list and the percentage of reference books by subject were identical to that reported in 1934. In 1945, $750 was stipulated for Junior College library expenditure for new titles. The budget for periodicals was increased somewhat. Library loans remained unchanged.[70] The librarian, as of 1946, was employed jointly by the Hershey Estates and the College. Also, at the suggestion of Tillinghast, all departmental books were catalogued in the Library.[71]

The expenditures for laboratory equipment and supplies for the first eight years was included in the 1946 report. The greatest outlay was in the first

---

[66]Dr. Charles C. Tillinghast, "Report On Inspection of Hershey Junior College," April 27, 1943, Middle States Association of Colleges and Secondary Schools.

[67]*Ibid.*

[68]Derry Township Public Schools, "Board Minutes," March 8 and April 12, 1944.

[69]Derry Township Public Schools, "Board Minutes," September 11, 1946.

[70]"Data Presented For Consideration Of The Commission On Institutions Of Higher Education for Re-evaluation After 3-Year Period," The Middle States Association of Colleges and Secondary Schools, November 22, 1946, pp. 20–23.

[71]*Ibid.*

three years and the least in the last two. In 1938-1939, $8,500 was spent for equipment and supplies and in 1945-1946, $500 was expended.[72]

No additional science laboratories were reported in the 1946 "Data." Cabinets for students' laboratory equipment were added to the chemistry laboratory. Also, the drafting laboratory was permanently located in the Community Building. Home economics, formerly taught in a laboratory, was assigned to a large room in the high school building which was converted into a home economics laboratory.

The 1946 "Data" submitted to the Commission included the following statement regarding the anticipation of a new building:

> . . . The war has prevented our building program. . . . .
> . . . .
> Our job is incomplete but with a new era approaching we expect to enlarge our quarters and exceed the 1943 recommendations given us.[73]

It is interesting to note that it was suggested during Breidenstine's administration that the Junior College move to the Women's Club or the Hotel Hershey.[74] Another interesting idea was to have Lebanon Valley College, located approximately 12 miles east of Hershey, move to Hershey and become Hershey College.[75] Apparently these proposals were not considered seriously.

Administrative Organization

It was explained that the Hershey Junior College was an integral part of the Derry Township School System and, therefore, the Board of School Directors was responsible for the institution. The Dean, the chief administrative officer of the College, reported to the Board through the Superintendent of Schools.

The fact that the College was financed by private endowment (Mr. M. S. Hershey and The M. S. Hershey Foundation) served to complicate the administrative organization of the Junior College, although this appeared not to be a serious problem in the early years of the College. Nevertheless, the Board of Managers controlled expenditures.

It should be emphasized that the Derry Township School Board assumed the responsibility for the governance of the Junior College as a result of Mr. Hershey's having decided to found the institution and have the School Board administer it. Although the planning for the Junior College extended over a three-year period, the Board of Managers of the Foundation, personnel of The Hershey Industrial School, and the Superintendent of Schools and the School Board were involved. The actual decision to found the College was made only months before it opened. As a consequence, the School Board had little time to devote to the details of opening the institution.

---

[72] *Ibid.*
[73] *Ibid.*, pp. 42-43.
[74] A. G. Breidenstine, personal interview, July 27, 1967.
[75] Frederick D. Miller, personal interview, July 26, 1967.

Figure 4. Hershey Community Center—Home of the Hershey Junior College

It must also be emphasized that the members of the School Board were elected to serve the public elementary and secondary schools. Although the Junior College, grades 13 and 14, was considered to be an extension of the secondary school, the Board could not have been expected to have the experience or the interest in governing an institution of higher education. In 1943, three of the seven members of the Board had attended college and/or professional school, one attended a business college, and three had no post-high school education.[76]

Not insignificant was the fact that matters which pertained to the Junior College were considered along with those of the elementary and secondary schools. Items concerning the Junior College were interspersed among the minutes of the elementary and secondary schools. From a study of the minutes, it appears that the Board made little if any distinction between the two levels of education with respect to policy decisions.

The fact that the Junior College utilized the facilities of the Community Building, administered by the Hershey Estates through a Director of the Community Building, was another complicating factor in the administration of the Junior College. Furthermore, it was necessary to share certain facilities of the secondary schools. Decisions with respect to room and time scheduling had to be approved by all concerned.

Basic policy with respect to eligibility for admission to the College in terms of residence and total enrollment was established and controlled by the Board of Managers. This authority, coupled with the Managers' right to approve expenditures, in effect, gave the Board of Managers a decisive role in the governance of the College.

It has already been explained that Dr. A. G. Breidenstinc was a highly respected and able Dean. His personality—open, outgoing, and friendly—made him ideally suited to be the first Dean of the College. The effectiveness of the Hershey Junior College program, in terms of student accomplishment and state and national recognition which accrued to the institution, is testimony of his administration. In spite of the several factors which complicated the administration of the College, Breidenstine was given a rather free hand in establishing the new Junior College. Mr. Hershey's active interest in the College, until his death in 1945, was probably a boon to Dean Breidenstine and the institution.

Based on accounts from people who knew Dr. Breidenstine and Dr. Baugher, the two men enjoyed a cooperative and productive working relationship. Equally important, both Breidenstine and Baugher were well known by residents of the community and they, in turn, knew the community. Good "public relations" was important to the success of the institution.[77]

---

[76]"Data Presented For Consideration Of The Commission On Institutions Of Higher Education of the Middle States Association . . . , 1943," *op. cit.*, pp. 34–35.

[77]Mr. and Mrs. John C. Lanz, personal interview, July 27, 1967. Mr. Lanz was a member of the Hershey Junior College faculty from 1949 through the closing. Mrs. Lanz (nee Hoerner) served as Secretary and Registrar from 1944 to 1952.

Dr. Baugher was replaced by Mr. Raymond H. Koch in April, 1942.[78] Koch's manner was apparently more pretentious than that of Baugher. It is interesting to note that, as of July, 1943, Mr. Koch made it a practice to give a report of the Junior College to the Board under the title "Dean of Junior College Report."[79]

Figure 5 shows the basic organization of the Derry Township School System and how the Junior College fit into the structure. (The organization chart was submitted to the Middle States Association in both 1943 and 1946.)[80]

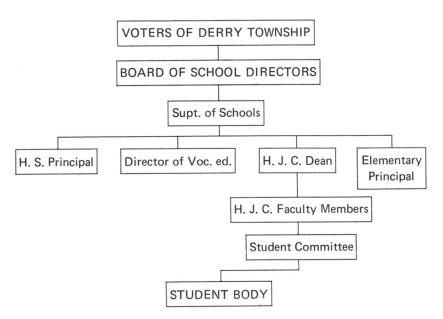

Figure 5. Derry Township Public School System Organization Chart

The following definition of the responsibilities of the Board of Trustees, faculty, and administration was submitted to the Commission on Higher Education:

> The rules and statutes are exactly similar to those recorded in the *School Laws of Pennsylvania* relating to the School Directors, the principal, and the supervisory officers. In the Junior College, the Dean serves in the capacity of the principal and the Superintendent of Schools as the chief executive officer.[81]

---

[78] Derry Township Public Schools, "Board Minutes," April 14, 1942.

[79] Derry Township Public Schools, "Board Minutes," July 12, 1943.

[80] "Data Presented For Consideration Of The Commission On Institutions Of Higher Education of the Middle States Association of Colleges and Secondary Schools," March 25, 1943, p. 4.

[81] "Data Presented For Consideration Of The Commission on Institutions Of Higher Education of the Middle States Association . . . , 1943," *op. cit.*, p. 32.

The following describes the academic and administrative responsibilities assigned to members of the faculty (other than the Dean):

> One faculty member is charged with the supervision of all student funds, another as dean of women, another as adviser of alumni and follow-up, one has charge of all student convocations, one handles all publicity, one supervises the college store and serves as coordinator of retailing in the stores, the history professor is in charge of civilian defense for the college. All of the Junior College department heads have charge of curriculum coordination down through the high school and the junior high school.[82]

Responsibility for student discipline in the case of routine regulations and minor infractions was handled by the Committee of Student Government. Final responsibility was vested in the Dean.[83]

Breidenstine advanced reasons for the addition of a Registrar in the same 1945 report. The appointment of a Registrar-Secretary, Kathryn Hoerner Lanz, was approved by the Board on May 8, 1946,[84] after the Board of Managers had considered the additional expenditures the appointment would represent.[85] (There was no extra compensation for the additional responsibility.)

The question of the relationship between the Hershey High School and the Junior College was one of both educational philosophy and administration. The following statement by Breidenstine to the School Board also underscores his continuing effort to provide new facilities for the Junior College:

> . . . Perhaps with the war in its present stages it isn't too early to again consider the proposed Senior Education Building. Several years ago about half of a year was devoted to detailed study on this problem. One major consideration always centered about the question—How much distinction and separation should exist between the High School and the Junior College? As can be expected opinion ranged all the way from complete separation in buildings to complete unification. Since 1938, however, several important observations can be recorded. Numerous cases of poorly adjusted students from both high schools made good in Junior College. This is not necessarily a junior college virtue; it is more a-beginning-again—another chance. This is also the opinion of present junior college experts.[86]

Breidenstine went on to quote Carl E. Seashore who argued that:

> The advantages of a complete break between high school and Junior College far outweigh the advantages of continuity. The strong arguments are based upon having a college faculty as opposed to a high school faculty. The laboratories and libraries are of a collegiate type; extra-curricular activities are distinctly different; recognition of the necessity of a break from the laissez-faire attitude so characteristic of the high school to a freshly motivated collegiate attitude, the necessity of maintaining a new type of relation with reference to

---

[82] *Ibid.*, p. 33.

[83] *Ibid.*

[84] Derry Township Public Schools, "Board Minutes," May 8, 1946.

[85] Derry Township Public Schools, "Board Minutes," March 13, 1946.

[86] A. G. Breidenstine, "Annual Report of the Hershey Junior College to Superintendent Raymond H. Koch," July, 1945, p. 5.

cooperative progress, and the recognition of the fact that these two years represent characteristically the storm and stress period of adolescence in which guidance programs should be favored. . . .[87]

In a similar report of December 10, 1946, Breidenstine strongly recommended that:

The Junior College should be made public in the sense that non-residents may be admitted for a tuition fee. . . . Such a change in our present policy would in no way alter admission of Hershey Industrial School graduates and Hershey High School graduates.[88]

Breidenstine had long argued for a liberalization of the residence eligibility policy. In the same report he suggested that admission should be handled in the Dean's office, by the Dean or Registrar, rather than by the Admissions Committee.[89] (Admission policy will be considered in greater detail in a subsequent section of this chapter.)

Although the Hershey Junior College experienced a sharp increase in enrollment in 1946-1947, which placed additional demands on the College, a review of the "Board Minutes" and Dr. Breidenstine's reports suggests that, starting about 1944-1945, the School Board and the Foundation Board of Managers became increasingly involved in the administration of the College. The Boards were consulted for decisions on items that would normally have been the prerogative of the chief administrative officer of the institution.

Breidenstine alluded to the increasing difficulty of administering the College in a letter written shortly after his resignation had been tendered. Reference was also made to the entanglements with other organizations of the community.

This Hershey position is very strenuous. It requires that the dean teach all the psychology, counsel students, handle all administrative affairs, and fit the entire organization into a previously designed community. Now that I have resigned from my position, scores of local citizens intend to ease the lot of the dean and free his hand in administration.[90]

Faculty

Plans with respect to the number, qualifications, and hiring of the first faculty of the Hershey Junior College have been reviewed. The individuals comprising the first faculty, with their academic backgrounds, were listed in a foregoing section.

Because some members of the faculty were employed part-time and included on payrolls other than or in addition to the Junior College, it is difficult to provide an accurate accounting of bona fide, full-time Hershey Junior College faculty members.

---

[87]*Ibid.*, citing Carl E. Seashore, *Junior College Movement*, pp. 79–80.

[88]A. G. Breidenstine, "Annual Report of the Hershey Junior College to Superintendent Raymond H. Koch," December 10, 1946, p. 2.

[89]*Ibid.*

[90]Letter from A. G. Breidenstine to Dr. Ralph D. Owen, Temple University, April 2, 1947.

However, during Dean Breidenstine's tenure (1938-1947), six Junior College bulletins were published and they list all members of the faculty without distinguishing part or full-time status. (Bulletins were printed annually for the first two years and biennially from 1940 to 1944; for the 1944-1945 academic year a separate "War-Time Edition" was printed; no bulletin was printed for 1945-1946; and a biennial edition was printed for 1946-1948.) Notations by the Dean in the bulletins provide an unofficial count of the number of the faculty who devoted full-time to teaching: six in 1938-1939; eight from 1939-1944; seven from 1944-1946; eight from 1946-1947; and nine from 1947-1948.[91]

The following table includes the total number of faculty (excluding the College physician and the secretary) listed in each edition of the bulletin through the 1944-1945 edition. Entries for 1946-1947 were taken from the 1946 data presented to the Commission on Institutions for Higher Education. The highest degree earned by each faculty member is also shown in the table.[92]

TABLE 3

NUMBER OF FACULTY AND HIGHEST DEGREE
1938-1947

Bulletin Issue	Faculty		Doctorate	Masters	Bachelors	Less Than Bachelors
	Total	Teaching				
1938-1939	21	7	4	7	9	1
1939-1940	24	8	3	10	8	3
1940-1942	24	8	3	10	8	3
1942-1944	28	8	1	15	11	1
1944-1945	28	9	1	17	9	1
1946-1947	22	8	1	14	6	1

According to the bulletins, miscellaneous records, and "Board Minutes," a reasonably accurate tabulation of the total number of individuals who served the Junior College throughout its history on a part-time or full-time basis can be reported. Approximately 111 individuals have served as professional personnel of the College from 1938 through its closing in 1965.[93] (Appendix A lists all Junior College faculty who were included in a bulletin of the College, the year of appointment, and title or academic discipline.)

During the 1938-1947 period during which Breidenstine was Dean, a total of 69 people served the Hershey Junior College in some capacity. Of this number, 32 devoted full-time to their job for one or more years. Seven people were on a leave of absence for one or more years (particularly during the war period to meet their military obligation) and these leaves are not re-

---

[91] *Hershey Junior College Bulletin, 1938-50*, (bound volumes).
[92] *Hershey Junior College Bulletin, 1938-40, 1950-1960; Hershey Junior College Information Bulletin, 1960-62, 1962-64, 1964-66*.
[93] *Ibid., 1938-1966*.

flected in their inclusive dates of service to the Junior College. Several of the 69 served as substitute teachers for those faculty members who were on leave of absence.

Several faculty committees functioned during the 1938-1947 period. They included: Admissions, Convocation, Curriculum (changed from Instruction), and Placement. The Admissions Committee included several members of the Derry Township School Board. The Superintendent of Schools served as an ex-officio member of all faculty committees.

By 1942, an Alumni Association Committee was organized. Harry K. Young was its first President; Avis E. Ensminger, Secretary-Treasurer; and Professor Harry K. Lane served as its Adviser and Director of Follow-up.[94]

Mentioned previously was the formation of a Student Committee the year the College opened. As of 1942, the Dean of Women was named as Adviser of this committee.[95]

Also in 1942, with the appointment of Raymond B. Koch as Superintendent, a "Superintendent's Cabinet of the Hershey Public Schools" was formed. Its membership consisted of the following: the Superintendent, the Dean of the Junior College, the Principal and Assistant Principal of the Hershey High School, Director of the Hershey Vocational School, the Principal of the Hershey Grade School, and the School Psychologist.[96] The purpose of the Cabinet was "to coordinate the work of the school district and to discuss plans and philosophy which will resolve into school policy."[97] (The writer has located no records of the deliberations of these committees.)

A number of faculty members assumed extra duties such as: book store manager, director of public relations, committee chairman or member, club or committee adviser. However, there were a few members of the faculty who were charged with specific administrative duties in other than academic, athletic, or recreational areas. During the 1938-1947 period, administrative responsibility was assigned to certain individuals as indicated by their titles. Luella M. Umberger was appointed Professor of Foreign Languages and Dean of Women in 1939.[98] (Dr. H. H. Hostetter was also listed as College Physician in the 1939-1940 *Bulletin* although he served in that capacity the first year. He remained the physician throughout Dean Breidenstine's tenure.)[99] As of 1942, a School Psychologist and Director of Testing was listed in the *Bulletin*. She served the public schools of the school district.[100]

Prior to the 1946 edition of the *Bulletin*, Junior College personnel were listed under the heading "Faculty." The 1946-1948 issue included the head-

---

[94] *Hershey Junior College Bulletin, 1942-1944*, p. 7.
[95] *Ibid.*
[96] *Ibid.*
[97] Derry Township School District, Duties of Administrators, (members of "Superintendent's Cabinet").
[98] *Hershey Junior College Bulletin, 1939-1940*, p. 6.
[99] *Ibid.*
[100] *Hershey Junior College Bulletin, 1942-1944*, p. 6.

72

ing "Administration and Faculty" although members of the administration were not actually listed separately. The 1946-1948 *Bulletin* lists Kathryn E. Hoerner as "Registrar-Secretary" indicating that she assumed the duties of the Registrar as well as those of Secretary to the Dean.[101]

Faculty members were not commonly designated by the titles of "Assistant Professor" or "Associate Professor." The title "Assistant Professor" was given to two part-time teachers the first year. No teacher was appointed as "Associate Professor" during Dr. Breidenstine's tenure. A relatively few teachers held the title "Instructor in . . ." or "Instructor of. . . ." The title was awarded more frequently at the end of Breidenstine's tenure and to teachers of technical subjects.

The following terms were the ones generally used to designate both the rank and title of Junior College personnel: "Professor of . . .", "Assistant in . . .", "Supervisor of . . .", "Director" or "Assistant" and "Director of . . .", "Librarian" or "Assistant Librarian," "Coach of Athletics," "Dean," "School Psychologist," "Registrar-Secretary," and "Secretary to the Dean."[102]

Faculty appointments and reappointments were made by the School Board upon the recommendation of the Dean.[103]

Junior College faculty members enjoyed several employment benefits. As an integral part of the public school system, Junior College employees were eligible to participate in the Pennsylvania Public School Employees Retirement program.[104] However, the matter of tenure was never clearly defined, and the faculty never had this benefit assured.[105]

Provisions for sabbatical leave were similar to those which applied to the public schools. In general, ten years of satisfactory service was required for eligibility.[106] A sick leave policy for Junior College faculty was established in 1940 by the School Board.[107]

Junior College faculty salaries tended to be $200 higher than those of Hershey High School teachers with comparable academic preparation and teaching experience.[108]

Teaching loads of the faculty during the 1938-1947 period were typical of those in other colleges at that time. The teaching loads of eight full-time Junior College instructors during the 1939-1940 academic year ranged from 13 to 17 semester hours; the average load was 15.1 semester hours. The average student load per teacher was 56.5 with a range of 34 to 102

---

[101] *Hershey Junior College Bulletin, 1946-1948*, p. 7.

[102] *Hershey Junior College Bulletin, 1938-1950.*

[103] "Data Presented For Consideration Of The Commission On Institutions Of Higher Education of the Middle States Association . . . , 1943," *loc. cit.*

[104] *Ibid.*

[105] A. G. Breidenstine, personal interview, July 19, 1967.

[106] "Data Presented For Consideration Of The Commission On Institutions Of Higher Education of the Middle States Association . . . , 1943," *loc. cit.*

[107] Derry Township Public Schools, "Board Minutes," February 12, 1940.

[108] Derry Township Public Schools, "Board Minutes," May 12, 1943.

students.[109] By 1946–1947, the average teaching load had increased to 16 to 18 semester hours.[110] Class size was reported to have ranged from 4 to 30.[111]

The Hershey Junior College faculty routinely attended meetings such as faculty meetings.[112] Faculty members were encouraged to attend other meetings and participate in organizations, including the Parent-Teachers Association. The advantages of membership in professional organizations, including the Hershey Education Association, Pennsylvania State Education Association, and the National Education Association, were emphasized. The membership of the Hershey Education Association included teachers and administrators of the elementary and secondary schools and the Junior College.[113] Committees of the Association included the following: Legislative, Social, Professional, Flower, Publicity, and Executive.

Under Dean Breidenstine, faculty-administration relationships were considered excellent and morale was high. These were important factors which contributed to the firm establishment and success of the Hershey Junior College from 1938 to 1948.

The Academic Program

Changes in Purposes and Admission Requirements

The initial purposes and admission requirements of the Hershey Junior College and their close interrelationship have been discussed. A study of the records and the bulletins issued during Dr. Breidenstine's administration indicate the purposes changed little.

The closing section of the 1939 "Brief Submitted in Support of Application to State Council" in support of the College's application (for accreditment by the Council) elaborated on the purpose of the College. The following statements were made with respect to "Future Plans":

1. Within the near future it is our hope to have a building of our own so designed that the work of a modern junior college can function efficiently.

2. It is necessary for us to make more permanent arrangements for a future financial program of the College and we aim to fulfill our opportunities in this respect.

3. We aim to strengthen our college very definitely in the field of Technical Education through a cooperative affiliation with industry.

4. It is our hope to expand the program of General Education, placing particular stress on courses related to Home Arts, Citizenship, and Personal Adjustment. Our program in this respect is in a pioneer stage but already we have experienced the satisfaction of filling a need that has long remained unsatisfied.

---

[109] "Brief Submitted in Support of Application to State Council, 1939," *op. cit.*, p. 13.

[110] "Data Presented For Consideration Of The Commission On Institutions Of Higher Education of the Middle States Association . . . , 1943," *op. cit.*, p. 15.

[111] A. G. Breidenstine, letter to writer, June 9, 1970.

[112] Hershey Junior College Faculty Meeting, September 9, 1942 (agenda).

[113] Hershey Education Association Minutes, 1942–1943.

5. We are at present making a close study to determine just what relationship should exist between grades 11 and 12 and the Hershey Junior College.

6. We need to effect still further the integration of junior college education on the adult level.

7. It is our hope to so relate the Hershey Junior College to the community that it may in every respect serve as a Life Institute to the youth and adult population that it serves. We fully appreciate our traditional obstacles but we are also cognizant of the challenges and unique opportunities.

8. It is a well-known fact, fully appreciated by all of us, that Pennsylvania is already overloaded with certain types of higher educational institutions. We clearly see, however, that many worthy students are not now cared for by the traditional higher institutions. In the area of the present gap of our educational system we hope to render our greatest service. We have no ambitions to compete with the established senior colleges but hope to effect such a program that a greater number of our youths and adults may have the advantage of higher education now offered to a relative few.[114]

A sixth purpose was added to the original five (see Chapter III, page 41) as of the printing of the 1942-1944 *Bulletin*. It reflected the general concern with and involvement in World War II:

To provide guidance and experience essential in our national emergency and to cooperate with the reserve organizations of the armed forces.[115]

After the war ended, this purpose was modified to reflect the College's interest in and concern for the veteran: "To provide guidance and testing services for veterans who are students of the Junior College."[116] This purpose was later broadened when it was modified to read: "To provide vocational and moral counselling and guidance for students of the Junior College."[117]

Although no formal "objectives" of the College were announced until Dr. Varnum H. Fenstermacher became Dean, an objective was stated in answer to the question posed by the Commission on Institutions of Higher Education as to the College's chief objective. The answer provided read:

The chief objective is to furnish upper secondary education including grades 13 and 14 for the high school graduates of Derry Township. The education provided shall include transfer courses and terminal courses.[118]

The Commission also inquired if any significant change in the College's stated purposes was contemplated in the near future. The reply indicated no changes were planned "except to continue to enroll as many returned veterans as our capacity will permit."[119]

Admission requirements of the Hershey Junior College directly reflected the wishes of Mr. M. S. Hershey and the provisions of The M. S. Hershey

---

[114] "Brief Submitted in Support of Application to State Council, 1939," *op. cit.*, pp. 25-26.

[115] *Hershey Junior College Bulletin, 1942-1944*, p. 8.

[116] *Hershey Junior College Bulletin, 1946-1948*, p. 4.

[117] *Hershey Junior College Bulletin, 1948-1950*, p. 5.

[118] "Data Presented For Consideration Of The Commission On Institutions Of Higher Education . . . , 1943," *op. cit.*, p. 36.

[119] *Ibid.*, p. 2.

Foundation. The basic admission requirement was, in fact, a residence requirement. It will be recalled that students were eligible to attend the Junior College who were graduated from the Hershey High School, The Hershey Industrial School, and residents of Derry Township who had been graduated from other secondary schools. The Hershey Industrial School students had to be "recommended for admission by the authorities" of the School. In addition, an unwritten agreement between the Junior College and The Hershey Industrial School guaranteed the admission of "recommended" orphan boys. This gave The Hershey Industrial School de facto control over the admission of its students.[120] (Mr. Hershey's wishes with respect to the admission of graduates of the orphan school to the Junior College were presumably, not contested. The "Board Minutes" include a report by Dr. Baugher that Mr. Hershey "intended to keep sending some of the Industrial School boys to the Junior College.")[121]

Questions of eligibility with respect to the residence requirement were considered by the Admissions Committee which included the Dean, the Superintendent, a professor, and three members of the School Board.[122] As early as January, 1939, questions regarding the interpretation of the residence requirements arose. At the first Board meeting Dr. Breidenstine attended after his appointment as Dean, he presented the cases of two students who did not technically meet the residence requirement.[123] The applicants were denied admission. In a report to the Superintendent, Breidenstine stated that throughout the 1938–1939 academic year a total of 57 ineligible, non-resident students had applied for admission.[124]

Early in 1941, Dr. Baugher also brought to the attention of the Board a question of admission eligibility.[125] By December of that year the School Board held a special meeting with Mr. Hershey at his home to discuss Junior College policies. From the following entry in the "Board Minutes" it may be assumed that some thought was given to the relaxation of the residence requirement:

> Mr. M. S. Hershey expressed the wish that students from Derry Township should be admitted with free tuition to the Junior College but that students from other districts should be charged tuition, the details of the plan to be worked out with Mr. Crouse.[126]

At the February 11, 1942 meeting of the Board it was decided that the Committee on Admissions should be revised to include the Superintendent of Schools, the Dean of the Junior College, the Principal of the High School, and

[120] Frederick D. Miller, personal interview, July 26, 1967.

[121] Derry Township Public Schools, "Board Minutes," January 11, 1940.

[122] *Hershey Junior College Bulletin, 1938–1939*, p. 6,8.

[123] Derry Township Public Schools, "Board Minutes," January 12, 1939.

[124] "The Day Student Body of the Hershey Junior College, Report to Dr. J. I. Baugher," November, 1939.

[125] Derry Township Public Schools, "Board Minutes," May 5, 1941.

[126] Derry Township Public Schools, Special Meeting, "Board Minutes," December 26, 1941.

two Directors of the Board. At the same meeting a report on Junior College entrance requirements was given by the Committee of the Board which was previously appointed at the December, 1941 special meeting. The following resolution, signed by M. S. Hershey, by Ezra F. Hershey, Attorney in Fact, was read and passed. It, in effect, restricted admission to the Junior College because graduates of schools outside Derry Township were denied admission to the Junior College after the 1942-1943 academic year.

> Resolved, that commencing with the academic year 1942–43 the student body of Hershey Junior College be limited to graduates of the Hershey High School whose families are bona fide residents in Derry Township and graduates of The Hershey Industrial School recommended by The Hershey Industrial School; provided that any resident of Derry Township, approved by the Committee on Admissions, may attend evening sessions; and provided further that graduates of the Hershey High School, who are members of the class of 1943 and who are not residents of Derry Township may complete the academic year 1942-1943.[127]

The above resolution failed to include Junior College students who were enrolled in the evening program. That section of the resolution was, therefore, amended to read:

> Resolved, . . . and provided further that graduates of the Hershey High School, who are members of the class of 1943 and evening school students who are not residents of Derry Township, may complete the academic year 1942-1943 or their present evening school course of study.[128]

Apparently the Board was presumed upon to modify the residence requirement to permit residents of the Township, but graduates of non-Township secondary schools, to attend the College. Also, with the further amending of the above resolution, employees of The Hershey Industrial School and the Public Schools became eligible to attend evening classes.

> Resolved: that commencing with the academic year 1942-1943 the student body of the Hershey Junior College be limited to graduates of an approved secondary school whose families are bona fide residents in Derry Township and graduates of The Hershey Industrial School recommended by The Hershey Industrial School; provided that any resident of Derry Township or professional personnel of The Hershey Industrial School or Derry Township Public Schools, approved by the Committee on Admissions, may attend evening sessions; . . .[129]

The above resolution, as amended, was included in the 1942-1944 *Bulletin*.[130]

The war prompted many colleges in the United States to adopt an "early admission" plan whereby exceptional high school students could enter college prior to their scheduled graduation date. At Dean Breidenstine's suggestion, recommended high school seniors, upon completion of three and one-half years of secondary school study, were granted the privilege of enrolling in

---

[127] Derry Township Public Schools, "Board Minutes," February 11, 1942.
[128] Derry Township Public Schools, "Board Minutes," August 10, 1942.
[129] Derry Township Public Schools, "Board Minutes," August 27, 1942.
[130] *Hershey Junior College Bulletin, 1942-1944*, p. 9.

college at mid-year.[131] Shortly thereafter, the local newspaper reported:

> Hershey Junior College this week welcomed a new class of freshmen who left high school at mid-year to enter the accelerated educational program sponsored by the colleges of the country. Twenty-five freshmen were registered, with more probably requesting admission before February 1, according to Dean A. G. Breidenstine. . . . .
>
> The new group will receive their high school diplomas after the completion of a year of college work or upon entrance in the armed forces. . . .
>
> Emphasis has been placed on the courses relating directly or indirectly to the war effort.[132]

Dean Breidenstine was not content with past successes of the College. He wished to have Hershey Junior College become a superior institution. Consequently, he made what in his professional judgement were sound recommendations for the future. The following excerpts from a 1944 Report reflect his concern over the admission requirements and their effect on the progress of the College:

> By careful planning and management now, Hershey Junior College can become the educational model of the Eastern United States, reflecting honor upon all who have had any part in its establishment. Lack of adjustment to new demands of our time may cause it to decline in service and growth.
>
> As a record to date it is of interest to know that more than 150 persons have been turned away because of ineligibility under the residence ruling. Most of these would have gladly paid regular tuition fees. Yearly the Hershey High School graduates are separated as to residents and non-residents. None of the non-residents can possibly join their fellow classmates in Junior College. Boys now in the service write in asking if by any chance it could be that after they have fought a war for us they may be denied entrance into Junior College upon their return. Faculty members now thousands of miles away in battle express concern for their institution when they hear of the number turned away. Army officers living in Hershey for the last three years cannot enter because under army regulations they must retain their former residence to insure complete records. Hershey employees living in Hershey for the last two or three years are often minors and hence may be non-residents legally. Dozens of these were shocked to find that in no way can they have access to the college opportunities of Hershey. Many of these could improve their skills and become better clerks, stenographers, and business employees if given further training, to say nothing of the enthusiasm their training would create in favor of Hershey and its industries and facilities.
>
> Having stated the problem confronting us, I feel that the School Laws of Pennsylvania should be brought to shed light on the problem. Section 401 of the Law gives the school board the privilege to establish "such schools—as they in their wisdom may see proper to establish—as an integral part of the public school system in the district." The Junior College was thus established and approved by the State Public Schools, however, [sic] accept resident students tuition-free and charge a prescribed tuition for nonresidents. Section 1409 of the Law says: "The board of school directors of any school district in the Commonwealth may permit any nonresident pupil to attend the public

---

[131] Derry Township Public Schools, "Board Minutes," January 13, 1943.

[132] "Hershey Junior College Aids Students Of High School," *Hotel Hershey High-Lights*, Vol. X, No. 31, January 30, 1943, p. 1.

schools in its district, upon such terms as it may determine, subject to the provisions of this act." Herein lies the power to limit enrollment when it has achieved its optimum level. The amount of tuition to be charged is defined in section 1441 of the Law and can be calculated as now for nonresident students attending Hershey High School.

Breidenstine closed his report with the following recommendations. He believed the first proposal was preferable to the second.

1. Make Hershey Junior College a public junior college in the present day definition of "public" with the School Law of Pennsylvania serving as a guide for admission, and nonresident tuition.
   Such a change in policy would in no way alter the admission of H.I.S. graduates, nor would it limit the number which could be admitted.

2. Open Hershey Junior College to H.I.S. graduates, Derry Township residents, Hershey High School graduates who have been through the last three grades of Hershey High School, and nonresident employees living in Derry Township who have been successfully employed for one year. Charge tuition to the nonresident groups in the above classification. For the present, military personnel residing in Hershey should be admitted for the tuition of nonresidents.[133]

The educational needs and the admission of veterans was considered by the Hershey Junior College. It is reasonable to assume that President Franklin D. Roosevelt's comments on the decisive role the junior college could play in the education of the returning veteran had an important part in authorizing the admission of veterans to the Hershey Junior College. The following article, "Roosevelt On The Junior College," appeared in a 1944 issue of the *Hotel Hershey High-Lights*:

The junior college has now become a robust youngster in the family of American educational institutions. My particular interest at present centers in the part that the junior college may play in providing suitable education for many of the returning soldiers and sailors. These men and women will wish, in many cases, terminal courses which combine technical or other vocational preparations with courses which assure a basic understanding of the issues confronted by them as Americans and world citizens. It seems possible, . . . that the junior college may furnish the answer to a good many of these needs.[134]

By September, 1944, Dean Breidenstine encouraged the School Board to consider favorably the admission of World War II veterans who did not otherwise meet the admission residence requirement. Upon presentation of the matter to the Board, through the "Junior College Dean's Report," the following plan was formulated:

It was the concensus of opinion that the superintendent should draft recommendations on post war plans to be presented to Mr. M. S. Hershey asking about admitting veterans to the junior college, expenses to be paid out of the veterans' fund and at the same time explain to Mr. Hershey how the junior

---

[133] A. G. Breidenstine, "Report On Hershey Junior College," Fall, 1944.

[134] "Roosevelt On The Junior College," *Hotel Hershey High-Lights*, Vol. XI, No. 39, March 25, 1944, p. 2.

college and the community could be benefited if the program of operation and admissions to the junior college were placed on the same basis as the public schools are generally conducted.[135]

The decision concerning the above was made by Mr. Hershey and reported at the December 13, 1944 Board Meeting:

Mr. M. S. Hershey's reply through Mr. Paul Witmer, to the report given to him on the junior college was that we will not liberalize the admissions at this time.[136]

It is noteworthy that a "Junior College Standing Committee" was established at the same meeting. The Committee of three, appointed by the President of the Board, was "to serve as advisers to the junior college admissions committee pertaining to the residence of those persons being examined for admission.[137]

It is significant that the lowest total enrollment of the Hershey Junior College was recorded in the 1945–1946 academic year. Thirty-nine full-time and 29 part-time or a total of 68 students were enrolled.[138] This low enrollment was mainly attributable to the fact that many high school graduates were entering military service. Other young men were forced to withdraw from the Junior College. It may be assumed that this fact prompted a reconsideration of eligibility requirements and the adoption of a more realistic policy. An indication of the change in policy was the public announcement that students, in addition to the "early admission" students would be admitted at mid-year. The release stated:

Hershey Junior College will follow its wartime policy of accepting new students at mid-term in order to prepare more high school graduates for wartime responsibilities, says a statement issued this week by Dean A. G. Breidenstine.[139]

Coincident with the increase in mid-year admissions, the decision that the admission eligibility restriction would be waived for veterans was announced. The Headline of the *Hotel Hershey High-Lights* read, "Hershey Junior College Waives Residence Requirements For Male World War Veterans." The article continued.

Hershey Junior College, through agreements with the Derry Township School Board and the College Committee on Admissions, has waived residence requirements for men who served in World War II.

Formerly all entering students were required to be residents of Derry Township. Now male veterans from any locality may enroll in the college, the Veterans' Administration being charged with tuition and cost of supplies, it is pointed out by Dean A. G. Breidenstine.

---

[135] Derry Township Public Schools, "Board Minutes," September 13, 1944.

[136] Derry Township Public Schools, "Board Minutes," December 13, 1944.

[137] *Ibid.*

[138] "Student Enrollment and Staff Members—September 30 Annually," personal files of V. H. Fenstermacher.

[139] "Hershey Junior College To Accept Students At Mid-Term," *Hotel Hershey High-Lights*, Vol. XII, No. 29, January 13, 1945, p. 1.

There are no resident requirements for veterans, but all others must live in
Derry Township to be eligible to enroll with free tuition.[140]

Breidenstine was pleased with the increase in enrollment within a two-week
period that resulted from the change in the requirement and he reported
"morale was never better."[141] Records show that of a total student body of
152, there were 64 veterans attending the Junior College during the
1946-1947 academic year.[142]

Few academic requirements for admission to the Junior College were
established. Except for students admitted at mid-year of their senior year,
students were required to be graduates of "a standard four-year high school" or
to be "recommended for admission by the authorities of The Hershey Industrial School." Students were also required to have completed 16 Carnegie
units of academic work. Students who entered the Lower (transfer) Division
of the Junior College were required to have earned a "B" average in high
school and be recommended by their senior teachers. To enter the Technical
and General (terminal) Divisions, students were required to have a "C"
average.[143]

Students whose academic background was considered marginal were sometimes admitted on probation. An average of 11.5 percent of the entering
student body were admitted on probation during the first five years of the
College.[144] The Commission on Institutions of Higher Education cautioned
the Junior College about the practice of admitting so high a proportion of
students on probation. Tillinghast wrote:

> Continued care should be given to the matter of the admitting of incoming
> freshmen. If the report is correctly interpreted as it seems to indicate that
> more than 10% of the incoming freshmen have been admitted on probation,
> this fact constitutes a situation to which careful attention should be given.[145]

The practice was sharply curtailed and after mid-year, 1943, no students were
admitted on probation during Dr. Breidenstine's administration except for
five percent in 1945.[146]

Great emphasis was placed on appropriate division and course placement of
admitted students. Placement was based on a conference between each
student and the Dean and on the results of psychological and placement tests
administered for that purpose. Proper placement and general orientation to
the Junior College was also facilitated through the required freshman course
in "Integration."

---

[140] "Hershey Junior College Waives Residence Requirements For Male World War
Veterans," *Hotel Hershey High-Lights*, Vol. XIII, No. 30, January 19, 1946, p. 1.

[141] "Enrollment Record To Date, Hershey Junior College, July, 1946."

[142] "Student Enrollment and Staff Members—September 30 Annually," *loc. cit.*

[143] "Data Presented For Consideration Of The Commission On Institutions Of Higher
Education of The Middle States Association of Colleges and Secondary Schools,"
March 25, 1943, p. 3.

[144] *Ibid.*, p. 4.

[145] Dr. Charles C. Tillinghast, "Report On Inspection of Hershey Junior College,"
April 27, 1943.

[146] "Data Presented For Consideration Of The Commission On Institutions Of Higher
Education . . . , 1943." *op. cit.*, p. 4.

The foregoing section reveals that the original purpose of the Junior College remained unchanged during Dean Breidenstine's tenure. The desire of the College to provide educational opportunity for veterans was incorporated in the purposes. On the other hand, considerable time and effort was devoted to admission requirements from the residence eligibility standpoint. The several changes reflected concern for the returning veteran and, more importantly, the total enrollment of the Hershey Junior College. It is interesting to note that Mr. Hershey was consulted when important admission decisions were to be made.

Rules and Regulations

The various rules and regulations governing the total academic program of the College were formulated by the time the first bulletin was printed. Registration procedures stipulated that students failing to register within the assigned period would be assessed a late registration fee and have to secure permission to register from the Dean. Likewise, the Dean's permission was required to change a course schedule within the first two weeks of the semester. Changes after the two-week period required the common consent of the Committee on Instruction. Matriculated students were required to obtain written permission from the Dean to withdraw from classes.[147]

The traditional grading system was used. A, B, C, and D were passing grades; the four "nonpassing" grades were: E (condition), F (failure), Inc. (incomplete), and W (withdrawn). Students were permitted to remove the deficiency represented by an E grade during the first two weeks of the following semester. Courses in which a grade of F was received had to be repeated. Incomplete grades could be removed by the end of the first month of the following semester. A grade of W was assigned if a student withdrew from the course while his work was satisfactory. An average grade of C was required for graduation.[148]

In addition to the grading system described above, three grades of accomplishment were awarded. Accomplishment was defined as "the ratio of achievement to capacity." The grades were: S (satisfactory), I (inadequate), and U (unsatisfactory).[149]

Class periods were 55 minutes in length; laboratory periods were 60 minutes long. The College calendar consisted of two 17-week semesters.[150]

Students were required to attend classes as scheduled. Except for a reason such as illness, absences were not excused. Students were penalized one honor point for each unexcused class absence in excess of the credit hours of the course. Absences from industry on the part of students who were enrolled in the Technical Division were handled in a similar manner. The *Bulletin* stated:

> If absences or the lack of a spirit of cooperation on the part of any student interferes with the relationship established between the College and the indus-

---

[147]*Hershey Junior College Bulletin, 1938–1939*, p. 9.
[148]*Ibid.*, pp. 12–13.   [149]*Ibid.*, p. 13.   [150]*Ibid.*, p. 12.

tries, the student will be required to withdraw from industry; and if sufficiently grave, according to the opinion of the faculty, the student will be required to withdraw from College.[151]

Provision was made for students attending the evening session to register for courses on a credit, noncredit, or audit basis. Class attendance and other regulations were similar to those of the day session. Evening students were limited to a schedule of six credit hours per semester. It was possible for an evening session student to complete degree requirements, with careful scheduling, in approximately five years.[152]

As was planned before the College opened, 64 credit hours (and 64 honor points) were required for graduation from the General College Division; 68 hours and points were required for graduation from the Lower Division. Thirty credit hours were required to be advanced to sophomore standing.[153]

Students eligible for graduation were required to participate in commencement exercises unless excused by the Administrative Committee.[154] Diplomas were awarded until the Junior College was authorized to confer the Associate Degree.[155]

Any student who desired to withdraw from the Junior College was required to file an application and be formally dismissed by the Dean.[156]

No significant additions or changes in the above rules and regulations were made during the nine years Dr. Breidenstine was Dean of the Hershey Junior College.

The Curriculum

The basic curriculum, as envisaged before the Hershey Junior College opened, was described briefly in Chapter III. The curriculum offered from 1938 to 1947 will be considered in more detail here.

From 1938 to 1946, as many as four different curricula were offered in the three divisions of the College. The three divisions were: the General College Division, the Lower Division, and the Technical Division. Enrollment in a particular division was based on a student's interests, aptitudes, high school records, and other guidance information obtained through counseling. Students were permitted to elect courses in a second division but were, thereby, subject to the requirements of both.[157]

The General College Division curricula were "terminal" programs. Course offerings were designed "for students who enter for cultural development and specific personal improvement."[158] The description of this division in the

---

[151] *Ibid.*, pp. 13–14.
[152] *Ibid.*, pp. 14–15.
[153] *Ibid.*, p. 15.
[154] *Ibid.*
[155] "Data Presented For Consideration Of The Commission On Institutions Of Higher Education . . . , 1943," *op. cit.*, p. 29.
[156] *Hershey Junior College Bulletin, 1938-1939*, p. 16.
[157] *Ibid.*, p. 8.
[158] *Ibid.*, p. 11.

Bulletin of the College explains the purpose and the underlying philosophy of the curricula.

> Most students, however, should be primarily concerned about their future welfare in the average vocation of life. A new significance must be attached to the work and life of the so-called average man, without whom no country can prosper. In this area of education the possibilities are boundless and unrestricted; hence, students will be judged more on personal improvement than on traditional norms and standards. A student in this division has a right to expect to find reasonably adequate answers to questions such as these:
>
> (a) What must a worthy citizen of the present age know in order to participate wisely in our American democracy?
>
> (b) How can I become an efficient home administrator and fulfill my obligations as a parent?
>
> (c) What must I know about my everyday job to have enough on the margin for enrichment of honest toil?
>
> (d) How can I become capable of artistic appreciations so that my free-time activities may make life colorful and enjoyable yet not extravagant?
>
> (e) What must I know about other people and their lands in order to become tolerant and considerate of their viewpoints?
>
> (f) How can I develop a sane and workable philosophy of life?
>
> (g) What must I do in order to maintain or regain a strong healthy body?
>
> (h) To what social institutions should I give my wholehearted allegiance?
>
> These questions and others of a more specifically individual nature, if answered only in part, are worth more in the building of a life than many of the more restricted outcomes from some of the traditional courses frequently pursued.
>
> To be sure the questions here raised are not entirely new to the alert graduate of a high school. It is equally true, however, that a lifetime spent in the solution of these vital life problems does not produce a complete answer to any one of them . . .[159]

Two curricula were offered within the General College Division: a General Curriculum and a Secretarial Curriculum. There were no modifications in the general description of the General College Division during Dean Breidenstine's administration. The following outlines list the required and elective courses of the two basic programs.

GENERAL CURRICULUM[160]

FRESHMAN YEAR
Courses Required

	Credits
Contemporary Economic Problems	−3
Contemporary World Affairs	3−
General and Remedial English	3−3
Integration	3−
Life Psychology	−3
Recreation Education	1−1
Pennsylvania Commonwealth	3−3

---

[159]*Ibid.*   [160]*Ibid.*, p. 17.

Additional Courses Open

	Credits
Art Education	2–2
Music Education	2–2
Theatre Arts	2–2
Writing Arts	2–2

Maximum Credit Hours—18

SOPHOMORE YEAR
Courses Required

	Credits
Euthenics Education	3–3
Human Development	
Personal Adjustment	
Income Management	
Selecting a Home	
Human Biology	3–3
General Biological Concepts	
Health and Disease	
Preventive Medicine	
Public Health	
Literature Today	3–3
Recreational Education	1–1
The American Nation	3–3

Additional Courses Open

	Credits
Art Education	2–2
Music Education	2–2
Theatre Arts	2–2
Writing Arts	2–2

Maximum Credit Hours—18

SECRETARIAL CURRICULUM[161]

FRESHMAN YEAR
Courses Required

	Credits
Contemporary Economic Problems	–3
Contemporary World Affairs	3–
General and Remedial English	3–3
Introduction to Business	3–3
Recreational Education	1–1
Secretarial Science I	4–4

Additional Courses Open

	Credits
Accounting I	3–3
Art Education	2–2
Music Education	2–2
Theatre Arts	2–2
Writing Arts	2–2

Maximum Credit Hours—18

---

[161] *Ibid.*, p. 18.

SOPHOMORE YEAR
Courses Required

	Credits
Literature Today	3–3
Recreational Education	1–1
Secretarial Science II	4–4
Selling and Marketing	2–2

Additional Courses Open

	Credits
Accounting II	3–3
Art Education	2–2
Music Education	2–2
Theatre Arts	2–2
Writing Arts	2–2

Maximum Credit Hours–18

Students enrolled in the Secretarial Curriculum were permitted to offer several hours of free secretarial services to professional men of the community each week. They also gained practical experience by working in the Junior College bookstore. These work experiences were not, however, integral parts of the curriculum.

The Lower Division curriculum was the "transfer" program of the Junior College. According to the *Bulletin:*

> The Lower Division courses, with slight modifications, are the traditional courses of the first two years of a liberal arts college. The offerings of this division are sufficiently broad to afford almost perfect articulation with the upper division of most liberal arts colleges. If, by the end of the freshman year, students select the senior college in which they wish to pursue higher work, much can be done to avoid transfer difficulties. Students in this division are expected to conform to the highest standards of our best senior colleges in class work. Only those who maintain an average grade of "B" will receive the Dean's recommendation for transfer.[162]

Three curricula were offered within the Lower Division: Pre-Healing Arts, Pre-Business Administration, and Pre-Engineering. The basic course outline of the division is shown below.

LOWER DIVISION[163]

FRESHMAN YEAR
Courses Required

	Credits
Expressional English	3–3
Integration	3–
*Language	3–3
or	
*Science	4–4

*Required of all Pre-Healing Arts Students

[162]*Ibid*., p. 12.   [163]*Ibid*., p. 19.

86

Life Psychology	−3
† Mathematical Analysis.	4−4
or	
† Mathematics of Finance	2−2
Recreational Education	1−1

Additional Courses Open

	Credits
Accounting I	3−3
Art Education	2−2
† Business Organization	2−2
‡Descriptive Geometry	−3
‡Engineering Drawing.	3−
History Survey	−3
Music Education	2−2
Theatre Arts	2−2
Writing Arts	2−2

Maximum Credit Hours−18

SOPHOMORE YEAR
Courses Required

	Credits
† Business Statistics	2−2
Language	3−3
‡Differential and Integral Calculus	4−4
ⁿᵇScience	4−4
Principles of Economics	3−3
World Literature	3−3

Additional Courses Open

	Credits
Accounting II	3 3
Art Education	2−2
‡Marketing.	2−2
‡Mechanics.	2−2
Music Education	2−2
The American Nation	2−2
Theatre Arts	2−2
Writing Arts	2−2
World Resources	2−2

Maximum Credit Hours−19

---

*Required of all Pre-Healing Arts Students
† Required of all Pre-Business Administration Students
‡Required of all Pre-Engineering Students

A cooperative sales program was an integral part of the curriculum. Dr. Breidenstine announced in December, 1941, that students in Sales and Marketing, under the direction of Professor William M. Kishpaugh, would work in the Hershey Department Store and Pomeroy's and Sears-Roebuck in neighboring Harrisburg.[164]

---

[164]"Hershey Junior College Has Co-operative Sales Program," *Hotel Hershey High-Lights*, Vol. IX, No. 25, December 20, 1941, p. 4.

The Technical Division, like the General College Division, was designed as a "terminal" rather than a "transfer" program. The *Bulletin* stated:

> The Technical Division courses meet the needs of those students who are interested in the technical phases of trades. Graduates of the vocational high school and other graduates who desire to become noncommissioned officers of industry should take the courses of this division. Students in this division are expected to spend one-fourth of their time during the sophomore year in industry, actively engaged in the vocation of their choice. The class work of the Technical Division is less formal than that of the other two divisions but nevertheless the students must, here as in all cases, do work comparable with ability in order to continue in the Junior College.[165]

The description of the Technical Division program remained unchanged through 1946. The basic course outline follows:

TECHNICAL DIVISION[166]

FRESHMAN YEAR
Courses Required

	Credits
Industrial Science I	3-3
Psychology of Industry	2-2
Recreational Education	1-1
Related Mathematics I	2-2
Technical Drawing I	1-1
Technical English I	2-2

Additional Courses Open

	Credits
Art Education	2-2
Music Education	2-2
Theatre Arts	2-2
Writing Arts	2-2

Maximum Credit Hours—18

SOPHOMORE YEAR
Courses Required

	Credits
Industrial Science II	3-3
Industrial Survey	2-2
Recreational Education	1-1
Related Mathematics II	2-2
Sociological Principles	2-2
Technical Drawing II	1-1
Technical English II	2-2
Technology	2-2

---

[165]*Ibid.*, p. 12.
[166]*Ibid.*, p. 21.

Additional Courses Open

	Credits
Art Education	2–2
Music Education	2–2
Theatre Arts	2–2
Writing Arts	2–2

Maximum Credits Hours–18

Note: [Included under Technical Division.] The number of course credit hours lost by employment in industry during the sophomore year, equals the number earned in industry.

Of the offerings of the three divisions, those of the Technical Division experienced the most problems. The "industrial" or cooperative program, in particular, encountered difficulties. As indicated in the outline above, this division combined both the practical and the theoretical in a "work-study" program. Students enrolled in the Technical Division spent a total of nine weeks in industry during the sophomore year.[167]

The first indication of trouble was found in the "Board Minutes" of the first year. Apparently a conflict of interest developed between regular employees and Junior College students who were gaining experience in industry. The following report to the Board by the Derry Township Public School Director of Vocational Education verified that a "public relations" problem had developed:

> Complaints have come to him asking that especially boys from the Industrial School be excluded from the shops on account of taking work away from some working men. No definite source for these complaints could be established, therefore, no action was taken by the board.[168]

The "Board Records" of The Hershey Industrial School verify the problem and suggest that it was the Junior College students from The Hershey Industrial School who were involved. The minutes state:

> We had a recent change in the cooperative plan that was started at the beginning of the school year, whereby the Junior College boys taking advanced courses in their trades were working out in industry. On Monday, January 16, these boys were returned to the shops . . . on the hill, [The Hershey Industrial High School] and will continue for the balance of the season. There are four printers, two electricians, and one plumber. This concerns the Hershey Industrial boys only. The boys from the public schools . . . have been transferred to the vocational shops in the public school.[169]

Dr. Breidenstine acknowledged that the cooperative program was hampered from the beginning.[170] Although the 1939–1940 through the 1946–1948

---

[167]"Brief Submitted in Support of Application to State Council, 1939," *op. cit.*, p. 6.

[168]Derry Township Public Schools, "Board Minutes," January 12, 1939.

[169]Richard H. Rudisill, *op. cit.*, p. 44 citing "Milton Hershey School Board Records," January 19, 1939.

[170]Letter from A. G. Breidenstine to writer, June 9, 1970.

Bulletin indicated that the Technical Division curriculum provided for work experience in industry, the program actually functioned as described in The Hershey Industrial School "Board Records" from 1939 on. (It should be noted that the school district offered a separate evening technical program.)

The three divisions of the Junior College were continued through Dean Breidenstine's tenure and described in the bulletins; however, "typical programs" of study tended to replace the basic divisional outlines. The three included in the *Bulletin* most frequently were Business Administration, Engineering, and Liberal Arts.[171] The last *Bulletin* printed during Breidenstine's administration included the following 18 "typical programs":[172]

Medical Technology (Type One and Type Two)	Secretarial Sciences
	Pre-Healing Arts
Elementary Education	Pre-Law
Secondary Education	Pre-Osteopathy
Ministry	Dentistry
Nursing	Journalism
Engineering	Kindergarten Education
Mechanical Engineering	Veterinary Medicine
Business Administration	Chiropody

The list of individual courses offered by the Junior College was not extensive in number, but it was comprehensive in that courses were offered in the major academic disciplines. A total of 62 different courses, by title, level, and number, were offered as of the first year. Within the 62 courses, 48 different subject titles, listed below by discipline, were included in the first *Bulletin:*[173]

Contemporary World Studies	Selling and Marketing
Contemporary Economic Problems	World Resources
Contemporary World Affairs	*English*
Drawing	Expressional English
Descriptive Geometry	General and Remedial English
Engineering Drawing	Literature Today
Technical Drawing	Technical English
Economics and Business	World Literature
Accounting	Writing Arts
Business Organization	*Euthenics*
Business Statistics	Euthenics
Introduction to Business	*General Arts*
Marketing	Art
Principles of Economics	Music
Secretarial Science	Theatre Arts

[171] *Hershey Junior College Bulletin, 1948-1950*, pp. 48-50.
[172] *Ibid.*, pp. 38-40
[173] *Hershey Junior College Bulletin, 1938-1939*, pp. 23-24.

History and Government
  History Survey
  Pennsylvania Commonwealth
  The American Nation
Languages
  French
  German
  Latin
Mathematics
  Differential and Integral Calculus
  Mathematical Analysis
  Mathematics of Finance
  Related Mathematics I and II
Psychology and Integration
  Industrial Survey

  Integration
  Life Psychology
  Psychology of Industry
  Technology
Science
  Biology
  Comparative Anatomy
  General Chemistry
  Human Biology
  General Physics
  Industrial Science
  Mechanics
  Recreational Education
Sociology
  Sociological Principles

Some courses initially offered were dropped or revised; others were added. A tabulation of the courses listed in the 1946-1948 *Bulletin* indicates that the number and extent of the course offerings had changed little during the first nine years of the College. A total of 60 individual courses were listed; 45 subject titles were included within the offerings.[174]

"The Investigative Paper" became a sophomore graduation requirement according to the 1942-1944 *Bulletin.* Although listed as a course of instruction, it carried no semester hour credit. The description of the requirement follows:

> Rather than write extensive papers in all subject fields, the student concentrates his attention upon his particular field of interest to produce a mature study of value to himself and to others interested in his field of inquiry.

> The paper is the result of an intensive study of a phase of the student's field of greatest interest. The paper is written under the direction of the instructor in the field and of the English instructor. The program for the preparation and writing of the paper follows: first, selection of fields of interest; second, selection of specific topic for investigation within the field; third, preparation of a tentative bibliography for readings; fourth, preparation of a tentative outline for the paper; fifth, criticism and revision of the first draft; sixth, presentation of the final draft. Uniformity in the presentation of the study is obtained through the medium of a style sheet.

> The final papers, together with a bibliography, are bound in a volume known as SOPHOMORE STUDIES.[175]

Another noteworthy addition to the curriculum was included in the 1942-1944 *Bulletin.* Courses in "Writing Arts" were offered the first year of the Junior College but it was not until the 1942-1943 academic year that the *Literary Artisan* was mentioned in the *Bulletin* as the medium through which students in the course published their best creative efforts.[176] The *Literary*

---

[174] *Hershey Junior College Bulletin, 1946-1948*, pp. 21-24.
[175] *Hershey Junior College Bulletin, 1942-1944*, pp. 30-31.   [176] *Ibid.*, p. 31.

Artisan proved to be an interesting and informative publication. In it was recorded much of the early history of the Hershey Junior College.

At least one remedial program was inaugurated during the first nine years. A noncredit English laboratory was organized during the 1945-1946 academic year to offer assistance to students requiring help in oral and written English and those with reading problems. Appropriate tests were administered to all students to determine whether they should avail themselves of the services offered through the English laboratory. Several faculty members assisted in the operation of the remedial program.[177]

The foregoing review of the curriculum of the Junior College during Dean Breidenstine's administration shows that emphasis was placed on "terminal" programs rather than those designed to enable students to transfer to senior institutions. This was, of course, the intent of the founder of the College and consistent with the early plans for its program. In fact, the Lower Division curriculum was purposely deemphasized. In commenting on the students planning to continue their education, Dean Breidenstine, in his speech at the opening program of the College, said:

> The Lower Division Courses satisfy their needs, while we have no desire to ignore the wishes of these students, believing in the democratic ideal of education, they nevertheless do not receive our chief consideration. To make the Lower Division Courses our first task would mean the creating of just another college in a State that now probably has an overabundance of this type.[178]

The seal of the Hershey Junior College symbolized the curriculum, as well as the founder, the date of founding, and the institution's status as a public institution. Breidenstine described the seal as follows:

> In the center, the capital letter "H" stands for Hershey. Without the vision and material assistance of Mr. M. S. Hershey, the Hershey Junior College could not have come into existence. Surrounding this central idea are the four symbols depicting the curricula of the Junior College. Starting at the top of the "H" is the lamp of knowledge, a symbol of the Lower Division Curriculum with those courses which are preparatory to further work in senior colleges and universities. To the right are the quill and scroll, used jointly to represent courses in business, such as accounting and shorthand. The cog wheel at the base of the seal is symbolical of the Technical Division with courses in science, mathematics, physics, technical skills, and industrial problems. The globe on the left has come to be the symbol of the General Division offering courses of a cultural nature such as art, music, literature, drama, and writing. It also represents all those subjects, which give one a world outlook (such as geography and social studies). Lately it has come to be used to stand for all college courses pursued by students who aim at personal development, but not at similar courses beyond the junior college level.

---

[177] Report on English Laboratory, personal files of A. G. Breidenstine.

[178] "Offerings of Hershey Junior College," A. G. Breidenstine, speech at Opening Program, September 14, 1938.

The date at the bottom is the year of the founding of the Junior College. While it is true that for at least five years prior to 1938 Hershey Junior College existed in the minds of many far-sighted Hershey men and women, August, 1938, is historically the month and year of its actual beginning.[179]

Figure 6. The Seal of the Hershey Junior College

Recognition

State, regional, and national recognition was extended to the Hershey Junior College early in its history. This recognition rightly caused students, faculty, and administration to take deep pride in their institution. The Hershey community, likewise, was justified in its satisfaction with its newest institution.

On May 31, 1938, a formal application for approval by the Council of Education of the Commonwealth of Pennsylvania was filed with the Superintendent of Public Instruction and on October 12, 1939, the Junior College submitted "organizational status and descriptive materials" to the Council in support of its application for accreditment. An inspection of the Junior College on May 9, 1939, was made by an official of the Department of Public Instruction.[180]   The Junior College was approved by the State Council on Education on December 1, 1939.[181]   The Derry Township "Board Min-

[179]Dr. A. G. Breidensinte, "The Hershey Junior College Seal," *The Literary Artisan*, Vol. V., No. 2, February, 1944, p. 4.

[180]"Brief Submitted in Support of Application to State Council, 1939," *op. cit.*, pp. 1-4.

[181]*Biennial Report of the Superintendent of Public Instruction For the Two-Year Period Ending May 31, 1940*, Commonwealth of Pennsylvania, Department of Public Instruction, Harrisburg, Pennsylvania, pp. 15-16; *Items of Business, Journals of Meetings and Annual Report of the State Council of Education*, Secretary, July 1, 1937 to June 30, 1938, p. 110.

utes" of December 11, 1939, show that Dr. Baugher reported the approval to the Board and he advised:

> This is an important step in the history of the College and means that the colleges of Pennsylvania should accept our students with credit for the first two years.[182]

An application dated December 13, 1938 was filed for associate membership in the American Association of Junior Colleges.[183] Approval for membership was granted one year later.[184]

In 1942, further State recognition was extended to the Hershey Junior College when on September 21, it was approved by the Department of Public Instruction, Teacher Education and Certification Division.[185]

Of crucial importance to any collegiate institution is approval of its initial application for accreditation by the appropriate regional association. In an October 8, 1940 letter to the Secretary of the Middle States Association of Colleges and Secondary Schools, Dr. Breidenstine expressed interest in having the Junior College evaluated by the Commission on Institutions of Higher Education.[186] The "Data for Consideration of the Commission on Institutions of Higher Education" was prepared and submitted on March 25, 1943.[187] Dr. Charles C. Tillinghast, Acting Secretary of the Commission visited the Junior College on April 15, 1943 and on April 30 Dean Breidenstine was notified that the Junior College was placed on the list of accredited members of the Association for a period of three years.[188]

With this accreditation an important milestone in the history of the Junior College was reached. In lauding the Junior College on its initial accreditation, the *Hotel Hershey High-Lights* reported:

> This accreditment achievement within a six year life history of the Hershey Junior College makes it the first accredited public junior college in the Eastern United States.[189]

Data were presented to the Middle States Association on November 22, 1946, for reevaluation after the three-year period. The College maintained its status as a fully accredited junior college.[190]

---

[182] Derry Township Public Schools, "Board Minutes," December 11, 1939.

[183] Letter from Mr. Jack Gernhart, Administrative Assistant to the Executive Director, American Association of Junior Colleges, to the writer, August 7, 1967.

[184] "Important Dates In History of Hershey Junior College," *The Literary Artisan*, Vol. 2, No. 4, May, 1941, p. 9.

[185] Letter from Henry Klonower, Director, Teacher Education and Certification, Pennsylvania Department of Public Instruction, to A. G. Breidenstine, September 21, 1942.

[186] Letter from Frank H. Bowles, Secretary, Middle States Association of Colleges and Secondary Schools, to A. G. Breidenstine, October 11, 1940.

[187] *Ibid.*

[188] Letter from Charles Tillinghast, Acting Secretary, Middle States Association of Colleges and Secondary Schools, to A. G. Breidenstine, April 30, 1943.

[189] "Hershey Junior College Opens For Its 7th Season On September 5; Evening School Program," *Hotel Hershey High-Lights*, Vol. XII, No. 5, July 29, 1944, p. 1.

[190] "Report On Inspection Of Hershey Junior College," Charles C. Tillinghast, April 27, 1943, p. 2.

On March 4, 1944, Dr. Breidenstine announced that the Junior College had been granted institutional membership in the American Council on Education, thereby further distinguishing the institution. By that date the Junior College was also admitted to membership in the, then, American Association of Collegiate Registrars.[191]

Another recognition which increased the standing of the Hershey Junior College was the New York State Education Department's registration of the curriculum on November 29, 1944. This registration indicated that:

> Any pre-professional courses completed in Junior College can be applied toward a license for practice in New York. This is a major achievement and should interest prospective doctors, lawyers, veterinarians, pharmacists, dentists, chiropractors, and laboratory technicians.[192]

The attention of school administrators across the country was drawn to the accomplishments of the Hershey Junior College in 1945. In the May, 1945 issue of *The School Executive*, the Junior College was voted as having an "unusual" and "noteworthy junior college program."[193]

The Junior College and Dean Breidenstine, in particular, were especially pleased with the national public recognition it received in 1946. The October 1, 1946 issue of *Look* magazine contained an article titled, "The Hope of American Education." Included as a section of the article was "an honor roll of 100 of the country's best public schools, selected by state superintendents and other prominent educators."[194] Among the list of 100 outstanding schools selected were 14 junior colleges, including the Hershey Junior College. It was the only two-year institution on the list representing Pennsylvania and the eastern United States.[195] The distinction was announced in the *Hotel Hershey High-Lights* in the front page article, "Junior College Listed On Public Schools Honor Roll." It was reported that 296 public junior colleges were then in existence in the United States.[196] The Hershey Junior College in existence for only eight years, had been acclaimed one of the very best in the nation.

The Extracurriculum

The activities included in the first year program have already been considered. Here the extracurriculum from 1939 to 1947 will be examined.

Several student publications were produced by Junior College students. One that proved to be of early and continuing value to the Junior College and

---

[191] "Hershey Junior College, In Its 6th Year, Wins American Council On Education Membership," *Hotel Hershey High-Lights*, Vol. XI, No. 36, March 4, 1944, p. 1.

[192] Letter from J. Hollis Miller, Associate Commissioner, New York State Education Department, to A. G. Breidenstine, November 19, 1944.

[193] *The School Executive*, Vol. 64, No. 9, May, 1945, p. 35.

[194] Harlan Logan, "The Hope of American Education," *Look*, October 1, 1946, p. 21.

[195] "Honor Roll of American Public Schools," *Look*, October 1, 1946, p. 40.

[196] "Junior College Listed On Public Schools Honor Roll," *Hotel Hershey High-Lights*, Vol. XIV, No. 14, September 28, 1946, p. 1.

its students was *The Literary Artisan*. The magazine, issued periodically, was written and designed by both day and evening students enrolled in the course Writing Arts.[197]   Members of the faculty and others made contributions to the publication.   The first issue was published in November, 1939, and the 19 members of the Writing Arts class contributed to it.   *The Literary Artisan* had a dual purpose:

> First, to provide the medium for the publication of materials produced by the members of the Writing Arts class; and second, to interpret the work of the Hershey Junior College to the community which it serves and to the institutions which are engaged in similar endeavor.[198]

The Literary Artisan was published regularly until it was decided to publish a College newspaper frequently and the *Artisan* infrequently.[199]

The first issue of the Junior College newspaper, *The Format*, was printed in the spring of 1947.   Professor Harry F. Bolich was the first adviser to the newspaper staff.   The third issue of the paper announced Dr. Breidenstine's resignation and was dedicated to him.[200]

Through the Student Committee, Hershey Junior College students had an opportunity to participate in the government of the institution from the beginning.

> The Student Committee, elected from the student body at large, reflects student opinion and cooperates with the administration in dealing with student problems of the College. It also serves under the direction of the faculty chairman of the Social Committee in the arranging of parties, picnics, and other social functions. Its duties in matters of deportment are of minimum significance at this time. Any student causing deportment problems may for sufficient reasons be dismissed from college. If thus dishonorably dismissed, he may not reenter until at least one semester has elapsed and then only upon the approval of the faculty and the Student Committee.[201]

The Literary Artisan elaborated on the function of the Student Committee:

> The duties of the Student Committee are varied. As a spokesman of the students, it plans all of the college social functions throughout the year. The accounts and handling of student activity money are under its management. In general this body integrates the ideas and activities of students and of the college faculty and directors.[202]

There were no changes in the function of the Student Committee during Dean Breidenstine's administration except that, as of the 1942-1944 *Bulletin*, it served under the Dean of Women rather than the faculty chairman of the Social Committee in arranging social events.[203]

---

[197]"Hershey Junior College Issues Magazine 'Literary Artisan'," *Hotel Hershey High-Lights*, Vol. VII, No. 21, November 25, 1939, p. 2.

[198]"Why The Artisan?", *The Literary Artisan*, Vol. I, No. 1, November, 1939, p. 1.

[199]Derry Township Public Schools, "Board Minutes," May 14, 1947.

[200]*The Format*, Vol. I, No. 3, May, 1947, p. 1.

[201]*Hershey Junior College Bulletin, 1939-1940*, p. 10.

[202]"Through The Halls," *The Literary Artisan*, Vol. II, No. 1, November, 1940, p. 22.

[203]*Hershey Junior College Bulletin, 1942-1944*, p. 11.

The freshman and sophomore classes were organized. Student officers were elected and members of the faculty served as advisers.[204]

Picnics, dances, teas, dinners, and other social functions were frequently held and well-attended. Starting the first year, formal dances and all-College dinners were held at Hotel Hershey. These functions were social highlights of each year.[205] At the 1947 Spring Prom held at Hotel Hershey, Dr. Breiden-stine was presented a wrist watch on which was inscribed "H.J.C. students of 1947.[206]

Weekly convocations were held in the Little Theatre of the Community Building. Students were expected to attend the programs which were de-signed for their interest and enlightenment. Program suggestions could be made to the Student Committee.[207] Each year was begun with a Freshman Convocation followed by an all-College picnic. Special "All-College Convoca-tions" were also scheduled periodically.

The conception of the student convocations was somewhat modified in the fall of 1946. Addresses were delivered by prominent individuals in their var-ious fields of activity. One of the purposes was to expose the students to a variety of vocations.[208]

Music, particularly vocal, held an important place in the Junior College ex-tracurricular program. Instrumental and vocal instruction was provided to in-terested students. A Boys' Glee Club, directed by Mr. Richard Neubert, was organized the first year. By 1940, 21 boys were members.[209] A Junior Col-lege Mixed Chorus was also organized in 1941 and by 1946 it consisted of 30 voices.[210] The "Vocaliers," a quartet, entertained at the College, in the com-munity, and at other locations in Pennsylvania.[211] A Junior College Dance Orchestra enjoyed high status among the various activity groups. Organized the first year and directed by Mr. Neubert, it played at many of the Junior College dances; in 1940, the orchestra consisted of 13 pieces.[212]

The first *Bulletin* stated that students interested in dramatics were to enroll in the course in Theatre Arts and that dramatics was considered a part of the curricular program.[213] Apparently a drama group, The Hershey Players, was organized early in the history of the College, became inactive, and was later revived.[214] A chapter of Delta Psi Omega, a national dramatic fraternity, had also been established by 1947.[215]

[204] "Directory," *The Literary Artisan*, Vol. I, No. 1, November, 1939, p. 16.

[205] Letter from A. G. Breidenstine to writer, June 9, 1970.

[206] "Spring Prom," *The Format*, May, 1947, p. 16.

[207] *Hershey Junior College Bulletin, 1939–1940*, p. 10.

[208] "Hershey Junior College Has 100% Increase in Enrollment; New Student Activities Added," *Hotel Hershey High-Lights*, Vol. XIV, No. 19, November 2, 1946, p. 1.

[209] "Through The Halls," *loc. cit.*   [210] *Ibid.*

[211] "Musical Groups Organized At Hershey Junior College," *Hotel Hershey High-Lights*, Vol. VIII, No. 19, November 9, 1940, p. 3.

[212] "Through The Halls," *The Literary Artisan*, November, 1940 *loc. cit.*

[213] *Hershey Junior College Bulletin, 1938–1939*, p. 10.

[214] "Hershey Junior College Has 100% Increase in Enrollment; New Student Activities Added," *Hotel Hershey High-Lights, loc. cit.*

[215] "'College Daze' Captivates Audience," *The Format*, May, 1947, p. 1.

A debating team was formed by 1941. Coached by Professor Robert B. Patrick, it competed with other institutions in the central Pennsylvania area.[216] The first intercollegiate debate was scheduled with Elizabethtown College on February 12, 1941.[217]

The first Annual Institute on State and Local Government was held during the 1939–1940 academic year of the College. The Institute was jointly sponsored by the social science department of the Hershey Junior College and the Hershey Senior High School. Robert B. Patrick and L. M. Brockman were the coordinators. Ten noted speakers were scheduled the first year. The purpose of the institute was explained in the first program:

> In our attempt to keep pace with the growing complexity of Local State Government as well as to satisfy an increased demand for first-hand information, the Institute on State and Local government has been created. This demand sprang from an interest among, not only students of the Senior High School and Junior College, but the citizens of Hershey and the surrounding communities.
>
> The men best qualified to satisfy this demand have been secured to speak on a single phase of the general topic in which they are expert.[218]

The Institutes were apparently well received.

"Senior Day" programs were sponsored annually by the Junior College. Invitations were extended to The Hershey Industrial and Hershey High School seniors who had an interest in the Junior College.[219] Programs consisted of speeches by students and faculty describing the Junior College program. Music, plays, dancing, games, and refreshments were also included in the "Senior Days."[220]

Athletics played an important part in the extracurricular program of the College. Intramural and intercollegiate sports provided students the opportunity to engage in physical activity and experience competition and cooperation. The athletic program also served to build school spirit and a sense of loyalty to the College on the part of the students and citizens of the community. Students were required to pursue successfully a minimum 15 credit-hour program of courses to be eligible to participate in interscholastic athletics.[221] This requirement was reduced to 12 credit-hours by 1942–1943.[222]

Basketball was probably the key sport in the interscholastic athletic program. As indicated previously, basketball competition began the first year under "Fritz" Miller, Coach. Dr. Breidenstine recalls the first opponent of

---

[216]"Junior College Debate On Union of United States and Britain," *Hotel Hershey High-Lights*, Vol. VIII, No. 38, March 22, 1941, p. 2.

[217]"Important Dates In History of Hershey Junior College," *loc. cit.*

[218]Program of The First Annual Institute on State and Local Government, Hershey, Pennsylvania, 1939–40.

[219]Derry Township Public Schools, "Board Minutes," February 12, 1940.

[220]Program from Second Annual Senior Day, Hershey Junior College, February 12, 1940.

[221]*Hershey Junior College Bulletin, 1938-1939*, p. 10.

[222]*Hershey Junior College Bulletin, 1942-1944*, p. 11.

the "Leopards" was probably the York Junior College.[223]   By the second year the team played a 15-game schedule with such colleges as Elizabethtown, Harrisburg Academy, Albright, Franklin and Marshall, Dickinson Junior College, Scranton-Keystone, Lebanon Valley, and Wyomissing Polytechnic. Eight wins and seven losses were recorded that year.[224]   The following year two new opponents appeared on the schedule: Bucknell Junior College and Penn State's Schuykill Undergraduate Center.[225]

Tennis was added as an intercollegiate sport in 1941 with Daniel Seiverling as the first coach.[226]   The first match was scheduled with the Patton Trade School.[227]   Tennis competition was discontinued for four seasons during the war years but resumed the spring of 1947 when matches were scheduled with York and Bucknell Junior College clubs.[228]   That year the Junior College won the Pennsylvania Junior College Athletic Association doubles championship.[229]

Golf was also organized during Dean Breidenstine's administration. Both singles and team matches were won by Junior College golfers in the 1947 Pennsylvania Junior College playoffs.[230]   As mentioned previously, the inclusion of football and baseball in the athletic program were considered the first year but they were not approved. There is no indication that Junior College students engaged in competition in these two sports.

The intramural athletic program was well developed from the beginning and facilities were ideal. In the fall of the second year archery was added to swimming, dancing, table tennis, badminton, and Ping Pong in the girls' sports program. The first archery contest was held on the lawn of the Women's Club.[231]   Swimming and field hockey were also added by 1946. The men's recreational program was also enlarged by that year.[232]

Delta Upsilon Kappa, an honorary fraternity, was established in 1940. Membership in the "Dukes," as the organization and the members were dubbed, was limited to 20 male students. The slogan of the group was "Through Truth Power." The purposes of the fraternity were to foster school spirit and lasting friendships, encourage scholarship, and to promote high standards of character. The "Dukes" sponsored several functions including an annual banquet in honor of the faculty. Awards were also presented to deserving students.

---

[223] Letter from A. G. Breidenstine to writer, June 9, 1970.

[224] "From The Leopard's Den," *The Literary Artisan*, Vol. I, No. 3, March, 1940, p. 23.

[225] "The Leopard's Den," *The Literary Artisan*, Vol. II, No. 1, November, 1940, p. 23.

[226] Derry Township Public Schools, "Board Minutes," May 22, 1941.

[227] "Important Dates In History of Hershey Junior College," *loc. cit.*

[228] "Hershey Junior College Team Re-enters Tennis Competition," *Hotel Hershey High-Lights*, Vol. XV, No. 4, July 19, 1947, p. 2.

[229] "Hershey Junior College State Champions," *The Format*, May, 1947, p. 4.

[230] "Hershey Junior College State Champion," *The Format, loc. cit.*

[231] "Junior College Girls Holding First Contest in Archery," *Hotel Hershey High-Lights*, Vol. VII, No. 20, November 18, 1939, p. 3.

[232] "Hershey Junior College Has 100% Increase in Enrollment; New Student Activities Added," *Hotel Hershey High-Lights, loc. cit.*

At the last Delta Upsilon Kappa convocation of the 1946-1947 academic year, the members unanimously elected Dean Breidenstine the first honorary member of the fraternity and he was presented with an engraved key.[233]

Harmless hazing of freshmen was practiced. A code of rules and regulations was established and published by the Committee on Freshman Rules. The code for the 1941 freshman class included several interesting stipulations. For example:

> All Freshmen (male and female) must at *all* times carry with them a toothbrush and at the request of *any* Sophomore illustrate how they brush their teeth. Last day, October 24.

> All Freshmen are to have chewing gum with them at all times to present to a Sophomore upon request. (Adams, Teaberry, Wrigleys or Dentyne) no other brands permitted. Last day October 17. Freshmen must *never* chew gum. Last day, February 12.

> All Freshmen boys must wear a dog biscuit as a tie for the first week ending October 17. This is then replaced by a black bow tie. Last day for black bow ties, February 12.

> Hair must be braided in two braids and pinned up on the top of the heads with no curls on top or in front. (Freshmen girls.)

> Must wear black lisle stockings with white elastic garters 1 1/2 inch below the knees. The garters must have a red ribbon bow 2 inches wide tied in the front. (2 weeks) No *blue* may be worn at any time. (Freshmen girls.)[234]

Two Junior College activities of special significance were baccalaureate and commencement exercises, especially those recognizing the first graduates of the institution. The "Board Minutes" of April 8, 1940 reveal that considerable discussion was devoted to the question of whether the Junior College should hold a separate commencement or a combined one with the Hershey High School. Dr. Breidenstine attended that meeting and reported that he had "very little criticism from the Junior College students concerning a joint commencement" and, "in general, there seemed to be a wholesome attitude toward such a commencement." It was decided that a joint commencement would be held.[235] The minutes of the following meeting indicate that the cost of the commencement speaker was also shared, 75 percent by the High School and 25 percent by the Junior College.[236]

The First Combined Commencement of the Derry Township Public Schools was held in the Hershey Community Theatre on May 29, 1940. A note in the program explained:

> This program includes the 33rd annual commencement exercises of the Derry Township High School and the first commencement of the Hershey Junior College.[237]

---

[233] "Delta Upsilon Kappa Annual Report and Duke Directory," 1947.

[234] "Freshman Codes," Committee on Freshmen Rules, Fall, 1941.

[235] Derry Township Public Schools, "Board Minutes," April 8, 1940.

[236] Derry Township Public Schools, "Board Minutes," April 15, 1940.

[237] Program from First Combined Commencement, Hershey Community Theatre, May 29, 1940.

The theme of the commencement was "Education for the Defense of American Democracy." There were speeches by both High School and Junior College students, musical selections by the Junior College Quartet and Glee Club and several solos. The Hershey Junior College Alma Mater was also sung. The commencement address was delivered by Dr. E. S. Evenden, Professor of Education, Teachers College, Columbia University. No awards or prizes were given. Diplomas were presented to High School and Junior College graduates by the President of the Board of Education, Mr. H. N. Herr. The program listed 37 Hershey Junior College graduates, seven women and 30 men, shown below:

William D. H. Black	George Lafferty
Wilmer G. Brandt	H. Chester Lawver
Paul E. Burke	William R. Linsley
Joyce Arlene Cake	Burdsall D. Miller
Marguerite Elizabeth Colbert	Leon E. Nark
Irwin K. Curry, Jr.	Charles Elwood Hess Schaffer
Ernest Clayton Doutrich	William Lester Faust Schmehl
George G. Dower	Lois Jane Seavers
Elizabeth Evelyn Eicherly	William C. Seibert
Avis E. Ensminger	Prowell M. Seitzinger
Harry Paul Forry	Richard F. Seiverling
Mary Joan Gasper	Paul McKinley Shiffler
Harold Long Godshall	Richard Vincent Showers
Lloyd H. Goodhart	Kenneth H. Smith
A. Marjorie Hantz	Robert D. Stewart
Robert McKay Haupt	Edwin Brandt Wagner
J. Wilmer Hershey	Elizabeth L. Whistler
Leonard John Kogut	Harry K. Young
Richard B. Zentmeyer	

Officers for the Class of 1940 were also listed:

Richard V. Showers, *President*
Paul M. Shiffler, *Vice President*
Avis E. Ensminger, *Secretary*
Leon E. Nark, *Treasurer*[238]

The first baccalaureate service, also combined, was held on May 26.[239] Baccalaureate services and commencements remained combined throughout Dr. Breidenstine's administration.

---

[238] Program from First Combined Commencement, *loc. cit.*
[239] "Important Dates In History of Hershey Junior College," *loc. cit.*

Enrollment and Student Achievement

There was some fluctuation in the enrollment of the Hershey Junior College during Dean Breidenstine's administration. The reader will recall that there was some question if the number of registrations would permit the opening of the College in 1938 but, fortunately, the final enrollment figure of 131 students (66 full-time, 65 part-time) actually exceeded the original estimates of about 80 students.[240] The ratio of men to women in the charter freshman class was two to one. Among the full-time student body, the ratio was approximately two and one-half to one.[241] Of the 66 entering, full-time students, 38 returned as sophomores the following year.[242]

Total enrollment grew steadily the first few years. By 1941, it topped 200 students, the highest during Dr. Breidenstine's administration. That year part-time enrollment (100) nearly equalled the full-time enrollment (102).

World War II, the restricted residence eligibility, and increased hiring by the Hershey Chocolate Corporation[243] caused sharp decreases in enrollment and by 1945 it had sunk to a total of 68 (39 full-time, 29 part-time), the lowest in the history of the College.[244]

With the first influx of 64 veterans in 1946, the enrollment jumped to 141, an increase of better than 100 percent over the previous year. All but 24 students were registered as full-time students that year. The enrollment of veterans resulted in the Junior College receiving its first tuition income as provided by Public Law 346 and Public Law 16. Veterans receiving "G.I." benefits who were high school graduates were admitted to the College regardless of residence.[245]

During Dean Breidenstine's administration, from 1938 through the 1946–47 academic year, the total enrollment was 1,212 (686 full-time, 516 part-time). During this period the ratio of men to women remained about two to one. Fifty-six percent of the charter freshman class graduated in 1940; only one less than the number of sophomores who enrolled in 1939 were graduated.[246]

During the first nine years the number of students who graduated closely paralleled the total enrollment figures. A high percentage of those students who enrolled as sophomores remained to graduate. The major exception to the pattern was in 1943-1944 when only five students out of an entering sophomore class of 22 were graduated. This was the lowest number of stu-

240 "Student Enrollment and Staff Members—September 30, Annually," personal files of V. H. Fenstermacher.

241 "Enrollment Record To Date," January 14, 1946, p. 2.

242 "Student Enrollment and Staff Members—September 30, Annually." Only full-time returning students can be reported because part-time (evening) students could not be easily classified as freshmen or sophomores and attrition among part-time students was relatively high.

243 "Enrollment Record To Date," loc. cit.

244 "Student Enrollment and Staff Members—September 30, Annually," loc. cit.

245 Hershey Junior College Bulletin, 1946-1948, p. 20.

246 "Student Enrollment and Staff Members—September 30, Annually," loc. cit.

dents to graduate in any year in the history of the institution. The highest number of graduates during Breidenstine's tenure was 42 in 1942. A total of 192 students in eight graduating classes were awarded diplomas by the Hershey Junior College.[247]

It has already been explained that students admitted to the Junior College during the early years were required to be graduates of The Hershey Industrial School or the Hershey High School or legal residents of Derry Township. Consequently, the large majority of the student body were graduates of the two local high schools.

Of the Hershey High School graduates from 1938 through 1946 who attended college, over half enrolled in the Hershey Junior College. During this period approximately 15 percent of all high school graduates in Pennsylvania attended college. A favorable 24 percent of Hershey High School graduates went on to institutions of higher education. Statistics on Hershey High School graduates and college attendance differ but it appears that an average of 14 percent of each graduating class enrolled at the Junior College.[248] In 1946, over 35 percent of Hershey High School graduates enrolled at the Junior College but this figure was inflated because it included a number of veterans who were graduates of the High School in earlier years. Nevertheless, a higher number of Hershey High School graduates could have been expected to take advantage of the opportunity to attend the Hershey Junior College at no cost.

The interest of The Hershey Industrial School boys in attending college was heightened when the Junior College opened. Typically, 15 to 20 boys out of classes of approximately 100 continued their education.[249] In a study by Olena and Hershey, it was reported that 30 orphan graduates enrolled at the Junior College in 1938, 21 of whom went on to graduate. This was the largest number to enroll in any one year. Approximately 127 Industrial School students matriculated at the College during the next eight years. The number and proportion of those Industrial School students who graduated from the College steadily declined through 1947. From 1938 through 1947, 61 or 46 percent of those Hershey Industrial School boys who enrolled in the Junior College graduated.[250]

The approximate distribution of Hershey Junior College students by secondary schools and residence is available for the 85 full-time students enrolled in 1940. Of the total, 37 percent were Hershey High School graduates whose residence was Derry Township; 25 percent were Hershey Industrial

[247]*Ibid.*

[248]O. H. Aurand *et al*, *A Study of the Schools of Derry Township Dauphin County, Pennsylvania, 1951-1952*, p. 133.

[249]"127 Graduates Of Hershey Industrial School Have Entered Colleges Or Universities," *Hotel Hershey High-Lights*, Vol. 10, No. 41, April 10, 1942, p. 1.

[250]Benjamin F. Olena and John O. Hershey, "Milton Hershey School Graduates in Hershey Junior College, 1938-1952," p. 5. Dr. J. O. Hershey is currently the President of the Milton Hershey School.

School graduates; 30 percent were Hershey High School graduates; and 7 percent were graduates of some other secondary school but were residents of Derry Township. In that year 73 percent of the student body were men.[251]

Dean Breidenstine was sincerely interested in the students who attended the Hershey Junior College—nongraduates as well as graduates. The College, with the assistance of Professor Lane, alumni adviser, spent considerable time and effort in conducting follow-up studies on its students.

The follow-up record of the Class of 1940 is interesting and informative. It indicated that of the 39 members, 21 became gainfully employed (with placement assistance from the College); 11 transferred to colleges and universities with advanced standing as juniors; three transferred to institutions after one year (one in music, one in veterinary medicine, and one in agriculture); two entered into nurses' training; and two became engaged in domestic work.

Among the institutions to which students transferred were the following: Albright College, Bucknell University, Duke University, Franklin and Marshall College, Lafayette College, Lebanon Valley College, Lehigh University, Pennsylvania State College, Shippensburg State Teachers College, Temple University, University of Pennsylvania, Virginia Polytechnic Institute, West Chester Teachers College. Students attending these institutions distinguished themselves in several areas: two became varsity athletes, one was elected president of the senior class, two became members of traveling glee clubs, one became associate editor of the yearbook, and one was named to the dean's list. Two students were reported to have withdrawn from college, one for poor scholarship and one for reasons of health.

Among the important positions held by students of the Class of 1940, six were shop inspectors in large industries, one was a receptionist at a university, one was a secretary to a personnel director, and two were Flying Cadets.[252]

The Junior College conducted a five-year (1940–1945) follow-up study of transfer graduates. Breidenstine reported that during that period 51 students transferred to 26 senior institutions. Of those, 23.5 percent earned honors, as follows: one, magna cum laude; two, cum laude; three, dean's list; four, senior honors; and two, second honor roll.[253]

During the period 1940–1946, 65 Hershey Junior College graduates transferred directly to 42 different colleges, universities, and professional schools. The two institutions enrolling the largest number of these students were Elizabethtown and Lebanon Valley. In addition, 43 graduates pursued graduate or advanced study at 28 institutions. Approximately 57 percent of all Junior College graduates between 1940 and 1946 transferred to a senior institution. It is also important to note that a significant number of students who

---

[251] Derry Township Public Schools, "Board Minutes," December 2, 1940.

[252] "Junior College Report to Board: Follow-up Record for Graduating Class of 1940."

[253] "Enrollment Record To Date," January 14, 1946, p. 4.

attended the Hershey Junior College for one year transferred to senior institutions.[254]

Junior College student records and graduation rosters were not categorized by academic division. An exception to this was the roster of the graduates of the Class of 1943. It revealed that the majority of students were enrolled in the Lower Division. The distribution was as follows: Lower Division, 13; General Division, 5; and Technical Division, 2.[255]

Dr. Breidenstine evaluated the success of Hershey Junior College students and the effectiveness of the instructional program by analyzing the grades earned in high school compared to those earned in the Junior College. In a study covering three years, 1940-1943, he found that students from the Hershey High School and The Hershey Industrial School experienced an average drop of one point (on a three-point system) in grades earned in the Junior College. Breidenstine's conclusions of the study which assessed grades and other matters associated with achievement of the Hershey Junior College are significant:

> The Admissions Committee has so carefully selected entering students that almost without question those recommended for Junior College have successfully pursued their courses in Junior College.

> There is no significant difference between recommended students from the Hershey High School and students from The Hershey Industrial School.

> As a general rule, students' grades in college are lower than the grades of the same student in high school.

> Hershey Industrial School students in Junior College are more select upon entrance than Hershey High School students.

> Twenty-five percent of the Hershey High School graduates in junior college either equalled or exceeded their former high school grade average. Fifteen percent of the Industrial School graduates either equalled or exceeded their grade average in Junior College.

> Ninety-five percent of the Junior College graduates who have transferred to senior colleges have pursued their further work satisfactorily.

> In so far as we have been able to discover, all Junior College job placements have been successful to date. Follow-up work was needed in three cases.[256]

---

[254] "Data Presented For Consideration of the Commission On Institutions of Higher Education, Middle States Association of Colleges and Secondary Schools," January, 1952, Section V: Outcomes.

[255] Graduating Class, Hershey Junior College, Class of 1943, May 23, 1943.

[256] "Summary Conclusions In High School and Junior College Achievement," [classes of 1940, 1941, and 1942], personal files of A. G. Breidenstine.

CHAPTER V

THE INSTITUTIONAL PROGRAM
1947-1965

The second Dean of the Hershey Junior College served from 1947 through the closing of the institution in 1965. During the latter period of his tenure, the administration of the College became increasingly complex. This Chapter, beginning with a review of the Dean as an administrator, is devoted to an analysis of the institutional program during the administration of the second and last Dean of the Hershey Junior College.

V. H. Fenstermacher, Last Dean

Varnum Hayes Fenstermacher was born in Reading, Pennsylvania, on August 8, 1908. After receiving his elementary education in Trenton, New Jersey, and attending the Chester High School, Chester, Pennsylvania, he enrolled at Technical High School in Harrisburg, Pennsylvania, from which he graduated in 1925.[1] An outstanding athlete, Fenstermacher earned nine high school varsity letters.[2]

At Shippensburg State (Teachers) College, Fenstermacher remained active in athletics and was President of the Varsity Club and the Student Government.[3] He earned the Bachelor of Science degree from Shippensburg in 1929. Dr. Fenstermacher attended Columbia University from which he was awarded the Master of Arts degree in 1933. In 1943 he was awarded the Doctor of Education degree from Temple University.[4]

Dr. Fenstermacher began his professional career in the Darby, Pennsylvania, school district where he taught social science and science and served as a coach from 1929 to 1931.[5] During the following 12 years, until 1943, he held the position of administrative assistant in the Norristown, Pennsylvania, school district. He also taught science and coached.[6]

During 1942, Dr. Fenstermacher also served the United States Signal Corps, Training Division, Philadelphia, Pennsylvania, as instructor and curriculum consultant.

---

[1] V. H. Fenstermacher, personal interview, February 23, 1967.
[2] "Dr. V. H. Fenstermacher," *The Format*, Vol. IX, No. 2, Winter edition, 1954, p. 3.
[3] *Ibid.*
[4] Varnum Hayes Fenstermacher, Personal Summary.
[5] "Dr. Varnum H. Fenstermacher of Norristown Named New Dean of Hershey Junior College," *Hotel Hershey High-Lights*, Vol. XV, No. 1, June 28, 1947, p. 1.
[6] "Know Your Faculty," *The Format*, Vol. XII, No. 1, October, 1957, p. 2.

In 1943 he entered the United States Navy Reserve, Bureau of Personnel, for which he served as Classification Officer at Newport, Rhode Island, Washington, D.C., New York City, Boston, and Norfolk. Fenstermacher remained in the Reserve until 1946 when he was employed by the Veterans Administration, Philadelphia, as Supervisor of the Vocational Rehabilitation and Education Services, Advisement and Guidance Division for the states of Pennsylvania, New Jersey, and Delaware.[7] Fenstermacher retired from the Navy as a lieutenant commander.[8]

Dr. Fenstermacher was elected to succeed Dr. A. G. Breidenstine as Dean of the Hershey Junior College on June 27, 1947.[9] There is no record that Dr. Breidenstine or the Junior College faculty played a part in the selection of Dr. Fenstermacher. However, in a personal letter to a colleague at Temple, Breidenstine indicated he felt Fenstermacher was "the best candidate."[10]

Dr. Fenstermacher's duties as Dean differed little from those of Dr. Breidenstine's. He served as Dean of the faculty and was responsible for admissions, discipline, budget preparation, testing and counseling, scheduling of classes, faculty, activities, overseeing the daily program, and interpreting the College to the community. Dr. Fenstermacher served as liaison between the institution and the governing bodies. He administered numerous tests including General Educational Development Tests, School and College Ability Tests, and College Entrance Examination Board tests.[11]

The 1963 evaluation committee described the Dean as having "perceptive control" and he was viewed generally as a very efficient, conscientious, meticulous administrator.[12] Decisions were made with deliberation and, once made, Dr. Fenstermacher changed them only after careful review. He maintained an excellent system of records and his reports, letters, and memoranda were clear and concise.[13] An examination of Dr. Fenstermacher's personal files reveals that he made exact notes of meetings with members of the faculty and administrative personnel of the public school system, the Hershey Estates, and The M. S. Hershey Foundation. He also made personal notes of his thoughts regarding matters which pertained to the Junior College program. Dr. Fenstermacher was genuinely interested in the Hershey Junior College.

To a great extent, Fenstermacher relied upon the use of written reports, information bulletins, and other records in communicating with the faculty, the superintendent, School Board, and Board of Managers. (An illness

---

[7] Varnum Hays Fenstermacher, Personal Summary.

[8] V. H. Fenstermacher, personal interview, February 23, 1967.

[9] Derry Township Public Schools, "Board Minutes," June 27, 1947.

[10] Letter from A. G. Breidenstine to Dr. Ralph D. Owen, Temple University, April 2, 1947.

[11] "Report of Evaluation Committee," Commission on Institutions of Higher Education, Middle States Association of Colleges and Secondary Schools, February 24–27, 1963, p. 2.

[12] *Ibid.*, p. 1.

[13] Mr. and Mrs. John Lanz, personal interview, July 27, 1967. Mr. Lanz was a member of the Hershey Junior College faculty and Mrs. Lanz served as secretary and registrar.

which affected his speech during the 1950-1951 academic year may have caused him to keep extensive notes and to rely more heavily upon written communication than he otherwise would have.)[14] In the opinion of the writer, communication was made difficult because of the complicated organizational relationship with the School District and the Board of Managers which necessitated Dr. Fenstermacher's resorting to written communications.

With increasing enrollment but without a proportionate increase in facilities, particularly from 1955 through the closing of the College in 1965, the task of administering the Junior College required the service of an efficient, respected Dean. He was assisted in the administration of the Junior College by the Secretary-Registrar and later, a Registrar and a Secretary. No other administrative personnel were added to the staff.[15]

Dr. Fenstermacher took an interest in the students of the College and he knew most of them by name. The students showed their regard for Dr. Fenstermacher by dedicating the second volume of the yearbook to him. The inscription read:

> We, the class of 1956, respectfully dedicate this volume of the HEJUCO to Dr. Varnum H. Fenstermacher, Dean of our College, in recognition of his many services and efforts toward its advancement.[16]

Leaving the Junior College the last year of its existence was not pleasant for Dr. Fenstermacher. Having served as Dean for 18 years, he was greatly disappointed in the decision to close the institution. Although he officially remained the Dean and acted as consultant to the Junior College through the final graduation, Dr. Fenstermacher was granted a leave of absence for the last semester[17] to accept an appointment to the Federal Office of Education in Washington.[18] Later he transferred to Charlottesville, Virginia, where he served as field representative of the Division of Student Financial Aid of the U. S. Department of Health, Education, and Welfare.[19]

The school paper, in reporting Fenstermacher's leave of absence, stated that his "valuable years of service and dedication to the College are appreciated by all."[20] W. Allen Hammond, a former Milton Hershey School principal and part-time Junior College English teacher, was named Acting Dean of the College effective March 15, 1965. Dr. Fenstermacher expressed to the faculty his sentiments on Mr. Hammond's appointment:

> Mr. Allen Hammond has been appointed to the position of Acting Dean of the College and will begin his duties on Monday, March 15, 1965. Mr. Hammond has accepted the duty in the spirit of cooperation and concern for the welfare

---

[14]*Ibid.*

[15]*Ibid.*

[16]*HEJUCO*, Vol. 2, 1956, p. 2.

[17]Derry Township Public Schools, "Board Minutes," December 14, 1964.

[18]"Dean at Hershey Takes U.S. Post," *The Evening News*, Harrisburg, March 12, 1965, p. 4.

[19]"Former Hershey Jr. College Dean Taken By Death," *Lebanon Daily News*, April 29, 1967, p. 2.

[20]"Fenstermacher Leaves," *The Format*, Vol. XIX, No. 5, May, 1965, p. 3.

Figure 7. Dr. V. H. Fenstermacher, Dean
Hershey Junior College
1947-1965

of the students, staff and citizens of the community. I cannot envision a better choice and commend him to you with perfect confidence for the continuation of policies and procedures during the remainder of the year.[21]

Dr. Fenstermacher was interested and active in professional educational organizations. He was particularly proud to have been elected president of the Pennsylvania Association of Junior Colleges in 1952. He also served as a member of the Executive Committee of the Association from 1949 through 1954. Fenstermacher was president of the Department of Higher Education, Southern District, Pennsylvania State Education Association during 1951. Membership was held by Dr. Fenstermacher on the State Advisory Committee on Education in 1952 and on College and Secondary School Evaluation Committees of the Middle States Association of Colleges and Secondary Schools, 1948-1953. He was also treasurer of the Junior College Council of the Middle States Association in 1949.[22]   Dr. Fenstermacher also held membership in the Pennsylvania State Education Association, the National Education Association, and the American Association of School Administrators.[23]

---

[21]"Information Bulletin," Vol. XXVII, No. 6, March 11, 1965. The "Information Bulletin" was an internal Hershey Junior College Administration-Faculty Communication.
[22]Varnum H. Fenstermacher, Personal Summary.
[23]"Know Your Faculty," *The Format, loc. cit.*

Dr. Fenstermacher was associated with the following fraternal, church, and service organizations:

Speakers' Bureau, Americans for Competitive Enterprise, Harrisburg
"75" Club of Pennsylvania
Swatara Council, Boy Scouts of America
Rotary International, Hershey
Derry Presbyterian Church, Hershey
Charity Lodge 190, F & AM, Norristown, Pennsylvania
Harrisburg Consistory[24]

Fenstermacher's hobbies and interests included athletics, outdoor activities, photography, and writing. He was an avid reader.[25]

Varnum Hayes Fenstermacher died on April 28, 1967 at Lebanon Veterans Hospital, less than two years after the last class had graduated from the Hershey Junior College.[26]

Facilities

The Community Center

The Hershey Junior College continued to utilize the facilities of the Community Center Building from 1947, when Dr. Fenstermacher assumed the position of Dean, through the closing of the College. No major changes with respect to the use of specific facilities took place during this period although some minor adjustments and additions were made. However, the overlapping use of the Community Building by various groups had the effect of complicating the administration of the Junior College program. (It will be recalled that the primary purpose of the Community Center Building was for the use and enjoyment of the residents of Hershey.) The complexity of the situation grew in proportion to the increase in Junior College enrollment and public Community Center activities. As a consequence, relations tended to become strained between personnel of the Junior College and the Community Center Building employees. In turn, officials of the Hershey Estates, directors of the School Board, and others became involved, directly or indirectly, in the administration of the nonacademic program of the Junior College.

The intricate relationship of the Junior College, through the Dean to the other individuals and organizations that had responsibility for the use of the facilities, is shown in Figure 8.[27]

The use of the Community Building and Women's Club social and recreational facilities by Junior College students presented problems. Eventually,

---

[24]"Former Hershey Jr. College Dean Taken By Death," *loc. cit.*

[25]"Know Your Faculty," *loc. cit.*

[26]"Former Hershey Jr. College Dean Taken By Death," *loc. cit.*

[27]"Data Presented for Consideration of the Commission on Institutions of Higher Education," Middle States Association of Colleges and Secondary Schools, January, 1952, n.p.

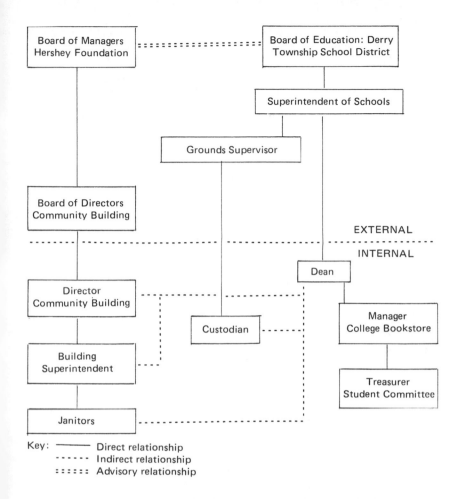

Key: ———— Direct relationship
      - - - - - Indirect relationship
      ꞊꞊꞊꞊꞊ Advisory relationship

Figure 8. Hershey Junior College Facilities Organization Chart

this led to required student membership in the Community Men's and Women's clubs. Prior to 1962, membership had been recommended but not required.[28]   Dues ranged from $6.25 in 1951 to $15.60 in 1963. Members were accorded "full Club privileges."[29]

As early as 1952 in Dean Fenstermacher's administration, the question of the use of a room in the Community Building as a social room for women students was considered. The following excerpt from a letter from Raymond

[28] *The Leopard: Student Handbook,* Hershey Junior College, 1961, p. 12.
[29] "Administrative Report," Hershey Junior College, April 30, 1951, p. 1; and "Student Information," December 13, 1963.

Koch, Superintendent of Schools, to Dean Fenstermacher reveals the general administrative problems that were developing and the concern over Club membership, specifically.

> It is suggested that the Dean of the College or the superintendent contact Ralph Hoar, Director, Community Building, requesting permission for the women students of the Junior College to use the Women's Club lobby as a social room during the day, or . . . a section of the lobby of the Community Club or the Little Theatre, as you suggested. Some place shall be found. It is recommended that the Dean of the College or the superintendent contact Mr. Hoar concerning the use of the Little Theatre for speech classes on Tuesday and Thursday at 1:00 P.M. and 3:00 P.M. It was suggested at the Board meeting that if all of the students at the Junior College were members of the Community Club much of this problem could be overcome, because as members of the Club, they would be entitled to its use without question. However, they took no action to require membership.[30]

It is of interest that the same letter reported the concern of the School Board regarding the number of high school students who were smoking on school property. The negative influence of the Junior College faculty and students was cited. The Superintendent's letter closed with the following admonition:

> Will you please instruct your faculty concerning regulations of smoking in the high school and ask them to cooperate in enforcing smoking regulations concerning Junior College students.[31]

Although the Community Center facilities were considered open to Junior College students, the Junior College Student Committee was billed for the use of the Social Room on February 2, 1953. The bill was later cancelled but Dean Fenstermacher advised the faculty that this event was a sign of future similar difficulties. As of that date, reservations for the use of Community Center facilities had to be made.[32]

About a year later, Dr. Fenstermacher included another item in the "Information Bulletin" concerning the use of the Community Center Building lobby by women students for the first time. The Dean suggested to the faculty that "a degree of decorum" was expected "which is perhaps in excess of the average found elsewhere." He explained:

> This is necessary because of the number of visitors who visit the school. This same mild control should be exercised on occasion in the matter of students using the elevator. It has been requested many times that the students refrain from use of the elevator. In this matter we are committed to cooperate with the officials.[33]

By 1956, the Student Senate passed a resolution asking for adoption of a policy allowing "all Hershey Junior College students to play cards in the Student Lounge with the stipulation that there be no gambling." At that time students had the use of the following Community Center facilities: room 207

---

[30]Letter from Raymond H. Koch to Dr. V. H. Fenstermacher, October 9, 1952.
[31]*Ibid.*
[32]"Information Bulletin," Vol. XV, No. 10, February 26, 1953, p. 1.
[33]"Information Bulletin," Vol. XVII, No. 8, December 2, 1954.

for "serious study"; room 211 as a social room for "light conversation"; the Lobby for lounging, study, and watching television; the Library for reference and study; the Game Room for recreation; and the Gym for swimming and athletics.[34]

In July, 1961, James E. Bobb, Chairman of the Board of Managers, wrote to Mr. Paul Curry, President of the Derry Township School Board, regarding the use of the Community Building lobby. A copy of the letter was sent to Dean Fenstermacher. The letter stated:

> As we have discussed from time to time, we should not like to have the same conditions arise as occurred with the college students last year by overflowing into the entire lobby of the Community Building. Situations which arise from some of the students create some very serious criticism by many who use the Community Club facilities and, of course, it was never intended that the entire lobby be utilized as a social room for the student body.
>
> We all recognize your increased enrollment creates need for additional facilities and we are therefore agreed to make available to the Junior College Room 214 on the second floor of the Community Building. By providing this extra space, it should enable your administration to provide lounging facilities on the second floor and confine the use of the Community Club lobby by the college students to the west end of the lobby which represents the area between the Library and the Little Theatre Lobby.
>
> I think with proper planning and presentation to the student body, this need not create any great conflict or condemnation towards the Community Club administration for the lobby facilities are available to the members at large as well as to other individuals who use the Club's facilities from time to time.
>
> I suggest Dr. Fenstermacher and Mr. Hoar get together to set up a plan which will create the least amount of friction when the students are advised of this arrangement.[35]

Of interest is the fact that the Derry Township School Board granted its approval on August 14 to assign room 214 as a lounge although no reference to Mr. Bobb's letter of July 14 was included in the "Board Minutes." The minutes read:

> Discussion on Junior College students using main lobby of Community Building as a lounge. Permission given by Board to have room 214 available for this purpose. This should relieve some of the congestion in the West end of the main lobby. Instructions were given that this room be equipped as a lounge.[36]

With the opening of the 1961-1962 academic year the overlapping use of the Club lobby and other facilities was, apparently, becoming critical. On September 9, Dr. Jacques, Superintendent of Schools, suggested that he and Dean Fenstermacher meet with Mr. Bobb to discuss several problems. Concerning the lobby, Jacques advised:

> We face a severe problem relative to the restriction of students in the lobby since we will have approximately 250 Junior College students in attendance

---

[34] "Information Bulletin," Vol. XVIII, No. 12, February 16, 1956.
[35] Letter from J. E. Bobb, Chairman, Board of Managers to Paul Curry, July 14, 1961.
[36] Derry Township Public Schools, "Board Minutes," August 14, 1961.

and we do not have adequate facilities for them during nonclass time. Perhaps a discussion relative to increased supervision might be of some value for all concerned.[37]

Dean Fenstermacher included the following statement, which revealed his feeling of increased helplessness over the worsening situation, in the September 19, 1961 faculty "Information Bulletin."

Today, the Community Club facilities have been taxed to capacity. There are outside groups meeting in the Community Theatre, Little Theatre, Dining Room and the Social Room. This is an example of the necessity for faculty supervision of the students using the lobby in competition with "guests." It has been made clear by edict that the guests are to be given preference in the use of facilities. Students are not to use the east end of the lobby at any time. Under the circumstances prevailing today it has been suggested that all students leave the lobby and use Room 214 for study, the Lounge for chatter and empty classrooms for sitting. This is obviously an unworkable condition but a certain amount of supervision is necessary to control and to establish the highest standards of decorum. Anything less will most likely result in an order of evacuate the lobby. On the positive side, faculty association with students on a companionable basis will bear fruit of cooperation, good feeling and pride in college life to a degree unobtainable in a classroom situation.[38]

On September 20, Mr. Bobb confirmed the conclusions of a meeting which was held to discuss the use of Community Building facilities. Concerning the social room and the use of the lobby, he stated:

We agree to permit you to use Room 214 as needed, but also be available for public meetings as arranged for between the Community Club Director and your Junior College Administrator. We also agree that the west end of the Community Club lobby from the Information Desk to the Cocoa Avenue side be available for use by your Junior College students provided, however, that proper conduct and attitude be assumed at all times by the students when using these facilities. Proper control shall be exercised between the Dean of the Junior College and the Director of the Community Club. If proper conduct cannot be maintained, this privilege may have to be revised.[39]

By the Fall of 1962, Community Center membership was required of all students although the collection of fees was postponed until November, 1963.[40] In a September, 1962 issue of the "Information Bulletin" Dr. Fenstermacher remarked:

All full time students are to be members of either the women's or the men's club. It might be considered that this is the rental of the property for a year by the students as well as the physical education services which are provided from the Club budget.[41]

---

[37]Letter from L. Eugene Jacques, Superintendent of Schools to Mr. James E. Bobb, September 7, 1961.

[38]"Information Bulletin," Vol. XXIV, No. 2, September 19, 1961, p. 2.

[39]Letter from J. E. Bobb to Dr. L. Eugene Jacques, Superintendent of Schools, September 20, 1961.

[40]"Statement of Understanding, Hershey Community Center and Hershey Junior College (Agreed upon by both the Center and College—November, 1962)," p. 1; and letter from V. H. Fenstermacher to John Zerbe, Director of Community Center, September 22, 1964.

[41]"Information Bulletin," Vol. XXV, No. 2, September 18, 1962.

It did not appear the required Club membership reduced the problems related to the overlapping use of the facilities.

The Library

The Public Library located in the Community Building served also as the Junior College Library throughout the history of the College. Its shortcomings were emphasized in the 1942 Middle States report and each subsequent report. Nevertheless, relatively little was done to correct the deficiencies of the Library.

Figure 9 shows the complicated relationship of the Junior College and the Community Center to the Library and its staff.[42]

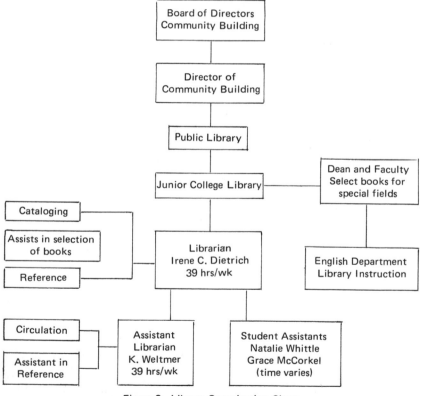

Figure 9. Library Organization Chart

[42]"Data Presented for Consideration of the Commission on Institutions of Higher Education," . . . 1952, n.p., *op. cit.*

The following description of material resources of the Library was provided in 1952 Middle States data:

> There is no special emphasis placed on any class of books in the library. The most recent additions have been in the fields of political science and philosophy. These two fields being the most recent changes in the curriculum are the weaker in number of volumes. Duplicates of books and special volumes are kept in classrooms for more intensive use. The more technical and specialized magazines are kept on tables in classrooms for ready use by students. The students use the more general periodicals in the Public Library. A special collection is that of bound volumes of the Congressional Record and Fortune Magazines which is kept on special shelves provided in the social studies department. A special collection of materials dealing with the life of Milton S. Hershey is kept in the Public Library.[43]

As of 1952, the Library contained 56 chairs and 10 tables. Some additional furniture was provided for casual reading. New shelving was installed in the reference section. The report acknowledged that "the lighting in this reference room is very poor" but the installation of fluorescent lighting was then being considered. The report conceded that the existence of front and rear entrances to the Library presented "the most difficult service problem" which resulted in the Library being used as a "thoroughfare," particularly in the late afternnon when the public school pupils entered the Library.[44]

The functions of the librarian, considered a member of the Junior College faculty, remained essentially unchanged from Dr. Breidenstine's tenure as Dean, and the faculty submitted requests for accessions according to the procedure earlier adopted. As of 1951, the library collection consisted of 2,943 volumes in the Reference Room and 13,700 volumes in the General Library or a total of 16,643 volumes. Junior College accessions from 1947 through 1951 totaled 820 volumes or an average of 164 per year. During the same period 85 volumes were discarded. The Junior College subscribed to 59 periodicals in 10 subject divisions.[45] During 1950-1951, an average of 18 outside loans were made per student and seven loans per faculty member. The Library was open 62 hours per week.[46]

The approximate annual Library budget for 1951-1952 was $750.00 or 1.3 percent of the total budget. From 1946-1947 through 1950-1951 an average of $865.00 per year, excluding salaries paid by the Hershey Estates, was spent on books, periodicals, binding, and supplies.

The "Report of the 1952 Visiting Committee" commented on inadequacies of the Library. The multi-purpose use of the Library by all age groups and the amount of confusion that resulted was noted. Training of the librarian was considered adequate, but the lack of any professional training on the part of the assistant librarian was considered a weakness. The practice of instructors gathering library-owned and personally-owned books and periodicals in separate classrooms rather than in the Library, was felt to reduce the teaching function of the Library. The Committee believed that this caused students to resort to the use of the libraries of private institutions in neighbor-

---

[43]*Ibid.*   [44]*Ibid.*   [45]*Ibid.*   [46]*Ibid.*

ing towns, thereby placing an additional burden on them. To provide needed study and working space for Junior College students, the Committee suggested certain tables or a section of the Library be assigned for their exclusive use and that as the collection and the enrollment grew a separate room in the College quarters be established. The appointment of a librarian whose full time would be devoted to College students was cited as being highly desirable. As a minimum, the Visiting Committee urged the assignment of a trained person whose "chief duty" would be that of providing service for the Junior College.[47]

In the summary of major recommendations the Committee suggested the College do the following:

Work to improve the library arrangements, so that there will be a separate room for junior college students to read and a full-time trained librarian to provide service for them.

Arrange for creation of a combined departmental library on the second floor, adjacent to classrooms of the junior college.[48]

The available records show that after the 1952 evaluation, little serious attention was given to the Library for ten years.

By 1958-1959, student dissatisfaction with Library conditions was being expressed. Ronald Keener, a student, wrote an article in 1958 which appeared in a later edition of *The Format*. The article satirized the Library and its patrons.

One may readily assume that one of the better places to pursue any undisturbed concentrated studying would be the local public library. Such a logical supposition might easily be based upon common belief (or misbelief) that the library would be the most likely place to afford the correct atmosphere for intense study. Indeed, is not the public library an institution widely characterized as the very essence of silence? Ah, but the foregoing conclusion is as erroneous and hasty a generalization as one is capable of making. . . . The public library might serve a useful purpose, but, as it is, this is the last place which might be considered conducive to study.

Mr. Keener concluded his article on a serious note:

Unfortunately, the library does not have the proper facilities to satisfy the heavy traffic of students from the High School, the Elementary School and Hershey Junior College. Often students are unable to find a place to study due to the crowded conditions. And the unavoidable shuffling noise of a crowd distracts one's attention so that concentrated efforts become trying events.[49]

In January, 1962, Dr. Jacques wrote to Mr. Bobb, Hershey Estates, emphasizing that the Library was "handicapped due to the lack of space." He suggested that it could be expanded by utilizing the space that had been vacated by the removal of the cafeteria from the Community Building.

---

[47]"Report Of The 1952 Visiting Committee," The Commission on Institutions of Higher Education, The Middle States Association of Colleges and Secondary Schools, April 15, 1952, pp. 11-12.

[48]*Ibid.*, p. 14.

[49]Ronald E. Keener, "Random Observations Viewed In The Library," *The Format*, Vol. XIII, No. 5, May 20, 1959, p. 4.

Jacques suggested that student use of the Community Building lobby would be reduced under the proposed plan but that it could be entirely eliminated by using the Community Building dining room as a student union.[50]

A meeting was held on February 23, 1962 to discuss the facilities of the Hershey Public Library. The librarian, Dr. Fenstermacher, and two outside library consultants attended. The functions and immediate needs of the Library were reviewed. The serious lack of space and the continued use of the Library as a thoroughfare was emphasized. The Committee proposed that a reference room could be established by partitioning the west end of the Club lobby, utilize the Social Room as an additional library facility, or move the Library to the dining room and kitchen of the Community Building cafeteria.[51] The committee report was later presented to the Community Club Board of Directors for their consideration.

A May, 1962 report of the Junior College Committee to the Derry Township Board of School Directors dealt with the continuing library problem. It stated:

> The committee discussed possible solutions for expanding the library facilities. They felt that since it was a cooperative program, a committee be appointed to make a thorough investigation with recommendations for a solution. This committee should be composed of the Junior College Committee, representatives from the Board of Managers and any other persons who may be deemed advisable.[52]

"The Self-evaluation Data of 1963," submitted to the Commission on Institutions of Higher Education of the Middle States Association, indicated that the total Library collection included 21,807 volumes, an increase of 5,614 over the 1952 number. Of the total collection, approximately 11,000 were considered applicable to the Junior College program. During the five-year period, 1957–1961, an average of 563 new titles were added and an average of 92 titles were discarded annually. The Junior College subscribed to 63 periodicals in six major subject divisions.[53]

The average annual expenditures for books and periodicals during the five-year period was $1,084, slightly over one percent of the total budget. From 1957 through 1961, full-time equivalent enrollment increased by approximately 100 students. Computations by Dean Fenstermacher show that the outlay per student decreased during the five-year period.[54]

Statistics on the use of the Library by students and faculty were not available for the 1963 report. The procedure regarding the selection of books was unchanged from 1952.[55] The Library contained 42 reference and bibliographical works and special collections on Pennsylvania History and Pennsyl-

---

[50]Letter from L. Eugene Jacques to Mr. James E. Bobb, January 18, 1962.

[51]Memorandum, February 23, 1962, personal files of V. H. Fenstermacher.

[52]Hershey Junior College Committee Report, May 2, 1962.

[53]"Report Of Self Evaluation," Hershey Junior College, to Commission On Institutions of Higher Education, Middle States Association of Colleges and Secondary Schools, February 24, 1963, p. 20.

[54]*Ibid.*, p. 21.   [55]*Ibid.*

vania-Dutch Literature. A collection of 175 records was reported and the purchase of a microfilm reader was noted. The *New York Times* was available on microfilm. Utilization of the Lebanon Valley and Elizabethtown College libraries and the State Library in Harrisburg was mentioned in the report.[56]

In answer to the Commission's question concerning student opinion about the Library, the following statement was included in the report:

> Junior College students seem to be satisfied with the present appearance of the library, but the recent addition of several sections of shelves in the main library tends to clutter. The library is attractive and the atmosphere conducive to study until 3:00 p.m., when the high school students use the library. The use of the library as a thoroughfare by students as well as adults is distracting.
>
> Ideally they would like to have their own library or, at the very least, to have a closed-off portion reserved for their exclusive use.[57]

It was also noted that the Library was inadequate for faculty members' personal research and professional activities.[58]

The deficiencies the Evaluation Committee found in the Library were strongly emphasized in the opening paragraph of its report on the Library:

> Improvement of the Library of Hershey Junior College is probably the most important item to which the administration of the college must give immediate attention.[59]

The Committee pointed out that it was erroneous to think that the Junior College Library "can be as successful and useful as it should be if it is part of the Hershey Public Library." The number of volumes useful for Junior College purposes was unclear to the Committee but the report suggested the number probably fell between 4,000 and 12,000. The report stated that "by any count, it is inadequate."[60]

The physical arrangements, the number of library professionals, and the fiscal, book selection, and other procedures were criticized. The report closed with the following pointed statement:

> The combination of a Public Library and a Junior College Library in one collection and one physical facility is *not* a recommended combination. A College Library collection is by definition of an intrinsically different qualitative nature than a Public Library collection. This is a fact which needs to be stressed and recognized as fundamental to a sound resolution of the present Library problem. The Junior College Library is to provide scholarly volumes and periodicals which are to support the work in the classroom and laboratory and which are seldom thought of as providing recreational or improvemental literature called for by the general public. Since the combination of Junior College and Public Library has now outgrown the space in which it is located, the time has come to face the problem squarely and to embark upon a program of development of a good college Library.[61]

---

[56]*Ibid.*, p. 24.   [57]*Ibid.*, p. 25.   [58]*Ibid.*
[59]"Report of Evaluation Committee," Commission on Institutions of Higher Education, Middle States Association of Colleges and Secondary Schools, February 24–27, 1963, p. 9.
[60]*Ibid.*   [61]*Ibid.*, p. 10.

The following specific recommendations with respect to the Library were offered by the Evaluation Committee:

1. A faculty committee should be created to conduct a full study for presentation to the Committee of Advisors of (a) what type Library facility and collection is most appropriate for our situation? and (b) what type of Library services do we need to support our educational enterprise?
2. It would be desirable to employ a qualified Library consultant to meet with the faculty committee and to assist in preparing its report.
3. Adoption of a program of rapid improvement of the Library by the Committee of Advisors acting in cooperation with the management of the community building in which the present Library is located.
4. At the same time that the study of the Library is being undertaken by faculty and administration, a faculty committee should be serving in an advisory capacity to the Librarian concerning needed additions to the collection, services to be rendered, statistics to be compiled, and other matters of operation and improvement.[62]

The personnel of the combined Library were commended as "a devoted and capable staff under competent professional administration and an efficient and appropriate circulation control system."[63]

Other Facilities

The coordination and use of the general facilities of the Community Building, including classrooms, became increasingly complex throughout Dr. Fenstermacher's administration. Several changes in the use of the facilities were made. In 1947, when Dr. Fenstermacher became Dean, the Junior College had the use of rooms 201 to 205 and 212 on the second floor, a book storage room, the lounge, the Library, the Little Theatre, and physical education facilities of the Community Building and the Women's Club.[64]

A Pennsylvania State College Survey Team, upon the request of the Derry Township School District and the Education Committee of The M. S. Hershey Foundation, did an extensive study of the Hershey Schools between December, 1951, and May, 1952. The report was made available in August, 1952.[65] The survey team considered the Hershey Junior College as it related to the Derry Township Public School System. Concerning the physical facilities of the Junior College, the team observed that "space is quite adequate in size but ill suited in its use." Staff and space sharing were also noted to result in administrative difficulties although this situation was considered to affect the High School more than the Junior College.

The report summarized the team's evaluation of the physical facilities as follows:

In general, members of the College faculty are satisfied with their classroom facilities and with College quarters. Facilities offered by the Community Building are, in fact, superior to those found on many College Campuses. But,

---

[62]*Ibid.*   [63]*Ibid.*
[64]V. H. Fenstermacher, personal interview, February 23, 1967.
[65]"Derry Township School News," Vol. 4, No. 3, February 6, 1953.

to the students the College atmosphere is lacking in a building which stands for recreation in the minds of many and which they must share with High School pupils.[66]

The description of the Junior College facilities and the explanation of policies governing their use, which were included in the data presented to the Middle States Commission on Institutions of Higher Education in 1952, closely paralleled that of the two previous reports during Dean Breidenstine's tenure. The plant and equipment were reported as being adequate for the program being offered but to better meet student and community needs, Dr. Fenstermacher felt that facilities required improvement.[67]

The "Report of the 1952 Visiting Committee" included a review of the function of the Community Building. The following observation was made:

> This set-up imposes some handicaps and inconveniences. The only facilities over which the college seems to have absolute control, so that they are available strictly for its own use, are a half-dozen classrooms, one office for the dean and the registrar, and the biology laboratory. It shares recreational facilities with all persons of the community who comply with certain qualifications for membership. It shares the facilities for instruction in the commercial branches, which are located on the same floor as the college, with the high school students. (The high school building itself is located approximately one hundred yards to the east of the community building, across a playground.) The college also shares with the high school the physics and chemistry laboratories, which are located in the high school building; the library, which is located in the community building, with the high and elementary school students and with the community in general.[68]

The Committee noted that except for the high school building, all College facilities, which were in an excellent state of repair and maintenance, were under the control of the Hershey Estates. Instructional units, laboratories, equipment and supplies were considered adequate but the problem of scheduling activities, which resulted from the need to share and the lack of space, was noted as a disadvantage. The Committee felt the situation could be improved through the provision of additional office facilities, lounge facilities for students, a meeting place for faculty and committees, and by partitioning a large classroom. The report on the general facilities concluded with the following statement:

> The administration seems to be aware of the disadvantages incident to the communal property arrangement and appears confident that improvement is in prospect through the erection of the new high school building which is now under consideration.[69]

Specific Middle States recommendations pertaining to facilities, other than

---

[66]O. H. Aurand *et al.*, *A Study of the Schools of Derry Township, Dauphin County, Pennsylvania, 1951–1952*, p. 131.

[67]"Data Presented for Consideration of the Commission on Institutions of Higher Education," Middle States Association of Colleges and Secondary Schools, January, 1952, n.p.

[68]"Report of the 1952 Visiting Committee," . . . Middle States, *op. cit.*, p. 11.

[69]*Ibid.*

the Library, included the following:

> Seek more classroom space in the community building, as well as place for conference rooms and for a student lounge.

> Press for elimination of sharing of facilities between junior college and the high school.

> Secure more adequate office accommodations for executive dean.[70]

By 1953, the Junior College retained the use of rooms 201 to 204 and two rooms on the fifth floor of the Community Building. Several rooms were made available to the Junior College as of 1954 when commercial High School classes were no longer held in the Community Building, thereby eliminating one phase of operation which caused scheduling and other problems.[71] Also in 1954, certain renovations were made in the Community Building which provided the Junior College with additional classroom space.[72]

Most welcome was the addition of new science laboratories in 1959. A biology and a chemistry laboratory, gifts of The M. S. Hershey Foundation, were installed on the fifth floor of the Community Building, the location of the former Hershey Hospital. A physics laboratory was also located in the room on the second floor of the Community Building previously occupied by the Biology Department. Prior to the installation of the laboratories, the Junior College shared biology and chemistry facilities of the Hershey High School and the physics classes were held in the science laboratory of the High School's vocational division.[73]

Another important addition to the academic facilities was made the following year. In November, 1960, a 15-unit language laboratory was installed in room 207.[74]

Prior to the 1960–1961 academic year, Milton Hershey School graduates who were attending the Hershey Junior College resided in Milton Hershey School homes named "Broad Acres," "Pinehurst," and "College Hall." Farm work was required of the orphan boys before College Hall was established by Dr. John O. Hershey in 1956. A hallmaster and an assistant hallmaster supervised the boys of College Hall. Much of the operation of the residence was delegated to the students through a Hall Council.[75]

As of September, 1960, Milton Hershey School graduates who attended the Junior College were housed on the fourth floor of the Community Club Building. Dean Fenstermacher's announcement of the new plan to the faculty is of interest:

> Undoubtedly there will be need for advice and counsel until these young men learn the rules of everyday conduct. Since this is their first experience of

---

[70]*Ibid.,* pp. 14–15.

[71]V. H. Fenstermacher, personal interview, February 23, 1967.

[72]Derry Township Public Schools, "Board Minutes," July 21, 1954; and Letter from J. E. Bobb and S. F. Hinkle, Trustees for The M. S. Hershey Foundation, to Carl Foreman, Chairman, Hershey Junior College Advisory Committee, July 21, 1954.

[73]"New Laboratories Show Progress At Hershey Junior College," *The Format,* Vol. XIV, No. 2, November 3, 1959, p. 1.

[74]"Information Bulletin," Vol. XXIII, No. 7, November 10, 1960.

[75]F. D. Miller, personal interview, July 26, 1967.

living alone, it is very likely that shades of the "town and gown" are in the offing. It has been mentioned already that the students are sitting on the front steps whistling at the girls, which is a good sport but it is apparently going to be frowned upon by the managerial group. More of the same type of behavior is quite likely to invoke comment from time to time.[76]

As many as 60 boys resided in the 26 rooms on the fourth floor. W. Lyndon Hess and Frederick D. Miller, the first basketball coach of the Hershey Junior College, served as hallmasters.[77]

Dean Fenstermacher and Dr. Jacques reviewed plans for the 1961-1962 academic year and, as a result, felt it advisable to present several problems to Mr. Bobb, Hershey Estates. Items included the use of Junior College classrooms by nonschool groups, provision to lock doors on the second floor, and demands on the physical education classes.[78] The following conclusions were reached in a meeting attended by Dr. Fenstermacher, Dr. Jacques, Mr. Bobb, and Mr. Hoar. The conclusions are not so important in themselves; rather it is interesting that decisions regarding such matters required a meeting of representatives of four different organizations. Excerpts from the letter follow:

It is agreed that when the Junior College classrooms are vacant and needed for other types of meetings that they be made available and any costs or operation needed to clean up the rooms after such meetings, if sponsored by the Hershey Estates, will be absorbed by the Hershey Community Club janitor staff. The Community Club will provide sufficient ash trays for the rooms during such usage for meetings.

We believe it unwise to lock all the doors on the second floor and as decided for a trial period, the classroom doors should be kept locked but other access doors to stairways and elevators be kept open at all times.

We will attempt to help police this area with our Community Club maintenance staff at times when the Junior College is closed. All parties concerned should be notified to report any trespassers to Mr. Hoar, who will take adequate disciplinary action.

Sufficient personnel and time will be effected to test the physical educational requirements for your Junior College classes at both the Women's Club and Community Club. This is an important part of college curriculum, and I assure you that we will provide the proper type of personnel supervision and participation in order to properly qualify the results in this phase of your educational program.[79]

In May, 1962, the Junior College Committee made several recommendations to the School Board regarding needed physical facilities. It was suggested the physics laboratory be remodeled and shelving installed. The Committee felt "a study should also be made of replacing some of the furniture which has been in use since the school opened." The partitioning of the main

[76]"Information Bulletin," Vol. XXIII, No. 2, September 7, 1960.

[77]"About the Hershey Junior College Men's Dormitory," *The Format,* Vol. XVII, No. 2, December, 1962, p. 3.

[78]Letter from L. Eugene Jacques, Superintendent of Schools, to James E. Bobb, Hershey Estates, September 7, 1961.

[79]Letter from James E. Bobb to L. Eugene Jacques, September 20, 1961.

office to provide storage and a private office for the Dean was also recommended.[80]

The "Statement of Understanding, Hershey Community Center and Hershey Junior College" of 1962 was, apparently, formulated in an attempt to reduce the administrative problems that had developed for both. The opening paragraph defined the relationship between the two organizations.

> The Junior College is administratively organized as an educational institution independent of the Community Center, yet it is required to function within a building and to use facilities administratively operated by the Community Center. In addition to the physical facilities, the Center provides library services and health, physical education and recreation instruction as a part of the College educational program. Only through close cooperation between the two chief executives of these separate organizations can the desired services be realized and problems be minimized.[81]

Three guidelines were established to bring about efficient, harmonious administration:

(1) The Director of Recreation of the Community Center and the Dean of the Hershey Junior College will keep in frequent contact with each other regarding the availability and care of facilities, the general conduct of students about the premises, and the services of the Center staff to the College program.

(2) The Chariman of the Recreation Board will meet with the Dean and the Recreation Director whenever it is deemed advisable.

(3) The Dean will be expected to meet with the Recreation Board for an annual evaluation of the College program as it relates to the use of the facilities and services of the Center. Additional meetings with the Recreation Board may be scheduled upon request of either the Dean or the Board.[82]

The responsibilities of the Dean and the Director of the Community Center were stipulated in the "Statement." The Dean was responsible for:

(1) All matters pertaining to the College curriculum, staff employed by the College, and the behavior of the students during the hours of activity scheduled by the College.

(2) The supervision of the College students in the lobby, library, and other areas about the building which are used by the students.

(3) The collection of membership dues for the Community Center from all students who do not hold regular membership cards and the forwarding of same to the Center.[83]

The Director of the Center was responsible for providing:

(1) Space, furniture, other facilities, and proper maintenances and limited janitorial services in keeping with the policies outlined from year to year by the Recreational Board.

---

[80]Hershey Junior College Committee Report, May 2, 1962.

[81]"Statement of Understanding. . . ." Hershey Community Center and Hershey Junior College. (Agreed upon by both the Center and College November, 1962), p. 1.

[82]*Ibid.*   [83]*Ibid.*

(2) Library services and health, physical education, and recreation services with qualified staff as per the instructional needs of the College.

(3) The scheduling of all meetings, conferences, etc., in close cooperation with the Dean when the facilities involved are those in regular use by the College.

(4) Assisting the College with the supervision of College students in the lobby, library, and other areas about the building which are used by the students.[84]

Finally, the "Statement" clarified which facilities were available to the College:

(1) Unless other arrangements have been made in advance with the Dean, the following facilities are available only for college use during the academic year.

  (a) The entire second floor of the building except room 217, and all of fifth floor except east corner, and the Kohr apartment.

  (b) The Little Theatre during the times when College activities have been previously scheduled in it.

(2) Facilities which are used jointly by the College and the community during the academic year include the library, physical recreation facilities as built into the schedule of instruction, the lobby, the Little Theatre, and other facilities of the Indoor Club.

(3) During the nonacademic portion of the year, Rooms 206, 207, 208, 212, 216, 501, and 502 are available only to the college.[85]

The 1963 "Report of the Self Evaluation" to Middle States included the following statement with respect to any impediment of the College's achievement of its objectives through the lack of funds, facilities, or equipment:

The attainment of institutional objectives is not seriously impeded in any respect by a lack of funds, facilities or equipment. There is at least a minimum level of tangibles to support and achieve the purposes of instruction. However, in certain areas of operation changes would be welcomed and in a few years will be necessary. Classroom space, offices or areas for teachers to conduct personal counselling and tutoring sessions, student lounging areas and the library fall into this category. All are susceptible to a solution within the building if so desired.[86]

The plans which had been made to meet the problems cited above were explained in the "Report."

These problems have been reviewed and discussed from year to year. Ordinarily the corrective action is approved as need becomes obviously apparent and forces the application of a solution. This observation undoubtedly is a result of the differences in viewpoint held by the operator of a program and the policy maker. This is a legitimate, and perhaps necessary, difference of opinion, but there can be little doubt that long range planning for the determination of policy would lead to more efficient operation in attaining the purposes for which the institution was founded.[87]

---

[84]*Ibid.*   [85]*Ibid.*

[86]"Report Of Self Evaluation," Hershey Junior College to Commission On Institutions of Higher Education, Middle States Association of Colleges and Secondary Schools, February 24, 1963, p. 32.

[87]*Ibid.*

The "Report of the Evaluation Committee," as did previous Committee reports, commented on the "advantages and disadvantages of . . . multiple occupancy" of the Community Building. It was observed that most of the facilities and equipment were good and the housekeeping excellent. The Committee called attention to several needs:

> On the main corridor of the second floor a piano teacher gives lessons all through the day, and the sound of the monotonous practicing by young students reaches far down the halls and, if not distracting to students, must be hard on the nerves of teachers.
>
> The Dean's office is crowded. He has no privacy for conferences, nor room for a meeting of more than three or four persons.
>
> One disadvantage from multiple use of the building relates to the use of the Little Theatre. Sometimes college groups or activities—chorus, music classes, convocations—have to be shifted to other quarters or have their meetings cancelled because outside groups are permitted to use this auditorium.
>
> There is little office space for teachers, and no laboratory space for student experimental work.
>
> Dean Fenstermacher is aware of the physical limitations of his plant. He has studied available space in the Community Building and elsewhere and has definite and suitable ideas about what can be done.[88]

The report included the following specific recommendations regarding general facilities:

1. Provide a soundproof room elsewhere for the piano teaching.
2. Provide the Dean with a larger office, one in keeping with his position and one affording both space and privacy when needed.
3. Study the space formerly used for the cafeteria and kitchens and utilize it to meet needs for space—library, lounges, etc.
4. Events in the Little Theatre should be scheduled in such a manner as to eliminate conflicts with college activities.
5. Rooms should be available for students who become ill.
6. Conference rooms or offices for faculty members should be sought.
7. A science laboratory for student research would be helpful.[89]

The section of the report devoted to resources closed with the following "general observations."

> The Librarian, the Physical Education Director, and the girls' Physical Education teacher are not on the college payroll, creating a potential sore spot in the realm of authority versus responsibility.
>
> A capital budget for Library and for equipment is needed.[90]

Paul D. Shafer was a member of the Middle States Evaluation Committee and a writer of the "Report" on the 1963 evaluation of the Hershey Junior College. Upon President Shafer's return to The Packer Collegiate Institute after the Junior College visitation, he wrote a personal note to Dr. Fenster-

---

[88]"Report of Evaluation Committee," . . . 1963, *op. cit.,* p. 5–6.
[89]*Ibid.,* p. 6.
[90]*Ibid.*

macher. The second paragraph of his letter is significant because it underscored the need for improved physical facilities.

> As you no doubt could infer from my report, I feel that you are running a good college. As an administrator, and as one who knows that all conditions are not perfect, I am particularly impressed by how well you do in spite of certain physical limitations, such as those faced in the Library.[91]

By September, 1964, it had been determined that the Hershey Junior College would no longer operate after that academic year. With the approval of the Hershey Estates, new organizations began to utilize the Community Building during the last year the College existed. Early in September, Dean Fenstermacher advised the faculty to anticipate increased confusion and the need for close supervision of students.

> The South Central Educational Television Broadcasting Station is housed on the fourth floor. Their 16 employees and equipment installation will add to elevator and other congestion. The Radio Station offices, on the fifth floor, employs four persons and adds to the problem. It will be a necessity to supervise student activity with more concern than had been required in past years.[92]

In the same bulletin Fenstermacher lamented on the state of readiness of the Junior College facilities.

> The usual resume of needed repairs was submitted last Spring for Summer action. A few items have been corrected but most have been neglected. Should you have a need for emergency repair, notify the office.

> The floors were not cleaned and waxed. Clocks have not been adjusted. Equipment may be misplaced. These and other minor problems may be corrected by notifying the office or suggesting solutions to Mr. Mathews, our Custodian.[93]

Later that month Dr. Fenstermacher wrote to Mr. John Zerbe, Director, Community Center, stating:

> Your decision to withdraw the services previously provided by the Community Center in the field of Recreational Education, comes at a most inopportune time.

Fenstermacher then reviewed the original provisions for the support of the college, the 1943 Middle States report by Tillinghast, the November, 1962 "Statement of Understanding" between the College and the Center (emphasizing the responsibilities of the Director of the Center), and, lastly, the conditions of the merger of the Junior College with the Harrisburg Area Community College. Dr. Fenstermacher closed his succinct letter with the following:

> It would appear that the instruction in Physical Education is properly a func- of the Community Center. This seems to be even more pertinent in relation to the fairly substantial increase in staff members for Recreational Education.

> I know you are plagued with problems, but I am hopeful of a solution which will permit the students to continue their past privileges.[94]

---

[91] Letter from President Paul D. Shafer to Dr. V. H. Fenstermacher, February 28, 1963.
[92] "Information Bulletin," Vol. XXVII, No. 1, September 9, 1964.
[93] *Ibid.*   [94] Letter from V. H. Fenstermacher to John Zerbe, September 22, 1964.

Administrative Organization

The underlying provisions for the founding, financing, and organization of the Hershey Junior College have been explained in the two previous chapters. Dr. Fenstermacher's manner, as an administrator, has also been considered. Changes in the Junior College administrative organization which took place during Dr. Vernum H. Fenstermacher's tenure are considered here.

The Pennsylvania State College survey team, previously mentioned, considered the Hershey Junior College to be a "distinctive feature" of the Hershey School System and "one that compares favorably with that of Junior Colleges anywhere, as does its faculty." The survey report declared the Junior College was a "unique institution" and, "controlled by the Derry Township Board of School Directors, it is a truly public institution." Concerning the administration of the Junior College, the survey team was of the opinion that "the administration seems to be all that could be desired and only special arrangements are deficient to any great extent."[95]

The survey team observed that the Junior College probably had "an obligation to popularize its appeal to high school students" in order to increase the number and proportion of local high school students taking advantage of the opportunity of obtaining a free, two-year college education. The Pennsylvania State College survey team concluded its analysis of the Hershey Junior College with the following statement:

> The College exercises a strong influence upon the work of the Hershey Public Schools. The survey staff respectfully suggests that this influence should be increased and improved.[96]

As an efficient administrator, Dr. Fenstermacher was interested in the findings of the survey team and urged the Junior College faculty and the School Board to give serious consideration to the recommendations included in the study. He included the following statement in his December, 1952, "Administrative Report" to the Board.

> The section of the Pennsylvania State College Survey of the Derry Township School District devoted to the Junior College discusses some interesting data. Many times the normal perusal of this type of material is provocative of discussion and on occasion of misleading conclusions. This report, and the report of the Middle States Evaluation Committee is well worth discussion beyond the time limitations of the formal meeting of the Board of Education. It would be a pleasure to meet with those interested in a full review of the two reports for the purpose of clarifying the elements of the reports and to implement the organization and the operation of the institution.[97]

The survey suggestion that the Junior College be popularized resulted in the printing and distribution of a brochure providing information about the

---

[95]O. H. Aurand *et al., op. cit.,* p. 130.

[96]*Ibid.,* p. 135.

[97]Hershey Junior College "Administrative Report," December, 1952 and January, 1953.

Junior College[98] and, later, the establishment of High School Visitation Days during which Hershey High School and Milton Hershey School students were hosted by the Junior College.[99]

The basic 1952 organization chart showing the relationship between the Junior College and the School District was identical to those submitted to the Commission in 1943 and 1946. The 1952 organization chart below, provides a detailed explanation (not included in the previous charts) of the relationship between the College and the School District, The M. S. Hershey Foundation, and the Community Building. It also reveals the complicated faculty structure with respect to full-time members, those who were "shared" with the Hershey High School and the Community Center, and those who were described as giving "associated time" to the Junior College.[100]

The 1952 data included an explanation that the Derry Township School District was the governing body of the Junior College:

> It is the responsibility of the Board of Education to determine and to author-ize the general policies of the institution, its organization, its administration, its maintenance and its general procedures for operation. In the discharge of these obligations the Board of Education follows the school laws as enacted by the General Assembly and recorded in "Bulletin 65, School Laws of Pennsylvania," Commonwealth of Pennsylvania, Department of Public Instruction, Harrisburg.
>
> This publication is the School Code which states that it is: 'To establish a public school system in the Commonwealth of Pennsylvania, together with the the provisions by which it shall be administered. . . .'[101]

The Superintendent of Schools was described in the Data as:

> The chief professional employee of the school district and the executive officer to the Board of Education. In this capacity the Superintendent reports the business of the Junior College to the Board of Education as part of the agenda of the regular monthly meeting. A committee composed of three School Directors is empowered: 'To serve as advisors to the Junior College Admissions Committees . . . .' and to examine problems pertaining to student admissions and enrollment.[102]

The Dean of the Junior College was described as:

> The chief professional employee of the institution and reports to the Board of Education through the office of the Superintendent of Schools. It is the responsibility of the Dean to conduct the affairs of the College in conformity with the general policies promulgated by the Board of Education and in ac-cordance with the purposes and objectives for which the institution was founded. Primarily this function included the planning and execution of the administrative details for the institution, the supervision of instruction, the well-being of the faculty and student body and attendance to those profes-sional meetings and conferences pertinent to the operation of the Junior College.[103]

---

[98] Derry Township Public Schools, "Board Minutes," January 14, 1953
[99] V. H. Fenstermacher, personal interview, February 23, 1967
[100] "Data Presented for Consideration . . . ," 1952, n.p.
[101] Ibid.
[102] Ibid.
[103] Ibid.

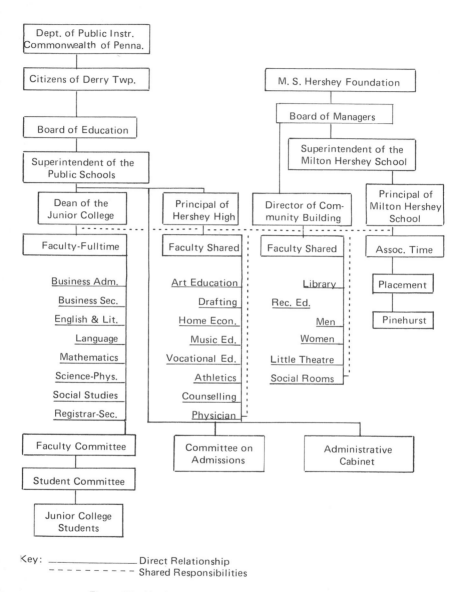

Key: _____ Direct Relationship
     — — — — — — — — Shared Responsibilities

Figure 10. Hershey Junior College Organization Chart.
"Data Presented for Consideration . . . ," 1952.

The function of the faculty and its relationship to the Dean were explained as follows:

> The Faculty is responsible for the subject matter instruction, and co-curricular activity and, through the Faculty and the Dean, the formulation and revision of the instructional program within the limits of established policy. Problems of interest in the administration of the institution are reported to the Dean through the Faculty Committee or informally and individually as is most often the procedure.[104]

It is worth noting that the "Report of the 1952 Visiting Committee" described the Hershey Junior College as follows:

> Hershey Junior College is unusual in that it is properly speaking a privately supported junior college functioning as a division of the Derry Township School District in Dauphin County, Pennsylvania. It is not chartered by the commonwealth but is under the administrative control of the Board of Education of the District, in accordance with the provisions of the School Laws of the Commonwealth of Pennsylvania.[105]

The following statement with respect to the "nature of the institution" is of particular interest.

> The operation of the college is so bound up with the other philanthropic interests of the late M. S. Hershey that it is not easy to apply to the institution some of the criteria commonly used to judge the value and efficiency of an educational institution of junior college rank. This observation is not meant to imply the existence of confusion or inefficiency. But the fact remains, that the set-up seems to a stranger unusually complicated.[106]

The Visiting Committee noted that the Dean believed in decentralization of administrative authority and he granted a great deal of autonomy to the various academic departments.

> The dean feels his main responsibility is that of keeping the wheels turning. He does not believe in any formal kind of supervision; . . . His philosophy of leadership does not include his having a major responsibility for the diagnosis of curriculum problems or for supervision of instruction; hence curriculum development is very informal.[107]

The secretary-registrar handled administrative transactions which were routinized. A major recommendation concerning definition of administrative duties was included in the report:

> Define more clearly the duties of the members of the administrative staff, especially with a view to the dean's being able to share with others the counseling functions which he now handles largely by himself.[108]

The Middle States Committee noted that members of the Junior College faculty tended to "transact their business through casual conversation and

---

[104] *Ibid.*
[105] "Report of the 1952 Visiting Committee," The Commission on Institutions of Higher Education, The Middle States Association of Colleges and Secondary Schools, April 15, 1952, p. 2.
[106] *Ibid.*
[107] *Ibid.*, p. 7.
[108] *Ibid.*, p. 14.

informal contacts" and the faculty (Faculty Committee on the organization chart) "Has not met regularly and records of its proceedings were not available.[109] It was recommended that the faculty be organized "so as to have regular meetings and accurate records kept of faculty decisions."[110]

Presumably the Visiting Committee had difficulty in deciding what role the Junior College should have played in the total Hershey community as the following comment suggests:

> Heavy emphasis is placed on operating a program "within the limits of established policy." In attempting to measure the extent to which Hershey Junior College meets its aims, it is important to remember that the public schools' approval is merely applied to a program designed "to enhance the vocational, cultural and professional educational opportunities with the community." When it is recalled that Hershey is an unusual community – with public clubs for men and women, public library, public swimming pools, community-planned entertainment and recreation, the junior college responsibility for participation in community affairs becomes so nearly unique that it is difficult to appraise by common criteria. It would appear that opportunities for recreation and entertainment are abundant in supply and easily available. These offerings relate to the student activities program and make it difficult to determine when it is best for the school to merge its efforts with the community's and when the college must identify itself as a separate institution.[111]

The above statement implied that the Committee believed that a certain amount of provincialism may have set in. It was recommended that the College "explore the possibilities of further development of the student activities program and the student health program.[112] Later, the Chairman of the Committee wrote to Dean Fenstermacher directing his "particular attention" to this recommendation. A report of any accomplishments in this area was requested prior to November, 1953. In the same letter Dean Fenstermacher was advised that the Committee voted to continue the accreditation of the Hershey Junior College.[113]

It has been mentioned earlier in this study that the 1952 Visiting Committee was, apparently, frustrated over not being able to obtain complete and accurate information with respect to fiscal operation and policies of the institution. Two recommendations were made which related to the finances:

> Devise some method of setting up simple books to record the financial facts connected with the operation of the college, so that *some* idea of actual costs may be arrived at.

> Arrange for keeping financial records so as to make it possible to compute on a realistic basis the approximate actual cost of operation of the Junior College.[114]

---

[109]*Ibid.*, p. 7.
[110]*Ibid.*, p. 14.
[111]*Ibid.*, pp. 7–8.
[112]*Ibid.*, p. 14.
[113]Letter From E. K. Smiley, Chairman of 1952 Visiting Committee to Dr. V. H. Fenstermacher, May 1, 1952.
[114]"Report of the 1952 Visiting Committee," . . . *op. cit.*, pp. 14–15.

It was also recommended that provision be made for an increase of salary for the Dean "in view of his heavy responsibilities and his twelve-month term of service."[115]

Following the receipt and study of the Middle States report, Dean Fenstermacher solicited comments from the faculty. At least two professors submitted comments and both concurred with the recommendation of the Visiting Committee that the faculty conduct regular meetings and keep minutes of the proceedings.[116] The professors' comments revealed their interest in establishing a more democratic, collegial organization.

On November 12, 1952, Dean Fenstermacher wrote to Dr. Smiley advising that the Middle States recommendations were subject to serious study and analysis. He pointed out that improvements had been made in the physical facilities, admission rules and regulations had been liberalized which resulted in a 30 percent increase in enrollment, and the faculty was devoting study to the Middle States report throughout the school year. The faculty, Fenstermacher reported, was simultaneously considering the recommendations relating to the instructional program.[117]

Dean Fenstermacher, as did Dean Breidenstine, gave serious thought to the most beneficial relationship of the College with the high schools of the community. For example, in January, 1953, Dean Fenstermacher proposed to the School Board and the faculty that the Junior College academic year open one week later than it previously did. He cited the fact that many students concluded their employment after Labor Day, many families observed the Labor Day weekend by traveling, students objected to starting the college year up to two weeks before their friends did, and a later opening would differentiate the Junior College from the High School. A detailed calendar plan was submitted[118] which was accepted and put into effect.[119]

The faculty also voiced their concern over the relationship of the Junior College with the secondary school. It was felt that the College's reputation would tend to suffer "by the subtle association" and the assumption, on the part of outside observers, that the Junior College was "a mere upward extension" of the secondary school. Further, this presumed relationship, the faculty believed, could prove a detriment to Junior College students wishing to transfer to other institutions.[120] This concern may have led to the authorization and appointment of a Junior College Committee (on Higher Education) in 1954. The body was a joint one, composed of two members of The M. S. Hershey Foundation Board of Managers, three members of the Derry Township Board of School Directors, and two members of the School

---

[115]*Ibid.*, p. 14.

[116]Memoranda from William Landis and John Lanz (Professors) to Dean V. H. Fenstermacher, n.d.

[117]Letter from V. H. Fenstermacher to E. K. Smiley, November 12, 1952.

[118]Hershey Junior College, "Administrative Report," January 1, 1953; and "Information Bulletin," Vol. XV, No. 9, February 5, 1953.

[119]Hershey Junior College, "Administrative Report," August, 1953.

[120]"Information Bulletin," Vol. 15, No. 13, March 25, 1953.

Administration, the Superintendent of Schools and the Dean of the Hershey Junior College.[121] The establishment of this committee was significant in that it was an attempt to bring together representatives of the three groups to improve communication and the administration of the College.

The first meeting of the Hershey Junior College Committee on Higher Education, held on February 5, 1954, was devoted to the general consideration of the "problems of the welfare of the Junior College" and "the place of the junior college in the educational world and in the community." The specific topic concerning rearrangement of classroom space was tabled.[122] Later the Committee became known as the Committee of Advisors.[123]

Raymond H. Koch, Superintendent of Schools, resigned at the close of the 1953–1954 academic year.[124] Dr. L. Eugene Jacques was elected to succeed Koch. Thirty-four candidates,[125] including Dr. Fenstermacher,[126] sought the position. The appointment of Jacques marked a somewhat different relationship between the Dean and the Superintendent in as much as Dr. Jacques adopted an attitude toward the Junior College which is best described as "laissez faire."

In 1955, the need for an additional classroom in the Community Building was made known during a Committee on Higher Education meeting. The following reply by Mr. Bobb of The M. S. Hershey Foundation, reveals the extent to which the Foundation's Board of Managers played a decisive role in the administration of the Junior College.

> It also was stated at that time you anticipated the enrollment may exceed one hundred fifty (150) students originally decided upon by the Board of The M. S. Hershey Foundation, however, if your enrollment this year exceeds one hundred fifty (150) students and they can be accommodated without changing the 1955–1956 budget, and without hiring an additional teacher beyond the extra teacher approved during our last meeting, the Board of The M. S. Hershey Foundation agreed that you may take in such additional students exceeding the one hundred fifty (150).
>
> Inasmuch as the School Board requested the use of only one additional room this term, and such accommodations will be made available, we believe you should start operation on this plan and if necessity requires the second room, your committee can discuss it with us.[127]

In September of 1955, the Board of School Directors voted that all matters pertaining to the Junior College were to be "cleared" through the Superintendent of Schools and presented to the Board in the "Dean's Report" each

[121] Letter from E. Morse Heisey, President, Derry Township District to V. H. Fenstermacher, January 19, 1954.
[122] "Information Bulletin," Vol. XVI, No. 14, February 17, 1954; and "Administrative Report," March 11, 1954.
[123] "Information Bulletin," Vol. XXIV, No. 6, March 27, 1962.
[124] Derry Township Public Schools, "Board Minutes," April 13, 1954.
[125] Derry Township Public Schools, "Board Minutes," May 31, 1954.
[126] Letter from Mrs. V. H. Fenstermacher to writer, July 8, 1970.
[127] Letter from J. E. Bobb, The M. S. Hershey Foundation, to L. Eugene Jacques, Superintendent, June 30, 1955.

month.[128]   This decision had the effect of reducing direct communication between the Dean and the Board.

It is noteworthy that the Junior College budget for 1958-1959 exceeded $100,000 for the first time in the history of the College. Full-time enrollment had reached 172 students by September, 1958.[129]

By 1962, the 25th anniversary of the Hershey Junior College, Dean Fenstermacher was prompted to emphasize to the School Board that the growth of the institution had resulted in the need for greater autonomy in the administration of the College. He wrote:

> Past reports have cited the problems and questions requiring solutions in order to indicate the best procedures to follow for the 1962-1963 college year—and planning beyond that year. There are certain problems, as noted in the March report and previous reports which seem to be overlooked and yet, their solution bears upon the efficiency level of the Junior College in direct and important phases of daily operation and future planning. The college has grown to a size and complexity requiring greater autonomy in order to solve the educational problems specifically applicable to the college program. Otherwise, the efficiency level of the college program will continue to fall, resulting in a loss of reputation and prestige which should never be permitted. Your discussion of this thought will be greatly appreciated.[130]

Apparently the Board concurred with the Dean's assessment of the situation and, possibly, with the earlier suggestions of the faculty. On April 6, 1962, the Board passed the following resolution:

> BE IT RESOLVED: At a combined meeting of the Junior College Committee and the Board of Managers the problems of Junior College administration were discussed. Merits of several plans were considered. It was decided it would be a beneficial move to separate the Junior College entirely from the High School. Under this plan, the Dean will be directly responsible to the Derry Township School Board and such committees as are established. This plan was deemed desirable to permit and facilitate more direct operation of the functions of the Junior College.[131]

The records do not reveal what effect this change had on the administrative organization of the Junior College. It is recorded that the faculty wished to meet with the Board of Advisors but it was difficult to arrange because of conflicts in the schedules of the advisors. One meeting was held in 1962 and another was scheduled for 1963.[132]

The data included in the "1963 Report of the Self-Evaluation Study" reflected the changes that took place in the administrative organization during the 10 years since the previous Middle States evaluation. Concerning the Committee of Advisors, the report explained that its function was that of the

[128] Derry Township Public Schools, "Board Minutes," September 19, 1955.

[129] Derry Township Public Schools, "Board Minutes," June 9, 1958.

[130] Hershey Junior College, "Administrative Report," April 9, 1962.

[131] Derry Township Public Schools, "Board Minutes," April 4, 1962.

[132] "Information Bulletin," Vol. XXV, No. 5, November 29, 1962; and "Report Of Self Evaluation," Hershey Junior College, to Commission On Institutions of Higher Education, Middle States Association of Colleges and Secondary Schools, February 24, 1963, p. 32.

Board of Trustees for the College. The Committee served to bridge the Board of School Directors and the Board of Managers. Composed of three members from the Directors, three from the Managers, and the Dean, the Committee of Advisors was responsible for the establishment, support, and general supervision of the College.[133] The Data emphasized that the "dual sponsorship" of the College demanded a degree of cooperative effort between the Board of School Directors, who had the duty and responsibility for the administrative functions, and the Board of Managers, who had "the authority and responsibility to administer the Trust for its designated purposes."[134]

Figure 11 shows the organizational plan under which the Junior College operated its last few years of existence.

The Report of the Evaluation Committee was critical of the manner in which the Committee of Advisors functioned. It stated:

> The meetings of this Committee of Advisors are not held on a regular schedule and some are quite informal. No adequate minutes of their meetings were available to the visiting committee. Since trustee interest, thoughtful consideration of problems and their expeditious solution, expressed support for the policies and actions of the Dean, or chief executive officer, are essential for an effective institutional program and for the planning that provides for its continuance—as well as necessary to prevent the Dean's feeling himself in a slough of frustration—lack of regularity and this informality, both in time and place of meeting and in the records of the meetings, are major administrative weaknesses. . . . There has been studying of problems and the solving of some; a modest amount of planning for the future has been done; but some of these plans are rather vague and have not been carefully considered and generally approved.
>
> Since the Committee of Advisors is now equally divided between two groups, one with power over program and the other with control of expenditures, consideration might be given to adding one to three additional public members to the Committee, with perhaps one member being a person who is active in college administration elsewhere. This is a suggestion for study rather than a recommendation.[135]

The Evaluation Committee found the responsibilities and activities of the Dean had changed little since the previous Middle States visit. No additional administrative personnel had been appointed; he was assisted only by a Secretary and a Registrar.

The following specific recommendations with respect to administration were offered by the Evaluation Committee:

> Another administrative officer is needed and should be appointed, his duties to be determined by the Dean.
>
> A better record should be kept in the administrative offices of all actions taken at meetings of the Committee of Advisors and the faculty, and of any other formal committees.
>
> The salary of the Dean should be increased substantially.

---

[133]"Report Of Self Evaluation," Hershey Junior College, *op. cit.,* p.v.
[134]*Ibid.,* p. 6.
[135]"Report of Evaluation Committee," . . . 1963, *op. cit.,* pp. 1–2.

136

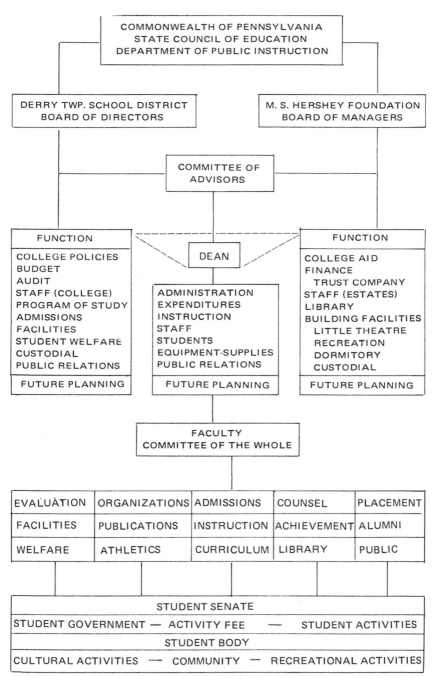

COMMONWEALTH OF PENNSYLVANIA
STATE COUNCIL OF EDUCATION
DEPARTMENT OF PUBLIC INSTRUCTION

DERRY TWP. SCHOOL DISTRICT
BOARD OF DIRECTORS

M. S. HERSHEY FOUNDATION
BOARD OF MANAGERS

COMMITTEE OF
ADVISORS

FUNCTION	DEAN	FUNCTION
COLLEGE POLICIES		COLLEGE AID
BUDGET		FINANCE
AUDIT		TRUST COMPANY
STAFF (COLLEGE)	ADMINISTRATION	STAFF (ESTATES)
PROGRAM OF STUDY	EXPENDITURES	LIBRARY
ADMISSIONS	INSTRUCTION	BUILDING FACILITIES
FACILITIES	STAFF	LITTLE THEATRE
STUDENT WELFARE	STUDENTS	RECREATION
CUSTODIAL	EQUIPMENT-SUPPLIES	DORMITORY
PUBLIC RELATIONS	PUBLIC RELATIONS	CUSTODIAL
FUTURE PLANNING	FUTURE PLANNING	FUTURE PLANNING

FACULTY
COMMITTEE OF THE WHOLE

EVALUATION	ORGANIZATIONS	ADMISSIONS	COUNSEL	PLACEMENT
FACILITIES	PUBLICATIONS	INSTRUCTION	ACHIEVEMENT	ALUMNI
WELFARE	ATHLETICS	CURRICULUM	LIBRARY	PUBLIC

STUDENT SENATE
STUDENT GOVERNMENT — ACTIVITY FEE — STUDENT ACTIVITIES
STUDENT BODY
CULTURAL ACTIVITIES — COMMUNITY — RECREATIONAL ACTIVITIES

Figure 11. Hershey Junior College Organization Chart. "Report of Self Evaluation," ...
1963, *op. cit.*, p. 14.

137

Consideration should be given by the Committee of Advisors to changing the the name of the chief administrative officer to President.

A handbook or statement or ordinances or by-laws or regulations concerning the powers, duties and responsibilities of the Committee of Advisors, the Dean, the faculty and the students should be prepared.[136]

There is no indication that any of these recommendations were acted upon before the College closed.

Faculty

Dean Fenstermacher maintained annual rosters listing "full-time," "part-time," and "ex-officio" members of the faculty. The Dean, Registrar-Secretary, and Secretary were included as full-time faculty members. Part-time faculty included such personnel as the librarian, basketball coach, and recreational education teachers. Ex-officio members included the Superintendent of Schools, the College physician, and Hershey Community Building employees who did not have teaching duties.[137] The faculty rosters for 1951–1952 through 1953-1954 also listed, under the heading "H. I. S.," or "M. H. S.," those Milton Hershey School staff members who had some indirect association with the Junior College.[138] As of 1954-1955, the "ex-officio" and Milton Hershey School personnel were combined and listed as "associated."[139] "Associated" faculty were so designated to distinguish their relationship from those members of the Junior College organization. They did not teach regularly scheduled classes, yet participated, to a greater or lesser degree, in the affairs of the College.[140]

Also included on the roster for 1954-1955 was the "Committee on Higher Education," which was changed to the "Board of Advisors" on the 1962 roster[141] and to the "Hershey Junior College Committee" on the 1964 roster.[142]

The biennial *Bulletin* for 1952-1954, and all succeeding bulletins of the College, differentiated full-time faculty from those who devoted less than full time to instruction. However, the several faculty roster classifications mentioned above were not included.[143]

During Dr. Fenstermacher's tenure as Dean, 1947 through 1965, 80 different people served the College in some capacity (teaching and non-teaching). Of this number, 37 individuals served full-time. The annual average number

---

[136]*Ibid.*, p. 3.

[137]"Hershey Junior College Faculty Roster, 1948–1949."

[138]"Hershey Junior College Faculty Roster, 1951–1952" and "1953–1954."

[139]"Hershey Junior College Faculty Roster, 1954–1955."

[140]"Data Presented For Consideration of the Commission On Institutions of Higher Education, Middle States Association of Colleges and Secondary Schools," January, 1952, n.p.

[141]"Hershey Junior College Faculty Roster, 1962–1963."

[142]"Hershey Junior College Faculty Roster, 1964–1965."

[143]*Hershey Junior College Bulletin, 1950-1960;* and *Hershey Junior College Information Bulletin, 1960-1962, 1962-1964, 1964-1966.*

of total faculty during this period was 27.9 with a range from 24 to 35. The full-time faculty average was 12.7 with a range from 10 to 19. Part-time faculty averaged 7.7 with a range from 6 to 11. Ex-officio, associated, or adjunct faculty averaged 7.5 and ranged from 5 to 9.[144]

The largest full-time faculty of 10 served the College during its last three years. The largest total faculty in the history of the College also served during the last year of operation; it numbered 35.[145] A statistical summary of the faculty from 1947-1948 through 1964-1965 is provided in Table 4.

TABLE 4

NUMBER OF HERSHEY JUNIOR COLLEGE FACULTY
1947-1965[a]

Year	Full-time	Part-time	Ex officio, Associated, or Adjunct	Grand Total
1947–48	11	8	7	26
1948–49	11	7	7	25
1949–50	10	9	6	25
1950–51	10	11	5	26
1951–52	10	9	8	27
1952–53	10	8	10	28
1953–54	10	8	10	28
1954–55	10	7	7	24
1955–56	11	8	7	26
1956–57	11	8	9	28
1957–58	11	8	9	28
1958–59	13	7	7	27
1959–60	14	*7	*7	*28
1960–61	14	7	7	28
1961–62	16	7	7	30
1962–63	19	6	7	32
1963–64	19	6	7	32
1964–65	19	8	8	35
	229	139	135	503

[a]"Hershey Junior College Faculty Rosters, 1947–1965."
(*estimated)

The number of full-time and part-time faculty, by department, was included in the 1952 Data submitted to the Commission. Departments and the number of full-time faculty in each were: English, 2; Social Studies, 2; Mathematics, 1; Science, 2; Business and Secretarial, 2; Psychology, 1; Languages and Philosophy, 1. Departments and the number of part-time faculty in each were: Art, 1; Music, 1; Home Economics, 1; Engineering Drawing, 1; and Recreational Education, 2.[146]

---

[144]"Hershey Junior College Faculty Roster, 1947–1965."   [145]*Ibid.*

[146]"Data Presented For Consideration of the Commission On Institutions of Higher Education," Middle State Association of Colleges and Secondary Schools, 1952, *op. cit.*

As was true during Dr. Breidenstine's administration, Junior College faculty appointments were made by the Dean with the approval of the School Board. By 1963, the faculty was characterized more by its diversity than its uniformity. Faculty members were being selected, primarily, for their "skill in instruction and ability to guide and implement the quest for knowledge among the students." The attributes of "effective teaching and effective leadership" were those sought in professors.[147] With few exceptions, full-time faculty were selected who had an earned master's degree and two years of teaching experience.[148] Of the 17 full- and part-time faculty in 1952-1953, the distribution of degrees was as follows: 5 bachelor's, 11 master's, and one doctorate. The age of 10 of the faculty fell in the 30 to 39 age bracket. Fourteen of the 17 were employed by the Junior College four to nine years.[149]

Compared to the 1952-1953 faculty, a higher proportion of the 1962-1963 faculty held a master's degree. Four of the members of the 1962-1963 faculty had recently attended National Science Foundation Institutes and two were candidates for advanced degrees.[150] Nineteen of the 21 part- and full-time faculty had completed the master's degree or better. The median age of the faculty was then 44 years.[151]

There was little faculty turnover during the three years prior to 1962-63. Only one resignation was submitted. During the same period four new positions were established, one of which was filled by a Hershey High School teacher.[152]

In the previous chapter it was explained that the traditional titles were not used to designate rank among the faculty at the Hershey Junior College. By the time Dr. Fenstermacher became Dean, the bulletin listed only two titles used to designate teachers of academic subjects. They were "Professor" and "Instructor." Other professional staff members held the titles of "Supervisor," "Director," "Coach," "Librarian," "Registrar-Secretary," and "Dean."[153] As of the printing of the 1950-1952 *Bulletin*, and throughout the history of the College, the titles "Professor" and "Instructor" were no longer used. Instead, only the name of the academic disciplines taught by the faculty were listed.[154] However, regular male teachers were addressed socially as "Professor."[155]

The policy with respect to faculty rank remained unchanged throughout the history of the College. However, during Fenstermacher's administration

---

[147]"Report Of Self Evaluation," . . . 1963, *op. cit.*, p. 66.

[148]"Information Bulletin," Vol. XIV, No. 8, February 28, 1952.

[149]"Data Presented For Consideration of the Commission on Institutions of Higher Education," . . . 1952, n.p.

[150]"Report Of Self Evaluation," . . . 1963, *op. cit.*, p. 79.

[151]*Ibid.*, p. 66.

[152]*Ibid.*, p. 77.

[153]*Hershey Junior College Bulletin, 1964-1966*, pp. 7-8.

[154]*Hershey Junior College Bulletin, 1950-1952, op. cit.*, pp. 7-8; and *Hershey Junior College Bulletin, 1964-1966, op. cit.*, pp. 7-8.

[155]John C. Lanz, personal interview, July 27, 1967.

"professional status" was achieved through appointment as a "department head" which carried some additional remuneration.[156] The 1963 Middle States Evaluation Committee noted that "the various departments of instruction operate without chairmen or directors." The Dean pointed out that their appointments were "informal."[157]

Provisions concerning tenure, retirement, sabbatical leave, and attendance at professional meetings changed little during the history of the College. Benefits to which the Junior College faculty were entitled paralleled those which applied to Pennsylvania school employees. The uncertainty regarding tenure was never clarified. The 1963 Evaluation Committee, as did previous ones, recommended the matter "should be cleared up."[158]

Junior College faculty members were encouraged to attend professional meetings although the amount budgeted for each expenditure was relatively low. Attendance was limited to one meeting a year. The policy and a suggestion by Dean Fenstermacher regarding professional meeting attendance was included in the faculty bulletin. The Dean regularly advised the faculty of known scheduled meetings.

> Staff members are permitted to travel to authorized meetings of professional organizations east of the Mississippi River. The budget item for travel is not great enough to permit every staff member to travel any distance. It will be wise to use the money for nearby professional visitation, to investigate and become familiar with methods used in other institutions for our own benefit as well as building friendships. All travel for which reimbursement is expected must be approved by the Dean prior to departure.[159]

The 1963 Evaluation Committee strongly recommended that faculty members be encouraged to attend subject-matter meetings in order that they keep abreast of developments in their academic fields.[160]

The percentage of faculty holding membership in the Hershey Education Association as well as the Pennsylvania State Education Association was high in the early years of Fenstermacher's administration.[161] After 1953, membership in the Hershey Education Association declined with the establishment of the Junior College chapter of the American Association of University Professors. The first officers of the chapter were: Norman Vanderwall, President; Elizabeth L. Taylor, Vice President; Paul E. Hofmann, Secretary-Treasurer.[162]

Teaching loads of the faculty grew heavier as the enrollment grew, particularly in the last few years of the College's existence. By 1962-1963, the faculty-student ratio, computed on the basis of 16 full-time faculty, was 1 to

---

[156] "Data Presented For Consideration of the Commission on Institutions of Higher Education," . . . 1952, *op. cit.,* n.p.

[157] "Report of Evaluation Committee," . . . 1963, *op. cit.,* p. 2.

[158] *Ibid.,* p. 3.

[159] "Information Bulletin," Vol. XXI, No. 2, September 18, 1958.

[160] "Report Of Evaluation Committee," . . . 1963, *op. cit.,* p. 8.

[161] V. H. Fenstermacher, personal interview, February 23, 1967.

[162] John C. Lanz, personal interview, July 27, 1967.

15. The median semester hour load was 14.4 and the median class (clock) hour load was 17.0.[163] The duties of a faculty member typically included the following: instruction—15 to 18 semester credit hours, 15 to 24 class sessions, two to four subject preparations; counseling—15 to 20 students; tutoring "as needed"; sponsorship of one student organization or a supervisory duty; and "cooperation and participation" in professional and student affairs.[164] The 1963 Evaluation Committee found teaching loads to be heavy when the number of hours devoted to guidance and counseling was considered.[165]

Hershey Junior College faculty salaries fell below the local and national averages during the last years of the College.[166] In March, 1962, the Faculty Committee of Hershey Junior College issued a statement requesting a revision of the salary schedule then in existence. The Committee made several proposals which it considered "applicable to the College as it is now composed, both by reason of its increased student enrollment and its enlarged faculty." In addition to the recommendation that a new minimum beginning salary be established commensurate with preparation and experience, the Committee proposed:

> . . . that the rate of annual increment and the maximum salary payment established for the rank of associate professors in the State Colleges of Pennsylvania be accepted for the teaching staff of the Hershey Junior College.
>
> . . . staff members attaining the doctorate should be given one extra increment following the awarding of the degree and two additional increments beyond the maximum established for the associate professor.[167]

Later, a letter from the Secretary of the Faculty Committee to Dr. Fenstermacher, with copies to the School Board, emphasized the dissatisfaction with the Board's procedures with respect to salaries. It read:

> The Faculty Committee is disappointed that the Board of School Directors has not advised this Committee of its action on the proposals made on March 2, 1962, for a salary schedule for the Faculty of the Hershey Junior College.
>
> Accordingly, the Faculty Committee has authorized me to send you a copy of the resolution it passed unanimously at its meeting on this date:
>
> (a) that the College Committee for the Board of School Directors begin early in the 1962–1963 academic year the preparation of an adequate salary schedule for the ensuing year.
>
> (b) that for the 1962–1963 academic year an increment of $300 be accorded each instructor on the Faculty; that, in addition, the minimum salary for those who are currently employed be established at $5500.

---

[163]"Report Of Self Evaluation," . . . 1963, *op. cit.*, p. 66.

[164]*Ibid.*, p. 81.

[165]"Report Of Evaluation Committee," . . . 1963, *op. cit.*, p. 8.

[166]Hershey Junior College "Administrative Report," June 11, 1962.

[167]The Faculty Committee of Hershey Junior College, Memorandum on Salary Schedule, March 2, 1962.

(c) that consideration be given Faculty members who are approaching retirement age by increasing their salary increments to enhance the retirement payments which staff members will ultimately receive.[168]

The Board did not accept the "across-the-board" proposal and did not reply to the other recommendations of the Committee.[169]

The 1963 Evaluation Committee concurred with the Hershey Junior College Faculty Committee. The report stated that salaries fell "below those required for good replacements" and that they "should be increased considerably." It was also recommended that the salary of the Dean "Should be
increased considerably."[170]

In March, following the receipt of the Middle States report, the Faculty
Committee again submitted proposals to the College Committee. They were:

1. that an annual increment of at least $300 be granted each member of the
   Faculty; that the increment be no less than that granted to teachers in the
   public secondary schools if such increment should exceed $300.

2. that a $5500, starting salary be established for newly engaged members of
   the staff, a sum that the College Committee may wish to increase if the experience and advanced preparation of the instructor warrant.

3. that a salary schedule be adopted, establishing minima, a rate of annual increments, and a progression according to which the annual increments will
   be granted.

4. that a sufficient fund be provided in the budget to enable members of the
   Faculty to attend conventions and professional meetings more frequently
   than has been possible heretofore.

5. that office space be provided for members of the Faculty who, with the
   exception of six, have no place in which to confer with students or to work
   during nonteaching hours.[171]

There is no record of any action taken on the proposals by the Board.

Various faculty committees were established during Dean Fenstermacher's
administration but they were included in the 1956–1958 *Bienniel* [sic]
Bulletin for the first time. The following committees were listed: Administrative, Alumni Affairs, Athletics and Recreation, Bookstore Accounts, Curriculum Planning, Cultural Activities, Counselling and Placement, Library,
Publications, Student Senate, Student Social Affairs, and Veterans' Records.[172] The last committee was excluded in the subsequent *Bulletin*.[173]

Eight standing committees were listed in the 1963 Self Evaluation Data:
Administrative, Alumni Affairs, Athletics-Recreation, Curriculum Planning,
Library, Placement, Publications and Student Welfare. They were designed

---

[168]Letter from Norman Vanderwall, Secretary of Faculty Committee to Dr. V. H.
Fenstermacher, May 29, 1962.

[169]Letter from Jefferson Barnhart, member Junior College Committee to Norman
Vanderwall, June 18, 1962.

[170]"Report Of Evaluation Committee," . . . 1963, *op. cit.*, p. 3.

[171]The Faculty Committee of Hershey Junior College, March 19, 1963.

[172]*Hershey Junior College Bienniel* [sic] *Bulletin, 1956–1958, op. cit.*, p. 8.

[173]*Hershey Junior College Information Bulletin, 1958–1960, op. cit.*, p. 6.

to provide the following:

> ... professional attention to problems in specific areas of the college program and, as a group, to meet the needs of the institution in the identification, control and solution of problems in any phase of the organization and operation of the college.[174]

In fact, they did not function as individual committees.

> Actually, the duties and responsibilities normally performed by the listed committees are accomplished by the work of the single unified Faculty Committee and in the regular staff meetings. From time to time the services of a listed committee or a special committee may be enlisted for intensive study, treatment and solution of a particular problem, duty, responsibility or a matter of personal group concern.[175]

In this connection, the role of the Faculty Committee was explained.

> The Faculty Committee operates as a fact finding body, a study and discussion group, and in an advisory capacity to the Dean in suggesting and recommending ways and means for the more efficient operation of the institution.[176]

The Evaluation Committee was, apparently, not satisfied with the system and made the following recommendation to the College:

> Some faculty committees should be created, especially one on the Library and one on curriculum, the first to be valuable to the Library in recommending accessions and stimulating the teacher of every course to list possible books for purchase, the second to assume a constant and steady scrutiny of the curriculum.[177]

A long-range planning committee was also suggested.[178]

The 1952 Middle States Visiting Committee praised the faculty as "active, energetic and interested in the college and its students. Instruction is done in a workmanlike way."[179] This finding was confirmed by student evaluation of the teaching techniques of Hershey Junior College professors. The elaborate rating system was devised by Dean Fenstermacher. A review of 1961, 1962, and 1963 student evaluations revealed that students liked their professors and felt they were effective. The faculty were, with very few exceptions, rated high. The purpose of the professor evaluations was explained to Junior College students in the instructions.

> This survey of student opinion is designed to identify major points of teaching effectiveness and to clarify areas of actual or potential differences of opinion in regard to the quality of instruction. The questionnaire is based upon the contention that the student's opinion of "good" or "effective" teaching is worthwhile in providing the viewpoint of the consumer of the instruction.
>
> This viewpoint, recorded in a serious mature and unbiased manner, can be of great value to the over-all educational program. Strengthening the effective

---

[174] "Report Of Self Evaluation," . . . 1963, *op. cit.*, p. 78.
[175] *Ibid.*   [176] *Ibid.*
[177] "Report Of Self Evaluation," . . . 1963, *op. cit.*, p. 3.
[178] *Ibid.*
[179] "Report of the 1952 Visiting Committee," *op. cit.*, p. 5.

and eliminating the ineffective areas of teaching will result in a higher level of satisfaction for student and staff member.

Signed opinions are preferred but you do not have to identify yourself. In any case, all papers will remain in a sealed container until after graduation and will be treated as private information unless permission is given to discuss it . . .[180]

Students were asked to rate each of their professors on ten qualities considered important to good teaching, on an A (high), B, C, D scale. The qualities were: (1) Organization of subject matter, (2) speaking ability, (3) ability to explain, (4) encouragement to thinking, (5) attitude toward students, (6) knowledge of subject, (7) attitude toward subject, (8) fairness in examinations, (9) tolerance to disagreement, and (10) instructor as "human being." The "most" and "least" effective instructional techniques and "most" and "least" liked subjects were also identified by the student respondents. Opportunity was also provided for students to rate the effectiveness of the student counseling system.[181]

The evaluation forms were collated and the responses subjected to detailed statistical analysis by Dr. Fenstermacher. Summaries were made available to individual faculty members for their consideration and the results were utilized in appraising the effectiveness of each member of the faculty.[182]

The Academic Program

Changes in Purposes

The underlying purposes of Hershey Junior College and subsequent changes in purpose during Dr. Breidenstine's administration have been reviewed in the previous chapters. The 1948-1950 *Bulletin*, the first issued under Dr. Fenstermacher, included the same six purposes that were stated in the 1946-1948 *Bulletin* with only one minor change. The statement that guidance and counseling services were provided for veterans was broadened to include all students of the Junior College. However, by 1950, the purposes were completely rewritten and reduced to a dual purpose "to provide an opportunity for the student."

1. To acquire one or two years of college training in school study, but with strict emphasis on the vocational, cultural and professional skill and knowledge required as preparation for employment or in anticipation of transfer to another college or university.

2. To develop a purposeful goal in life with the social intelligence, the civic responsibility and the personal culture gained through knowledge and co-operative living that will contribute most to useful citizenship in both private and public affairs.[183]

180"Student Survey of Teaching Techniques" and "Student Evaluation of Teaching Techniques," n.d.

181*Ibid.*

182V. H. Fenstermacher, personal interview, February 23, 1967.

183*Hershey Junior College Bulletin, 1950-1952*, p. 12.

This dual purpose was elaborated upon as follows:

PROGRAM—The public junior college is an institution whose success is measured by the extent to which it actually meets the many and varied needs of the individual student and the community it serves. The program of the Hershey Junior College, based upon a survey of these needs, provides the first two years of college instruction along with some advantages and opportunities noted hereafter.

—The student may choose his courses of study under supervision. The total program of study is arranged for each student in conference and in accordance with his present status, his potential ability, his educational objective and his need to prepare for immediate employment or continued study in another collegiate institution.

—A thorough preparation may be obtained for many semi-professional vocations which require no more than two years of training beyond the secondary school, but do demand knowledge and skill unattainable in the high school curriculum.

—Provision is made for a smooth and gradual transition from the secondary school to the college and university with the benefit of small classes insuring excellent instruction.

—The expenses of a college education are considerably reduced. It is estimated that it costs approximately $1,200.00 per year to attend the typical college. Living at home, the student reduces this expense to a minimum and has an additional two years to save toward the completion of his education.

—The breaking of home ties may be delayed until the advent of full maturity and the greater ability to successfully cope with the problems of establishing and becoming acclimated to a new and strange way of living. Immaturity accounts for the majority of those new entrants who withdraw from college before their junior year. Adequate preparation in the junior college, maturity and social competence tend to eliminate this factor.

—Students who completed a pattern of courses in the high school which do not meet the regular sequence required for admission in the professions may avoid delaying college entrance by correcting the irregularity and, at the same time, gain experience in study on the college level.[184]

As indicated in the following statement, the Junior College personnel who were responsible for providing the 1952 "Data to the Commission On Institutions of Higher Education" judged that the College program was fulfilling the purposes and objectives of the institution:

The present program, the organization of the college and the financial and physical facilities of the institution are adequate to accomplish the stated purpose and objectives. The scholastic achievement and the employment records made by graduates appears to substantiate this assertion as a valid statement of fact.[185]

Likewise, it was felt that the College program was meeting the needs of the constituency it served:

The institution was established to provide the opportunity, for those high school graduates who met the scholastic entrance requirements and who were residents of Derry Township, to complete the first two years of college in-

---

[184]*Ibid.*   [185]"Data Presented For Consideration . . . , 1952," *op. cit.*, n.p.

struction at home and with the benefit of free tuition. Within these limitations the Junior College objectives are in harmony with the needs of the selected student population.[186]

(In a hand-written statement by Dr. Fenstermacher, following the above quotation, he revealed that he believed the purpose should be broadened. He wrote, "It is, of course, difficult to justify the 'half free-half excluded' policy from a strictly educational viewpoint. The policy is educationally and community-wise short-sighted.")[187]

The Middle States Visiting Committee was, apparently, troubled over the College's belief that providing only one year of education was a justifiable purpose. The report stated:

> The Committee found no fault with the nature of the objectives but expressed some surprise at the idea of suggesting the possibility of a thirteenth year without a fourteenth ("one or two years of college training") . . .[188]

The Committee also observed the effect of the admission requirements on the broader purposes of the College.

> In carrying out its purposes, the college is limited by the admission requirements stipulated by the Board of Directors of Derry Township. The committee understands that the admission requirements, so far as geographical restrictions are concerned, have recently been liberalized. The effect of this liberalization has been the creation of "150 free tuition scholarships annually for the benefit of qualified secondary school graduates who are residents of, or dependents of persons employed in Derry Township. . . ."[189]

The first major recommendation made by the 1952 Visiting Committee was: Restudy the "Statement of Purpose."[190]

The 1954-1956 *Bulletin* contained a completely rewritten purpose. Although revised, the statement reflected the original purposes of the founder. It is noteworthy that the statement suggesting there was value in completing "one or two years" of post-secondary education before entering into employment was retained in the *Bulletin*.

> PURPOSE—The Hershey Junior College was founded for the purpose of providing the youth and citizens of the community with the opportunity to continue their formal education in areas of study beyond the scope of the traditional secondary school program.
>
> To realize this objective the curricular program of the college is organized:
>
> 1. To offer the first two years of college study for those students preparing to transfer to another collegiate institution with advanced standing.
>
> 2. To provide courses of study for those students expecting to terminate their formal education after one or two years of preparation for employment in a junior professional capacity in government, business or industry.
>
> 3. To provide a program of general education for the social, cultural and personal development of those students who desire college training for their

[186]*Ibid.*   [187]*Ibid.*
[188]"Report of the 1952 Visiting Committee," *op. cit.,* p. 3.
[189]*Ibid.*   [190]*Ibid.,* p. 14.

individual needs and the satisfaction inherent in a greater knowledge and understanding of local, national and world affairs.

4. To offer short units of subject matter, a single course or a combination of subjects in accordance with the interest and needs of those adults who desire to supplement their education by enrollment in the community division of college. These classes may be scheduled for the day or evening hours, on a credit or noncredit basis, when the demand warrants the inclusion of the subject in the college program.

5. To provide educational services for those individuals and organizations of the community who desire assistance in the fields of personal counselling, tests and measurements, vocational guidance, organization of special programs, and associated activities.[191]

The purposes of the College were further modified in the 1956-1958 *Bulletin* and, for the first time, formal objectives were stated. The close interrelationship of the purpose of the College and admission requirements is emphasized in the statement of purpose:

PURPOSE—The Hershey Junior College was founded for the primary purposes of: (1) providing the opportunity for the youth and citizens of the community to continue their formal education in fields of study beyond the scope of the traditional secondary school program and (2) to perpetuate this opportunity through the award of free tuition grants for those applicants who are both scholastically qualified and eligible for enrollment in accordance with the stipulations of the admission policy.

OBJECTIVES—The educational objectives of the college have been formulated to attain the purposes for which the college was founded and to provide a comprehensive program of instruction for students.

The curricular program of the College is organized:

1. To provide the opportunity for students to complete the Freshman and Sophomore years of training in preparation for transfer to another collegiate institution with advanced standing.

2. To provide a terminal program of study for those students who desire to complete their formal education after one or two years of training in anticipation of employment in a junior professional position in government, business or industry.

3. To provide a program of general education for those students who desire college training as further preparation for personal development and the satisfaction inherent in an advanced study and greater knowledge of the world and its affairs.

4. To provide a single course or sequence of courses for those adults who have need for additional preparation in a specific field of training offered in the community division of the college program.

5. To provide educational services for those individuals and organizations who may have need of assistance in personal counselling, tests and measurements, educational and vocational guidance, and similar activities within the province of the college program.[192]

---

[191] *Hershey Junior College Bulletin, 1954-1956,* p. 11.

[192] *Hershey Junior College Bulletin, 1956-1958,* pp. 13-14.

There was no change in the stated purpose and objectives of Hershey Junior College during the remainder of its history.[193]

Those Junior College faculty members who prepared the 1963 Self Evaluation Data carefully assessed the success of the institution's program in terms of its purposes and objectives. Among their comments are the following:

> The performance of the institution in helping students obtain those advantages for which it is designed is considered to be quite satisfactory in the judgement of the secondary school personnel, particularly the guidance teachers, who are acquainted with new entrant admissions and follow-up procedures. The college faculty considers the correlation between the overall objectives and the outcomes attained in terms of very good, outstanding and excellent. The same general reaction is voiced by graduates, the citizens of the community, the governing board, our colleagues in nearby colleges who are familiar with the facts through transfer students and professional activities.

> The purpose of the college in providing an opportunity for continuation of their education beyond the secondary school program at a minimum cost is reflected in the enrollment of a greater percentage of high school graduates as new entrants than is normal or average in Pennsylvania. The number who graduate from four year programs also exceeds the normal expectations. The low cost factor undoubtedly is a major factor, for it permits enrollment of students who could not attend under any other condition. It also permits the student to save his earnings during three summers prior to enrollment in the junior year. This factor has been responsible for a significant number of terminal students continuing their studies beyond the two year level. This circumstance also has an effect on the program of instruction directing attention to the transfer function with a corresponding reduction in emphasis on the terminal and the adult evening school programs.

> The restricted eligibility eliminates such usual services as a request from the nearby Olmstead Air Force Base for a training program for their military and civilian personnel. The same condition applies to the Pennsylvania State Police Academy. The trainees coming from all parts of the state are ineligible to attend should they prefer college level courses as a part of their instruction. This condition, in conjunction with a diminishing enrollment in the extensive evening program conducted by the local secondary school and the need for additional instructors for the day time college program resulted in a decision to concentrate the work of faculty members in the area of the full time, day school program. Part time students are, in most cases, adults who attend the day program of classes through adjustment of their obligations or hours of employment.[194]

The Commission on Institutions of Higher Education was advised that "no changes in the institution's functions, characteristics, or operations" were contemplated.[195]

The report of the 1963 Evaluation Committee included the following statement with respect to the College's purposes and objectives:

> The purposes and objectives of Hershey Junior College are well stated and appropriate for a junior college. They relate, however, only to the formal pro-

---

[193]*Hershey Junior College Bulletin, 1964–1966*, pp. 11–12.
[194]"Report Of Self Evaluation," . . . 1963, *op. cit.*, pp. 9–10.
[195]*Ibid.*, p. 10.

gram of instruction and educational services. Without overstressing its importance, perhaps some thought should be given to amending the statement of purposes and objectives to include reference to the many informal and helpful types of assistance designed to develop the personality, motivation and cultural awareness of students which are provided by faculty and staff through informal conferences, extra-curricular activities and friendly guidance.[196]

Changes in Admissions Policy

Residence eligibility for admission to the Junior College continued to receive considerable attention during Dr. Fenstermacher's administration. *The Literary Artisan* of May, 1950, was devoted to a review of Hershey Junior College from 1938 to 1950, "to recall the accomplishments and anticipations of the past, as well as the College's promise for the future."[197] The student magazine included a provocative, unauthored article, "Junior College Movement." The article closed with an analysis of the College's enrollment pattern and the suggestion that the admission policy should be revised.

> The first four years of the Junior College are notable for the increase in student enrollment from 66 to 102 full-time students. In August 1942 a firm policy governing admission of students was adopted. This, in conjunction with the war period, decreased the full-time student population during each of the following four years from 73 to 45 students. The return of men from the military service increased the enrollment for two years, but with their graduation a loss is recorded for the past two years. In the future, it is expected that the enrollment of full-time students will decrease slightly from the present low figure and remain more or less constant unless the admission policy is revised.

> A revision of the admission standards would require little more than a desirable re-interpretation of the requirements for enrollment now in force. This would allow graduates of the Hershey High School who are not residents of Derry Township and children of employees of the Hershey Estates and the Hershey Chocolate Corporation who are graduates of other high schools the privilege of enrollment in the Junior College if otherwise qualified for entrance. Should the admission requirements be changed to make this group eligible, the total student enrollment would increase by perhaps 50% and become stabilized at a number not to exceed about 125 students with the present facilities. The Junior College program would then reach all members of the community. This would be highly beneficial to those who are members of the service area of which Hershey is the center of employment and communal efforts. It would add another mark of distinction to those who caused Hershey to become known throughout the world and renowned in publications as the "Model Town."[198]

A month later Dr. Fenstermacher reported an anticipated September enrollment of 81 students. He further suggested that the admission policy

---

[196]"Report Of Self Evaluation," Hershey Junior College to Commission On Institutions of Higher Education, Middle States Association of Colleges and Secondary Schools, February 24, 1963, p. 1.

[197]"Prefatory," *The Literary Artisan*, Vol. XI, No. 1, May, 1950, p. 1.

[198]"Junior College Movement," *The Literary Artisan*, Vol. XI, No. 1, May, 1950, pp. 5–6.

should be revised to:

> ...allow bona fide non-resident tuition students who are graduates of Hershey High School and children of bona fide employees of the Hershey Estates, Hershey Chocolate Corporation and teachers who are professional employees of the local schools to enroll up to a stated limit in accordance with our facilities. ....[199]

(Fenstermacher had first suggested admission on a tuition basis in November of 1947).[200]

The residence eligibility requirements were revised in 1951 and *The Literary Artisan* article was given credit for helping to effect the important change.[201]

The Derry Township Board of School Directors had requested the Managers of the Foundation consider the admission policy. The reply by the Managers, reproduced below, announced the new, broadened admission policy and stipulated the maximum enrollment of the Junior College.

Hershey, Pennsylvania
April 6, 1951

The Directors of Derry Township Public Schools
Hershey, Pennsylvania

HERSHEY JUNIOR COLLEGE—ADMISSIONS

Dear Sirs:

The Managers of The M.S. Hershey Foundation have had before them your request for guidance relating to the broadening of the eligibility rules for admission to Hershey Junior College.

It has been stated that the present enrollment is sixty-five and that the facilities are sufficient for the enrollment of one hundred and fifty students, and further that if the enrollment is brought up to one hundred and fifty students the College would be of more real value to the Community and to the students themselves. It was suggested that one instructor would be reinstated and that this would be practically the only additional expense.

The Managers have been informed that the eligibility requirements at present are as follows:

> 'The student body of the Hershey Junior College is limited to graduates of an approved secondary school whose families are bona fide residents in Derry Township and graduates of the Hershey Industrial School, recommended by the Hershey Industrial School; provided that any resident of Derry Township or professional personnel of the Hershey Industrial School or Derry Township Public Schools, approved by the Committee on Admissions, may attend evening sessions.'

---

[199]Hershey Junior College, "Administrative Report," June 30, 1950.
[200]*Ibid.*
[201]"Data Presented For Consideration of the Commission On Institutions of Higher Education, Middle States Association of Colleges and Secondary Schools," Janaury, 1952, n.p.

In light of the above facts the Managers are of the opinion that the College should have more students, but in no event more than one hundred and fifty. The Managers favor the broadening of the eligibility rules of admission. With this in mind and answering your request, the Managers recommend the order of admissions be fixed as follows:

(1) Residents of Derry Township who are high school graduates or its equivalent and graduates of the Hershey Industrial School recommended by the Hershey Industrial School.

(2) Sons and daughters of employees of the Hershey Interests and sons and daughters of employees of the educational institutions in Derry Township, who are high school graduates or its equivalent, living outside of Derry Township.

(3) Sons and daughters of other persons employed in Derry Township, who are high school graduates or its equivalent, living outside of Derry Township.

We will appreciate it if you will advise us as to your final action on this whole matter and also if you will take up with us in writing any question you might have on the above recommendations by the Managers of the M.S. Hershey Foundation.

Very truly yours,

THE M.S. HERSHEY FOUNDATION

(Signed)   by P. A. Staples
Chairman[202]

The School Board unanimously adopted the new policy and the secretary was instructed to write a letter to the Managers "advising them of our action and thanking them for their interest and guidance in helping to make the junior college stronger and to be of more value to the youth of our community."[203]   Within the same month, Dr. Fenstermacher expressed to the School Board his pleasure with the new policy and he submitted a detailed admission policy and procedural statement as follows:

> The modification of the admission regulations is sincerely appreciated. The beneficial affects of this action will be reflected in a better balanced program in the Junior College along with increased student morale. Your efforts and final decision in effecting this desirable change are highly esteemed.
>
> Undoubtedly, there will be some questions arising in the initial stages of selecting students. It appears that they will pose no problem this Spring. Nevertheless, there will be a large number of inquiries when this is made known to the community. These questions will, of course, require answers, which fit with a general, and later a more detailed, pattern of principle and practice. The suggestions presented are offered for your consideration.
>
> 1. The free tuition awards to students should be known as M.S. Hershey Foundation Scholarships.

---

[202] Derry Township Public Schools, "Board Minutes," April 16, 1951. Letter from the Managers of The M. S. Hershey Foundation to The Directors of Derry Township Public Schools, April 6, 1951 was attached to "Board Minutes."

[203] *Ibid.*

2. The maximum number of scholarship awards granted annually shall be such as to allow for a maximum total enrollment of no more than 150 regular day students pursuing a course of study acceptable in fulfillment of requirements for graduation.

3. All applications for admission must be approved and the candidate recommended for the scholarship award by the Committee On Admissions.

4. The Committee On Admissions will award scholarships on a priority basis as follows until such time as conditions show need for a revision of procedure.

   A. To be eligible for consideration for a scholarship award the applicant: must present evidence of graduation from an approved secondary school or possess equivalent education as shown by standardized tests.

   B. Applicants will be rated with respect to scholastic achievement by determining their grade point average for all subjects undertaken in the tenth, eleventh and twelfth grades. Students with A average will be given first priority, B average second priority and C average third priority.

   C. Potential ability to profit from post secondary education as revealed by continued application to study and wholesome attitudes as shown by personality ratings and testimonial letters will also be considered in the final decision.

   D. Applicants for scholarships who possess the requisites noted in the preceding paragraphs will be considered for awards and admission to the Junior College in the following order of priority.

      (1) Residents of Derry Township, Dauphin County, Pennsylvania and graduates of the Hershey Industrial School recommended for admission by the administrators of the Hershey Industrial School.

      (2) Non-residents of Derry Township who are the siblings or legal wards of employees of the Hershey Interests and the non-residents who are the siblings or legal wards of employees of the educational institutions permanently located in Derry Township, Dauphin County, Pennsylvania.

      (3) Non-residents of Derry Township who are siblings or legal wards of persons who are regularly employed by a legitimate and recognized business or industrial enterprise located in Derry Township, Dauphin County, Pennsylvania.

5. Decisions of the Committee On Admissions shall be final and conclusive in the case of every individual application for an M. S. Hershey Foundation Scholarship.[204]

Dean Fenstermacher again expressed his satisfaction with the new admission policy in his report to the School Board:

> The recent announcement concerning admission regulations to the Hershey Junior College has been very favorably received. Printed postcard announcements were distributed to all Hershey Estates and Corporation employees to insure uniformity of information. Other local employers have been notified of this new opportunity for the youth of the community and it appears that the revision will ultimately result in increased good public relations within the entire area. Your efforts in accomplishing this most desirable change are sincerely appreciated by all.[205]

---

[204] Hershey Junior College "Administrative Report," April 30, 1951, pp. 1–3.
[205] Hershey Junior College "Administrative Report," May 31, 1951, p. 3.

News of the extension of free Hershey Junior College education to employees and dependents of employees of any enterprise permanently located in Derry Township was reported in the *Pennsylvania Labor Record.* The headlines read: "Hershey Enjoys Unsurpassed Education Opportunities" and "Free Junior College Open Now To All Derry Residents." (The new admission policy provided yet another means of attracting employees to Hershey.)[206]

The Hershey Junior College students were also encouraged with the prospects of increased enrollment as a result of the change in the residence requirement. "Populous J. C. Freshman Class Features Honor Students, Athletes," was the apt title of the "Special" lead article in the Fall Edition of the 1951 *Format.* The article reported:

> The Freshmen outnumber the sophomores almost 2 to 1 at H.J.C. this year.
>
> This large enrollment of freshmen may be partially accredited to the new eligibility rule passed by the Board of Education last spring.
>
> Present regulations permit students living outside of Derry Township to attend the Junior College, providing their parents or guardians are employed by the Hershey interests, or have established business or employment in Derry Township.[207]

The 1952-1953 *Bulletin* reflected the revised residence eligibility regulations. The admission requirements included:

1. Scholastic achievement record above average in the secondary school.
2. Recommendations attesting to desirable qualities in personality, character and leadership.
3. Potential ability to profit from college study.
4. Legal residence in Derry Township, or
   Employment of parent or guardian in Derry Township, Dauphin County, Pennsylvania.[208]

A personal interview, prior to final acceptance, was also required.

The following statement which appeared in the *Bulletin* indicates that a "selective" admission policy was not followed.

> The Committee On Admissions will review this data and the applicant will be notified of the decision. Applications should be filed at an early date since all scholarships are processed and granted in order of their receipt until the quota is completed. Applications for admission are then terminated for the school year.[209]

The broadened admission policy had the desired effect of increasing enrollment. Total fall, full-time enrollment had increased from 70 in 1950 to 97

---

[206] "Hershey Enjoys Unsurpassed Education Opportunities," *Pennsylvania Labor Record,* August, 1951, p. 8.

[207] "Populous J. C. Freshmen Class Features Honor Students, Athletes," *The Format,* Vol. VI, No. 1, Fall Edition, p. 1.

[208] *Hershey Junior College Bulletin, 1952-1954,* p. 12.

[209] *Ibid.,* p. 3.

in 1952. From 1953 on, total enrollment increased every year with one exception, 1957–1958.[210]

Evidence of the qualifications of the freshman classes of 1949 and 1950 was submitted to the Commission On Institutions of Higher Education in 1952. The statistics which were provided related students' high school rank with grades earned at the end of the freshman year. The information is shown below.

TABLE 5

HIGH SCHOOL RANK AND JUNIOR COLLEGE FRESHMAN
YEAR GRADE POINT AVERAGE[a]

FRESHMAN CLASS OF 1949		
High School Rank		First Year J.C. Average
Top quartile	34%	4% averaged between 2.5 & 3.0
2nd quartile	24%	10% averaged between 2.5 & 2.499
3rd quartile	22%	32% averaged between 1.5 & 1.999
Lowest quartile	9%	24% averaged between 1.0 & 1.4999
Not Ranked	11%	22% averaged below 1.0
FRESHMAN CLASS OF 1950		
High School Rank		First Year J.C. Average
Top quartile	46%	12% averaged between 2.5 & 3.0
2nd quartile	35%	19% averaged between 1.0 & 2.499
3rd quartile	19%	38% averaged between 1.5 & 1.999
		31% averaged between 1.0 & 1.499

[a]"Data Presented For Consideration . . . 1952," *op. cit.*, n.p.

The 1952 Visiting Committee emphasized the need to "recruit" additional students:

> The small enrollment tends necessarily to limit the opportunity for diversity of offerings in the various departments, even though the college is willing to offer courses for only two or three students. This fact suggests the possibility of some positive procedures of recruitment . . . Larger enrollment would ensure more effective class size in some courses, and would make additional electives possible.
>
> . . . .
>
> Students at Hershey Junior College come chiefly from two schools: Derry Township High School and Milton Hershey School, formerly The Hershey Industrial School. High school advisers at both schools help to select the students who apply for admission. The dean or one of the junior college instructors may appear before a group of seniors and explain the program, but recruitment is not a major activity of the junior college.[211]

---

[210]Students Enrolled and Staff Members—September 30, Annually," personal files of V. H. Fenstermacher.

[211]"Report of the 1952 Visiting Committee," *op. cit.*, pp. 4, 8. The name of The Hershey Industrial School was officially changed to the Milton Hershey School on December 24, 1951. However, various communications and reports continued to refer to the institution by its original name after December 24, 1951.

The following major recommendation concerning admission and enrollment was made by the 1952 Middle States Visiting Committee: "Make an active campaign for increase of enrollment in view of new admissions policy."[212]

Concerning the evaluation of applicants for admission the Visiting Committee observed that:

> Applicants are evaluated by the Admissions Committee with two divisions. One division ("The Trustees of the Milton [sic] S. Hershey Foundation") decides on citizenship eligibility, the other on scholarship qualifications. Admission follows the pattern described in the *Catalogue* and in the *Data*. Some students with less than a "B" average are admitted. Examination of their records show that some of these students earn less than a 1.00 ("C") average in college.[213]

The report made no recommendation with respect to admission procedure.

The admission policy with respect to residence eligibility was reconsidered and restated by the Managers of The M. S. Hershey Foundation. The following letter from the Managers to the School Directors was entered in the "Board Minutes." It clarified the eligibility of "employees."

Hershey, Pennsylvania
February 16, 1954

The Directors of Derry Township Schools
Hershey, Pennsylvania

HERSHEY JUNIOR COLLEGE—Admissions

Gentlemen:

On April 6, 1951, at your request, we recommended that the order of admissions to Hershey Junior College be fixed as follows:

(1) Residents of Derry Township who are high school graduates or its equivalent and graduates of the Hershey Industrial School recommended by the Hershey Industrial School.

(2) Sons and daughters of employees of the Hershey Interests and sons and daughters of employees of the educational institutions in Derry Township, who are high school graduates or its equivalent, living outside of Derry Township.

(3) Sons and daughters of other persons employed in Derry Township who are high school graduates or its equivalent, living outside of Derry Township.

Following a meeting of our Messrs. Hinkle and Bobb with representatives of your Board, at which meeting the eligibility rules of the College were discussed, they were further discussed by our Board. The managers recommend that you adopt the following order of admissions:

(1) Residents of Derry Township who are high school graduates or its equivalent and graduates of the Milton Hershey School recommended by the Milton Hershey School.

(2) Employees, and sons and daughters of employees of the Hershey In-

---

[212]*Ibid.*, p. 14.   [213]*Ibid.*, p. 8.

terests, and employees, and sons and daughters of employees of the educational institutions in Derry Township who are high school graduates, or its equivalent, living outside of Derry Township.

(3) Employees, and sons and daughters of other persons employed in Derry Township who are high school graduates or its equivalent, living outside of Derry Township.

Very truly yours,

THE M. S. HERSHEY FOUNDATION

(signed) P. A. Staples

Chairman[214]

In 1955, the Derry Township School Board established a policy regarding the "resident status of veterans of military service." Eligibility for free tuition status was to be determined "by evidence of six months' residence prior to date of enrollment in the Hershey Junior College." A provision was included whereby veterans charged tuition could apply for reclassification after six months had elapsed.[215]

By 1957–1958, total enrollment exceeded 150 students, and further increases were anticipated. Enrollment had increased 30 percent since 1955 whereas the full-time faculty had increased only 10 percent since 1953. This situation prompted Dr. Fenstermacher to explain to the School Board the necessity of increasing the size of the faculty. The faculty-student ratio in 1957-1958 was 1 to 15. Fenstermacher pointed out that a ratio less favorable than 1 to 14.5 would make it difficult to maintain the quality of instruction. He continued:

> . . . If budget limitations preclude employment of needed staff members, then it is suggested that quality be maintained by admitting the best prepared students with the greatest potential for success up to the pre-determined limit and rejecting applications of all others. This would be most unfortunate at this time of the year, for such a decision should have been made last year for this year when it was first mentioned for study. In the final analysis, an automobile will go so far on 9.7 gallons of gasoline and no further. A faculty of 9.7 [full-time] teachers can teach 126 students. Through efficiency and overwork this has been stretched to 150 students and can hardly be stretched any further.

> The present ratio of 1 to 15 is excessive and to add 30 students requires at least 2 full time teachers . . . .

> Should it be impossible to increase the budget outlay and it is considered desirable to enroll 180 full time students, it may be feasible to investigate the possibility of a $50.00 tuition fee, or the use of local school district tax revenues, or gifts and donations from other sources. This is a policy-making decision of great importance to students, staff, the college and eventually in the quality of instruction and the reputation of the institution, which will surely suffer by lowered quality of instruction and poorly prepared graduates.[216]

[214] Derry Township Public Schools, "Board Minutes," February 23, 1954.

[215] Derry Township Public Schools, "Board Minutes," August 8, 1955.

[216] Hershey Junior College "Administrative Report," June 9, 1958.

Admission and enrollment policy, as it related to space, faculty, and finances, remained a problem in 1962 as indicated in Dr. Fenstermacher's March, 1962 "Administrative Report."

> Applicants for admission September 1962.
>
> There are now 140 applications from the public schools and 52 from the Milton Hershey School under consideration for admission in September 1962. The 140 applicants include a number whose academic achievement is below the standard for acceptance and some, including a number from Milton Hershey, who will enroll elsewhere. Undoubtedly, other eligible and qualified students will apply between now and September. It is most difficult, if not impossible, to guess the exact number of new entrants under the provisions of the present admission system. The only method which provides some assurance of adequately gauging enrollment and therefore staff, curricula, facilities and finance, is to designate the number of new entrants to be maintained each year. Every student requires a fractional part of the staff, facilities and cost allowance which can be estimated fairly accurately, leaving the curricula or educational program in some degree of doubt.
>
> . . . .
>
> Some indication of the student population to be enrolled for 1962–1963 and succeeding years is highly desirable at this time to permit proper planning in light of the objectives and outcomes to be followed and attained . . . .[217]

Again, in June, Dr. Fenstermacher called to the School Board's attention the problems of increasing enrollment, and consequently, the need to enact a more selective admission policy:

> . . . .
>
> Every year it is necessary to dismiss a number of students for academic malingering or lack of ability or both. This year there are approximately a dozen students involved in this dismissal procedure. In practically all cases it would appear as if the academic factor was the more potent factor. In most of the cases the records show a very low high school grade point ratio, which indicates with the increasing enrollment we perhaps should be more selective in the original admission of students for in many cases we are actually doing the student and the family a disfavor of putting them into an environment where success is beyond their capacities.[218]

There were no important changes in the stated admission requirements of the College until 1962 when applicants for admission were required to submit the results of the Scholastic Aptitude Test of the College Entrance Examination Board. The addition of this requirement may have been prompted, in part, by the enrollment situation mentioned above.[219] There were no further changes in the admission requirements of the Hershey Junior College.[220]

The "Self Evaluation Data" submitted to the Commission On Institutions of Higher Education in 1963 confirmed that admission policy had not become more selective, in spite of the burgeoning enrollment which reached 250 during 1962-1963.

---

[217]Hershey Junior College "Administrative Report," March 12, 1962.
[218]Hershey Junior College "Administrative Report," June 30, 1962.
[219]*Hershey Junior College, Information Bulletin, 1960-1962, op. cit.,* p. 14.
[220]*Hershey Junior College, Information Bulletin, 1964-1966, op. cit.,* p. 14.

The academic qualifications and the personal characteristics of the new entrant students show little variation from year to year. This is an outcome of the admission policy which restricts enrollment to those who can qualify under the residence and dependency clauses of the admission regulations as well as the provision for satisfactory scholastic achievement.[221]

The data also reveal that great importance was placed on the personal recommendations of guidance counselors and teachers in judging the qualifications of applicants.

While the standardized data provide a foundation for judgement, the personal recommendations of the high school guidance directors and teachers provides a background appraisal the equal to, and perhaps, superior to the objective evidence. Since the great majority of the new entrants were graduated from a secondary school within a dozen miles of the college, personal observations are relatively easy to obtain and to evaluate in terms of the known reputation of the counselor for harsh or easy judgement. This condition is of great value in admissions for the counselors are aware of the college restrictions in enrollment and of the experiences of their students who were admitted, withdrew, graduated, transferred or were placed in employment.[222]

It was also reported that the School and College Ability Test (SCAT) and the Sequential Tests of Educational Progress (STEP) were administered to all students the first several days of the semester. Results were utilized in student counseling and course placement.[223]

Statistics on the distribution of intelligence quotient (I.Q.) test data of students who entered the Junior College from 1959 through 1962 show the median I.Q. for the four classes fell between 110 and 113. Median grade point averages earned at the Junior College by the same classes ranged from 2.58 to 1.70 (on a 4.0 system).[224]

Better indicators of potential for the 1961 and 1962 entering freshman classes were the results of the Scholastic Aptitude Test. The median verbal and mathematics scores for the 1961 class were 406 and 470; the median scores for the 1962 class were 423 and 478.[225]

The College reported to the Commission that, through experience, it had been found that:

. . . applicants whose test and achievement records fall in the lower third of the average standards maintained by secondary school graduates will encounter difficulty in the college program. Those applicants with records in the upper third, who apply themselves, have little difficulty in meeting their objectives. The middle third will be successful in an average college curriculum if there is no deficiency in motivation and good study habits.[226]

The Hershey Junior College accepted for admission what it considered marginally qualified or "risk" students. The justification of the practice was explained to the Commission's Evaluation Committee as follows:

The exclusion of all applicants in the category of marginal potential academic ability and of low average scholastic achievement would eliminate a share of

[221] "Report Of Self Evaluation," . . . 1963, *op. cit.*, p. 40.   [222] *Ibid.*
[223] *Ibid.*   [224] *Ibid.*, p. 41.   [225] *Ibid.*, p. 41a.   [226] *Ibid.*, p. 42.

those who will withdraw prior to graduation. It will also eliminate the two out of five admissions in this category who acquire a new sense of purpose and build a satisfactory achievement record leading to graduation, transfer, employment, as well as stable family and community relationships.

It appears wise to continue admission of marginal cases to "save" the twenty-one or so percent who achieve academic success resulting in later worthwhile contributions to society. To deny admission to this group of applicants would improve a statistic at the price of lost opportunity for those who would be successful in academic endeavors despite poor secondary school records. It appears not unwise to continue the policy of admitting a controlled proportion of marginal cases in accordance with the purpose of the college, "to elevate the standards of education–in Derry Township" through the education of its citizens.[227]

Financial aid resources normally have a direct bearing on admission. The unusual, if not unheard of, provision for tuition free education at the Hershey Junior College has been explained. However, the remission of tuition fees for Milton Hershey School boys was made possible through a separate program. Graduates applied for consideration as a candidate through the Milton Hershey School College Aid Committee. If accepted, students received a full scholarship to cover all expenses incurred. The financial support of the Milton Hershey School students was derived from the Milton Hershey School Trust Fund, previously explained, which is separate and distinct from The M. S. Hershey Foundation endowment. However, the Trust funds were not used to support the College program.[228]

Rules and regulations

Upon his appointment as Dean, Dr. Fenstermacher instituted several changes in rules and regulations, most of which related to academic matters.

At the time of enrollment, students were assigned a status based on "demonstrated readiness for college instruction in the field of his interest." Status was granted on three levels, "regular," "provisional," and "limited." Students who earned an average grade of A or B through tenth, eleventh, and twelfth grades, in all subjects required for enrollment in the chosen Junior College curriculum, were classified as regular students. Those who earned less than an A or B average or who presented an Equivalent High School Diploma were granted provisional status, but could be reclassified if they earned an A or B average during the first semester or a C average and a "satisfactory" accomplishment ratio by the end of the second semester. Marginal students who could not be granted regular provisional status were placed in limited status. Such students did not meet the regular requirements but were judged to have the potential to do junior college work. Upon removing any deficiencies and earning a C average and a satisfactory accomplishment ratio, regular status was granted at the end of the freshman year. All work satisfac-

---

[227]*Ibid.*, pp. 93–94.
[228]*Ibid.*, p. 51.

torily completed was applied toward graduation.[229] Limited status was discontinued by 1950[230] and the use of regular and provisional status was dropped as of the printing of the 1952-1954 *Bulletin*. Only the probationary status was maintained.[231]

Students who failed to earn the corresponding number of honor points and semester hours undertaken were placed on "scholastic probation." Probationary students who failed to remove the deficiency or to earn passing grades in 12 semester hours of credit in each semester could be withdrawn from the College.[232]

Students were required to have completed 31 semester hours of credit to be classified a sophomore. Those students registered for less than 12 hours were placed on limited status.[233]

Students approved to audit classes were limited to two courses in the day or evening sessions.[234]

Attendance at all scheduled classes and convocations was required of all students. The specific requirements remained the same as during Dr. Breidenstine's administration.[235] Likewise, the academic and "accomplishment" grading systems remained unchanged. However, an "Honors" designation was instituted whereby students who earned an average between 2.50 and 2.78 (on a 3-point system) were awarded Honors; those who earned an average of 2.78 or higher were awarded Highest Honors.[236] By 1952, the Honors designations were revised as follows: Special Honors (2.90-3.00), Honors (2.50-2.89), and Honorable Mention (2.20-2.49).[237] The option of completing an Investigative Paper was continued but limited to students who had earned averages of 2.0 or better and were approved by the Committee on Scholarship.[238] The name of the paper was changed to "Research Paper" by 1950.[239]

According to the 1948-1950 *Bulletin*, graduation requirements for students enrolled in the Lower and General Divisions were unchanged from the 1938-1947 period. The Technical Division, as such, was discontinued but a new Community Division (Evening School) was formally listed and students enrolled in the division were eligible to graduate upon completion of 60 semester hours of credit in an approved sequence of courses. Other graduation requirements remained unchanged.[240] As of 1950, a Certificate of Achievement was awarded to students who completed 30 semester hours and 30 honor points in an approved sequence of study in the day or evening programs. The certificate represented "the attainment of a specific educational

[229] *Hershey Junior College Bulletin, 1948-1950*, p. 15.
[230] *Hershey Junior College Bulletin, 1950-1952*, pp. 16-17.
[231] *Hershey Junior College Bulletin, 1952-1954*, p. 16.
[232] *Hershey Junior College Bulletin, 1948-1950*, p. 16.
[233] *Ibid.*   [234] *Ibid.*   [235] *Ibid.*   [236] *Ibid.*, pp. 15-16.
[237] *Hershey Junior College Bulletin, 1952-1954*, p. 17.
[238] *Hershey Junior College Bulletin, 1948-1950*, p. 17.
[239] *Hershey Junior College Bulletin, 1950-1952*, p. 18.
[240] *Hershey Junior College Bulletin, 1948-1950*, p. 18.

goal obtainable through one year of study."[241]   Students who completed a "regular, two-year program" were awarded the Hershey Junior College Diploma.   To qualify for the Diploma, students were required to earn a minimum of 30 semester hours and 30 honor points "in residence."   Work from other institutions was accepted toward Junior College graduation requirements.   In the case of veterans, credit was accepted for "equivalent subjects" in accordance with American Council On Education and Department of Public Instruction guidelines.[242]

The 1952 Middle States Association of Colleges and Secondary Schools Visiting Committee commented at some length on the "Accomplishment Mark" which the Committee described as "an unusual feature of the grading system" of the College. (The system has been described previously in Chapter IV.) It was noted that the Committee "was not able to find any evidence of weighting nor were the members able to form any adequate judgement as to the value to the student of this interesting device."   Further, the Committee was unclear regarding the application of the accomplishment mark within the total grading system.[243]   This concern was reflected in the following major recommendations to the College: "Work to iron out apparent inconsistencies relating to [the] number of credits required for [the] diploma and clarify the 'Accomplishment Mark.' "[244]

The 1954-1956 *Bulletin* explained the accomplishment mark "is an estimate of the student's scholastic achievement in relation to his potential capacity for scholastic success."   Results of various academic records and personal observation were used to estimate potential.   Students were advised that the accomplishment mark was part of their record but was not recorded on the official transcript unless requested.   However, students were advised that "students failing to receive an accomplishment mark of S [satisfactory] jeopardize their transfer recommendation."[245]

By 1956, the three-point grading system had been replaced by a four-point system.   Grades awarded were A, B, C, D, F and E (Incomplete-Conditions), and W (Withdrawal).   A grade of E was recorded as F if the deficiency was not removed within six weeks.   A grade of WF was recorded to indicate withdrawal from a course after three weeks of instruction without approval and if the student was failing the course.   The accomplishment mark system was, apparently, discontinued because it did not appear in the 1956-1958 *Bulletin*. The rules regarding probation and scholarship honors were changed to reflect

[241] *Ibid.*, p. 19.

[242] "Data Presented for Consideration of the Commission On Institutions of Higher Education, Middle States Association of Colleges and Secondary Schools," January, 1952, n.p.

[243] "Report of the 1952 Visiting Committee," The Commission on Institutions of Higher Education, The Middle States Association of Colleges and Secondary Schools, April 15, 1952, p. 6.

[244] *Ibid.*, p. 14.

[245] *Hershey Junior College Bulletin, 1954-1956*, p. 17.

the new grading system. "Dean's List" classifications were limited to "Honors" and "Distinction."[246]

On July 7, 1955, Dean Fenstermacher petitioned the State Council of Education, Department of Public Instruction, "to consider authorization of the use of the associate's degree, in place of the diploma of graduation, to signify the satisfactory completion of two years of college study."[247] On September 9, 1955, the State Council of Education granted approval for the Hershey Junior College to award the Associate in Arts Degree.[248] This important change was included in the 1956-1958 *Bulletin*. To qualify for the degree students were required to complete 68 semester hours of credit and maintain an honor point ratio above 2.00. The Certificate of Attendance was awarded to students who did not complete all degree requirements but who earned 60 credits and attended four semesters.[249]

The same *Bulletin* issue stated the regulation that to engage in co-curricular activities students had to maintain an honor point ratio of 2.00 and a minimum course schedule of 12 semester credit hours.[250] By 1962, elected officers of student organizations were required to maintain a minimum 2.20 average if membership was maintained in more than one co-curricular activity.[251]

There were no other significant changes or additions of the rules and regulations of the Hershey Junior College and the 1962 Visiting Committee of the Commission On Institutions of Higher Education offered no comments or recommendations with respect to the institution's rules and regulations.

The Curriculum

As has already been explained, the terminal course offerings of the academic program were strongly emphasized during the first decade of the Hershey Junior College. At about the time Dr. Fenstermacher became Dean, the thrust of the program began to change in favor of the transfer curricula. This was probably the result of a number of factors including the lack of facilities and the duplication of some technical programs by the vocational division of the school district. In addition, the socio-economic composition of the Hershey community was changing due to an influx of semi-skilled, skilled, and professional employees. Their children were more inclined to want to complete a baccalaureate degree and, consequently, there was more interest in Junior College transfer than terminal programs. Those students who were interested in the technologies required basic, general education courses to enable them to transfer to other institutions.[252]

---

[246]*Hershey Junior College Bulletin, 1956-1958*, pp. 19-20.

[247]Letter from V. H. Fenstermacher to Dr. Carl E. Seifert, Secretary, State Council of Education, Department of Public Instruction, July 7, 1955.

[248]Letter from Dr. Carl E. Seifert to V. H. Fenstermacher, September 19, 1955.

[249]*Hershey Junior College Bulletin, 1956-1958*, pp. 20-21.

[250]*Ibid.*, p. 19.

[251]*Hershey Junior College Information Bulletin, 1962-1964*, p. 18.

[252]V. H. Fenstermacher, personal interview, February 23, 1967.

In an attempt to revitalize the technical offerings of the Junior College, Dr. Fenstermacher and Robert Jacoby, Director of Vocational Education of the Hershey Vocational School, revamped the technical curriculum. The curriculum was intended to meet the need of the new technology. The rationale for the program was presented by Fenstermacher and Jacoby as follows:

> The vocational technical curriculum is designed to give terminal courses in the mastery of techniques and applied subjects in preparation for technical jobs involving aspects of supervision and control of men, materials or equipment. In addition, the program should provide for courses in general education which lead to a successful social, civic, personal and occupational living. Industries with which we maintain placement contacts for our graduates indicate the increasing need for technicians because of the growing complexity of mechanization, scientific processing, quality control and growth in organization problems and policies. They want our graduates for their immediate skill contribution but they also need and desire young men with better technical background and general understanding of industrial interdependence for specialized technical services and ultimate promotion. They need young men who have qualities of education, initiative and technical comprehension not usually found among their regular, loyal employees on the skilled level.[253]

The freshman year of the curriculum was described as an upward extension of the vocational-industrial program with special attention being paid to "individual interests and capacities." The two-year curriculum was outlined as follows:[254]

Freshman Year	1st Semester Hrs. per week	2nd Semester Hrs. per week
Drawing I–II	3	3
Technical Mathematics I	2	2
General Psychology	2	2
Industrial Orientation (5:13 to 6:00)	3	3
(Woodwork, Machine shop, Electrical, Sheet Metal, Printing)		
Expressional English	3	3
Principles of Economics	3	3
Technical Chemistry	4	4
Recreational Education I	1	1

Sophomore Year	1st Semester Hrs. per week	2nd Semester Hrs. per week
Drawing III–IV	3	3
Math Analysis	5	5
Business Accounting Survey	2	2
Industrial Laboratory (2 mornings per week)	8	8
Industrial Management	2	2
Sociology	3	3
Technical Physics	4	4
Recreational Education II	1	1

---

[253] "Suggestive Proposal For Establishment Of Technical Curriculum," p. 1, personal files of V. H. Fenstermacher.
[254] *Ibid.*, p. 3.

Announcement of the revised Hershey Junior College vocational-technical program was made in the *Hotel Hershey High-Lights* in August, 1948. It was explained that the program, to begin in the fall term of the 1948-1949 academic year, was designed "to meet the growing need for technicians whose qualifications lie between those of the skilled mechanic and the professional engineer." Dr. Fenstermacher pointed out the demand had doubled since pre-war days. The article also explained that:

> The program is flexible enough to allow outstanding students in the technical curriculum to elect courses that will qualify them for the regular pre-engineering program.[255]

Although the new technical curriculum was included in the 1948-1950 *Bulletin*, it was shown as a curriculum within the General Division. The Technical Division was discontinued as of 1948. The broad purposes of the General Curriculum remained unchanged; offerings were "designed for students who desire to complete their formal education in Junior College." The aim was to prepare students for employment and to provide a broad cultural background.[256]

Other curricula of the General Division included in the 1948-1950 *Bulletin* were the elective arts, secretarial, and clerical. The elective arts curriculum was "designed for the student who desires a special or unique program of study to meet a personal need." It provided the greatest latitude in the choice of subjects and could be adopted "to provide the necessary training for most of the semi-professional occupations, home-making, small business ownership and similar interests."[257] The intended purpose of the secretarial and clerical curriculum is self-explanatory and the subjects included in each were very similar.[258]

The Lower Division was continued and its basic purpose, "articulation with the curricula of senior colleges and universities," was unchanged from the previous nine years. The 1948-1950 *Bulletin* included such "typical programs" as liberal arts, engineering, and business administration.[259] Unlike earlier editions of the bulletin, the course offerings of the evening session were included in the newly-created Community Division—Evening School. Courses offered were determined by student demand, provided 10 students enrolled for each course. The regulations which applied to evening enrollment were essentially unchanged.[260]

An article which appeared in the local newspaper in September, 1948, reported on the decreasing evening session enrollment.

> At present there are fewer evening students enrolled than in past years. This is due, it is believed, to the fact that not all of the residents of the township are

---

[255] "Junior College To Offer Revised Vocational-Technical Program To Meet The Growing Need," *Hotel Hershey High-Lights*, Vol. XVI, No. 7, August 7, 1948.

[256] *Hershey Junior College Bulletin, 1948-1950*, pp. 22-23.

[257] *Ibid.*   [258] *Ibid.*, p. 23.

[259] *Ibid.*, pp. 19-21.   [260] *Ibid.*, p. 24.

aware of the scope and flexibility of the evening program and its ability to meet the needs of people with varied background and interests.[261]

In an attempt to bolster evening enrollment, Dean Fenstermacher wrote to employers in the Hershey area to ask their cooperation in making known the opportunities of the evening program.[262] Evening School bulletins which provided general information and listed course offerings were also distributed periodically.[263]

According to the 1948-1950 *Bulletin*, the College was then offering 67 different courses, by title, in nine departments in the day and evening programs.[264]

It should be emphasized that there was no interference in the operation of the academic program of the Junior College on the part of The M. S. Hershey Foundation. The faculty had freedom in the selection of texts, preparation of syllabi, and method of instruction.[265] Apparently there was an exception to this practice of non-interference in academic matters in 1950 when Dean Fenstermacher requested permission to add a course in Russian to the curriculum. This request was tabled and the following explanation was offered to Dean Fenstermacher by the Superintendent.

> It was the opinion of the Board that before establishing a course in Russian, their committee should convey this request to the Board of Managers and request their opinion concerning this matter.[266]

It was reported in the 1952 data submitted to the Commission on Institutions of Higher Education that responsibility for the evaluation of the instructional program was vested in the Dean but shared with the faculty. Uniformity of instruction was achieved through the following:

> ... informal discussions, examination of achievement grade curves, student interviews, the prepared syllabus of each course, the use of professional literature, conference between staff members and by appraisal of the problem in formal faculty meetings.[267]

The "Report of the 1952 Visiting Committee" commented on the appraisal of the curriculum as follows:

> In this small college in a comparatively small community (11,000) a natural, pleasant, informality prevails. Discussions about objectives, the curricula and the program in general are on a dean-instructor or instructor-instructor basis. . .
>
> The program is studied and revised chiefly through individual action and informal discussion. It would be well to introduce enough formality in this situation to ensure positive, continuous consideration of the curricula, lead-

---

[261] "Hershey Junior College Opens For Its 11th Academic Year," *Hotel Hershey High-Lights,* Vol. XVI, No. 13, September 18, 1948, pp. 1-2.

[262] Form letter, V. H. Fenstermacher, September 2, 1949.

[263] Hershey Junior College "Evening School Bulletin," 1949-1950.

[264] *Hershey Junior College Bulletin, 1948-1950,* pp. 19, 24-35.

[265] John C. Lanz, personal interview, July 27, 1967.

[266] Letter from Raymond H. Koch, Superintendent of Schools to V. H. Fenstermacher, December 14, 1950.

[267] "Data Presented For Consideration . . . 1952," *op. cit.,* n.p.

ing to definite action. It was noted by the Committee that "during the past year more attention has been devoted to the problem of relaxing the restriction on admission of students than on revision of the instructional program." Committee members wondered why these two problems could not have been tackled simultaneously, one being almost entirely administrative, the other instructional.[268]

"Distinctive instructional procedures" reported to the Commission included the use of audio-visual equipment and field trips to local museums, industries, and seats of government, including the Capitol at Harrisburg. Students in the business administration curriculum participated in a "short-term cooperative work-study program" in Harrisburg and local stores. Secretarial students engaged in "a long-term program" at the Hershey Chocolate Corporation offices during the last semester of the two-year program.[269] The Visiting Committee commended the College on its work-study program.[270]

The 1952 data submitted to the Commission on Institutions of Higher Education provided a tabulation of the enrollment in each major curriculum for the two-year period, 1950–1952. It was explained, however, that each student's program was individually tailored to meet his particular interests and long-range goals. Nevertheless, the following curriculum and the total, two-year corresponding enrollment in each shows that the "transfer" programs were in greatest demand: Business Administration, 37; Liberal Arts, 29; Secretarial, 19; Elective Arts, 11; Pre-Engineering, 10; Pre-Nursing, 8; and Technical Arts, 7.[271]

Grade distributions by department for the second semester, 1950–1951, were also reported to the Commission in 1952. The following table shows the pattern of grades awarded approximated the normal distribution curve.

TABLE 6

DISTRIBUTION OF GRADES SECOND SEMESTER 1950–1951[a]

Department	Grades				
	A	B	C	D	F
English	4	24	21	8	1
Social Studies	14	29	21	7	0
Mathematics	6	10	17	2	0
Sciences	2	11	17	2	0
Business & Secretarial	27	36	32	4	0
Psychology	3	4	6	0	0
Language	4	6	3	1	0
Art, Drafting and Home Economics	12	17	10	0	0

[a]"Data Presented For Consideration . . . 1952," *op. cit.,* n.p.

---

[268] "Report of the 1952 Visiting Committee," *op. cit.,* p. 4.
[269] "Data Presented For Consideration . . . 1952," *op. cit.,* n.p.
[270] "Report of the 1952 Visiting Committee," *loc. cit.*
[271] "Data Presented For Consideration . . . 1952," *op. cit.,* n.p.

The "Report of the 1952 Visiting Committee" questioned the necessity of the three instructional divisions and the objectives of each.

> ... The separation into Lower Division (transfer program), General Division (terminal program), and Community Division (adult-education program) is logical enough, but the committee felt that the distinction between "Lower Division" and "General Division" had little real significance outside the *Catalogue*.[272]

Dean Fenstermacher concurred with the Committee, stating that "the actual difference between the Lower and General Division sequences is related to transfer or terminal objectives." He also explained that the technical-terminal program was not then attracting many students but "probably would do so with shop work facilities."[273]

Concerning the different curricula offered by the College, the Committee wrote that they were:

> ... Suggestive rather than prescribed programs. Each student's program of studies is arranged through the guidance efforts of the dean who seeks to adapt the offerings to the needs of the individual. Only two courses—Expressional English and Recreational Education—are common to all suggested programs. Some study by the faculty of the second of the two stated objectives of the college and the implications of that objective might lead to a determination of additional courses that would be required of all students. These required activities—a core—could then be so presented in the *Catalogue*.[274]

Three major recommendations of the 1952 Committee with respect to the curriculum were:

> Examine [the] possibility of establishing a core of general education courses common to all curricula.
>
> Provide for continuous study and revision of the whole instructional program.
>
> Develop adequate syllabi for all courses.[275]

The 1956-1958 *Bulletin* made no mention of the Lower, General, or Community Divisions. Instead, the curriculum was explained under the general heading "Programs of Instruction." The *Bulletin* explained:

> All programs of study conducted in the Hershey Junior College are representative of the typical Freshman and Sophomore years of formal preparation and lead to the award of the Associate In Arts degree. Each program of study is designed to furnish the student with an opportunity to acquire a broad general education along with the initial specialization in the professional training required in the chosen major field of study.
>
> The sequence of courses in each curriculum has been planned to permit variations consistent with the students' secondary school preparation, interests, aptitudes, educational objective and the extent of formal education required. ... This flexibility in scheduling of classes does not, however, permit aimless selection of courses for whimsical reasons. The student will confer with the

[272] "Report of the 1952 Visiting Committee," *op. cit.* p. 3.
[273] V. H. Fenstermacher, handwritten note on page 3 of "Report."
[274] "Report of the 1952 Visiting Committee," *op. cit.*, p. 4.
[275] *Ibid.*, p. 14.

faculty counselor, submit the proposed schedule for review and obtain the approval of the Dean of the College before admission to class is authorized.[276]

Typical curriculum outlines rather than specific courses of instruction were included in the *Bulletin*. Expressional English and Recreational Education remained the only courses required of all Junior College students. The typical "Basic Curriculum" and the "Basic Liberal Arts" curriculum are reproduced below. The following explanation of the Basic Liberal Arts program was offered.

> This curriculum is arranged to provide the student interested in pre-professional preparation in the medical arts, mathematics and science with a substantial preparation for later specialization. It can be varied to satisfy the requirements of the undergraduate program as they exist in different localities.[277]

BASIC CURRICULUM[278]

Freshman Year	Credit	Sophomore Year	Credit
Recreational Education	1–1	Recreational Education	1–1
Expressional English	3–3	Literature	3–3
Effective Speech	2–2	Art and Music	2–2
Foreign Language	3–3	Foreign Language	3–3
Mathematics or Science	3–3	Science or Mathematics	3–3
Social Science	3–3	Social Science	3–3
Major Field Elective	3–3	Major Field Elective	3–3

BASIC LIBERAL ARTS[279]

Freshman Year	Credit	Sophomore Year	Credit
Recreational Education	1–1	Recreational Education	1–1
Expressional English	3–3	English and American	
French or German	3–3	Literature	3–3
Algebra-Trigonometry	3–3	Effective Speech	2–2
General Biology	4–4	French or German	3–3
General Chemistry	4–4	Principles of Economics	3–3
		General Physics	4–4
		General Psychology	3–
		Sociology	

Other typical curricula included in the 1956-1958 *Bulletin* were: Basic Engineering, Basic Teacher Training, Basic Healing Arts, Basic Business Administration, Executive Secretarial Curriculum, General Business Training, General Technical Training.[280]

The 1963 self evaluation data, submitted to the Commission on Institutions of Higher Education of the Middle States Association, reported that 10 curricula were being offered by the College. They are listed in the table

---

[276]*Hershey Junior College Bienniel [sic] Bulletin, 1956-1958*, p. 24. It is of interest that, for the first time, the inside title page of this *Bulletin* included the sub-title, "A Two Year Coeducational Community College." It appeared in each successive issue of the *Bulletin*.

[277]*Ibid.*, pp. 25–26.   [278]*Ibid.*, pp. 26–28.

[279]*Ibid.*, p. 26.   [280]*Ibid.*, pp. 26–28.

below which also provides enrollment statistics as of September, 1962.[281] These programs were offered the remaining two years of the College[282]

TABLE 7

ENROLLMENT BY CURRICULUM, CLASS, AND SEX
SEPTEMBER 1962[a]

CURRICULUM	FRESHMEN			SOPHOMORES			TOTAL		
	M	W	T	M	W	T	M	W	T
Basic	1	0	1	0	1	1	1	1	2
Liberal Arts	18	10	28	15	11	26	33	21	54
Science	3	0	3	1	0	1	4	0	4
Engineering	28	1	29	20	0	20	48	1	49
Healing Arts	7	5	12	1	1	2	8	6	14
Education	17	22	39	14	8	22	31	30	61
Business Administration	16	0	16	16	0	16	32	0	32
Secretarial	1	17	18	0	10	10	1	27	28
General Business	1	0	1	0	0	0	1	0	1
General Technical	2	0	2	1	0	1	3	0	3
Total	94	55	149	68	31	99	162	86	248

[a]"Report Of Self Evaluation," . . . 1963, *op. cit.*, p. 39.

The following explanation regarding students' enrollment in a particular curriculum was given:

> In most cases the student will be enrolled in a curriculum by title but if the sequence of studies requires alteration, the transfer student may be classified as enrolled in the Basic Curriculum, while the terminal student may be classified as enrolled in the General Curriculum. The lines of demarcation between the several curricula are not crystal clear and the situation is of little importance to the student, the college or the transfer institution for the facts are understood by all concerned.[283]

As these statistics show, few students were interested in the General Business and General Technical programs. The proportion of students enrolled in Liberal Arts, Engineering, and Education accounted for 66 percent of the total enrollment. The Education curriculum attracted more girls to the College; enrollment in that program increased 60 percent from 1955-1956.[284]

The 1963 self-study reported that no evening courses were being offered[285] nor were there any formal independent study programs, although the faculty encouraged students to do independent work. However, through acceleration in the secondary schools, six students had entered the Hershey Junior College

---

[281]"Report Of Self Evaluation," . . . 1963, *op. cit.*, p. 39.

[282]*Hershey Junior College Information Bulletin, 1964-1966*, pp. 23-27.

[283]"Report Of Self Evaluation," Hershey Junior College to Commission On Institutions of Higher Education, Middle States Association of Colleges and Secondary Schools, February 24, 1963, p. 38.

[284]*Ibid.*, p. 82.   [285]*Ibid.*, p. 46.

upon completion of their eleventh grade. Consideration was being given to the possibility of granting credit and placement for work completed in secondary school advanced placement programs.[286]

With respect to class size, the self-study stated:

> Experience with the problem of class size in the local situation with the typical student body enrolled over the past several years is overwhelming in favor of small classes. There is an advantage in the friendly student-staff relationship and the opportunity for probing and depth in discussion of topics leading to greater knowledge and enhanced self-assurance of competence in the subject-matter field.[287]

Dean Fenstermacher also explained that the above situation required superior teaching to upgrade average students, at the time of admission to the College, to above average students by the completion of the sophomore year.[288]

Commendation of the academic program and the faculty of the Hershey Junior College was offered by the Evaluation Committee of the Commission On Institutions of Higher Education in the following sentence: "It is in the area of instruction that the greatest strengths of Hershey Junior College are found."[289] The Social Science offerings were praised for the maintenance of "an excellent standard of instruction" and use of various teaching techniques. "Particularly noteworthy and commendable in the Social Sciences is the effective correlation of subject matter to current social, economic and political problems."[290] The Evaluation Committee similarly commended the instruction and program in the Humanities and Sciences.[291]

As mentioned previously, the greatest concern of the Visiting Committee had to do with keeping the faculty up to date in their subject matter fields and instructional methodology. Other recommendations with respect to the academic program included the addition of more opportunity to develop creative potential in English Composition and Literature, and increased use of audio-visual equipment.[292]

Recognition

Public recognition of the Hershey Junior College was extended relatively early in its history. State and initial Middle States Association of Colleges and Secondary Schools accreditations and the *Look* and *The School Executive* citations were extended to the institution during Dr. Breidenstine's tenure. These have been reviewed in the previous chapter.

Of significant importance during Dr. Fenstermacher's administration was the re-evaluation and continued accreditation of the College by the Commis-

[286]*Ibid.*, p. 85.
[287]*Ibid.*, p. 91.
[288]*Ibid.*
[289]"Report of Evaluation Committee," 1963, *op. cit.*, p. 6.
[290]*Ibid.*, p. 7.
[291]*Ibid.*, pp. 7–8.
[292]*Ibid.*, pp. 8–9.

sion On Institutions of Higher Education of the Middle States Association of Colleges and Secondary Schools. These reaccreditations were granted in 1952[293] and 1963.[294] Already noted was State Council on Education permission to grant the Associate of Arts Degree in 1955. Membership in the various professional organizations was continued.

In the opinion of the writer, probably the greatest recognition which came to the Hershey Junior College was at the time its closing was publicly announced. The demonstration of loyalty and devotion to the institution by the faculty, students, and the alumni as well as the general populace of the Hershey community, was testimony of the recognition extended to the College.

The closing of the Junior College will be considered in the last section of this Chapter.

The Extracurriculum

The extracurricular program of the Hershey Junior College continued to grow at a moderate rate during the 1947-1965 period. It is likely that it would have grown more rapidly had it not been for the fact that the College was a nonresidential institution. Furthermore, Hershey was planned to be a cultural and recreational center in itself. Students had the unusual opportunity to enjoy and profit by the many programs and activities of the community.

Publications

Several Junior College publications were produced during Dean Fenstermacher's tenure. *The Literary Artisan,* a magazine which contained original contributions by students, was published until about 1955 when it was discontinued in favor of the yearbook.[295] *The Format*, the College newspaper which was first published during the last year Dr. Breidenstine was Dean, became an important College news publication. It was published throughout the history of the institution. As of 1960-1961, "The Leopard's Pulse," a weekly news bulletin, was also being published. It listed events and activities of the College. Also included were jokes and a "Thought of the Week" contributed by the Student Christian Association.[296] *The Leopard* was the Junior College student-faculty handbook which was published periodically by the Student Senate. It contained general information about the College, including government, rules and regulations, activities, cheers, and the alma mater.[297]

---

[293]Letter from E. K. Smiley, Chairman (Evaluation Committee) to Dean V. H. Fenstermacher, May 1, 1952.

[294]Letter from Albert E. Meder Jr., Chairman (Middle States) to Dean V. H. Fenstermacher, June 28, 1963.

[295]Letter from Norman Vanderwall to writer, August 20, 1970.

[296]*HEJUCO,* Vol. VII, 1961, p. 20.

[297]*The Leopard: Student Handbook,* Hershey Junior College, 1954.

The first printed issue of *HEJUCO*, the Hershey Junior College yearbook, was published by the Class of 1955 and by each class thereafter. (The first issue was produced in 1954 as a mimeographed yearbook.) The following statement was included in the 1955 *HEJUCO:*

> The Class of 1955 feels that the air of permanence that is normally associated with the printed page will encourage students of future classes to surpass the efforts of the present editors, who in many ways are privileged to regard themselves as pioneers. . . . From these modest beginnings, the classes which follow will be able to expand and perfect the annuals they will develop.[298]

Professors Hiram Frysinger and Norman Vanderwall served as the first advisors to the yearbook staff.[299]

Organizations

The Student Committee was the dominant student organization throughout the history of the College. Members were elected from the student body by popular vote. The Dean of Women served as adviser to the organization. In cooperation with faculty representatives, they arranged and supervised the social, athletic, and other non-academic affairs of the Junior College. An activity fee was collected from all Junior College students and the Student Senate, consisting of six freshmen and six sophomores, appropriated the funds to the various activities.[300] All students had "the prerogative of participating in Community deliberations and of offering suggestions for the guidance of its members." The responsibilities of Junior College students, in general, and the Student Committee, in particular, were described as follows:

> Personal dignity, poise, self restraint and a sense of obligation for the rights of others are the paramount elements of human relations required of each student at all times. The Student Committee has the responsibility for the promulgation and supervision of such regulations as may be considered necessary or desirable for a democratic campus government consistent with these personal attributes and in accord with the demands for serious and successful academic achievement.[301]

The name of this governing body was changed to the Student Senate by 1952. By then, the Senate was sponsoring two formal dances a year and a number of informal dances, socials, teas, outdoor parties, and other functions which were held at Hotel Hershey, in the Social Room of the Community Building, or outdoors.[302] Later, the Spring Formal and other dances and social events were being held at country clubs and other locations in Harrisburg and nearby areas.[303] The annual Senate-sponsored Parents' Tea remained an important

---

[298] *HEJUCO,* Vol. I, 1955, p. 20.
[299] *Ibid.*
[300] "The Student Senate," *HEJUCO,* Vol. I, 1955, p. 18.
[301] *Hershey Junior College Bulletin, 1950-1952,* p. 15.
[302] *Hershey Junior College Bulletin, 1952-1954,* pp. 13-14.
[303] V. H. Fenstermacher, personal interview, February 27, 1967.

social event.[304] By 1961, the Senate was responsible for the Freshman Week Orientation program.[305]

Musical activities continued to increase throughout the history of the Junior College. By 1948 a Junior College Choir was organized by Professor W. Paul Campbell. It sang at community and College functions, such as the spring concert.[306] It consisted of 35 members in 1949. As of that year, the earlier Boys' Glee Club had become the Men's Glee Club.[307] The College Chorus and Orchestra gave recitals and sponsored and participated in the Annual Music Festival.[308]

One of the biggest events to be held in Hershey, Pennsylvania, was "The President's Birthday Party," in honor of President Dwight David Eisenhower and his wife. The party was held on October 13, 1953, and it was staged in the Hershey Arena and Stadium and in the "Big Top" tent loaned by Ringling Brothers-Barnum and Baily Circus. The Birthday Party was produced, directed, and staged by Fred Waring in the Sports Arena. The entertainment program was a musical saga of our country's founding, "The Song of America," presented by Fred Waring and His Pennsylvanians and an "All-Pennsylvania Schools Chorus of 1000." Included in the chorus of the pageant were vocal groups from the three Hershey Schools: the Milton Hershey School Glee Club, the Hershey High School Chorus, and the Hershey Junior College Choir. The Junior College Choir consisted of 47 voices. W. Paul Campbell was then the director of the latter two groups.[309] The opportunity to participate in this spectacular event was one of the greatest, if not the greatest thrill for the Hershey Junior College vocal group. An estimated 20,000 people attended the affair.[310]

It was also in 1953 that the College could boast of having a full orchestra with each musical section represented. The instrumental group consisted of three sophomores and 14 freshmen.[311]

The Hershey Junior Players, one of the oldest organizations of the College, continued to perform through the closing in 1965. The dramatic group presented the play "Good Housekeeping" in November, 1952.[312] A week later the Board of Education passed the following resolution: "Use of profanity shall be eliminated whenever possible in all high school and junior college plays."[313] Dean Fenstermacher, in his November "Administrative Report"

[304] Hershey Junior College "Information Bulletin," Vol. XX, No. 4, October 31, 1957, p. 1.

[305] HEJUCO, Vol. VII, 1961, p. 6.

[306] "The Hershey Junior College Choir," The Format, Vol. II, No. 3, February, 1948, p. 1.

[307] "Junior College Choir Program," The Format, Vol. VI, No. 1, December, 1949.

[308] Hershey Junior College Bulletin, 1950-1952, p. 16.

[309] "The President's Birthday Party," official program, October 13, 1953.

[310] "Real Dutch Treat For Ike," Hershey News, Vol. I, No. 1, October 1, 1953, p. 1.

[311] "Prof. Campbell's Dream Comes True," The Format, Vol. VII, No. 1, Fall Edition.

[312] Hershey Junior College "Administrative Report," November, 1952.

[313] Derry Township Public Schools, "Board Minutes," November 12, 1952.

commended the performance as a "professional performance of merit." He continued:

> It is regretted that the repetition of a single word, of not too uncommon profanity, on three or so occasions gave rise to some concern. It was not the purpose of the cast to shock anyone's sense of propriety. The mild use of the word "damn" seemed so inconsequential that little was thought of it.[314]

Fenstermacher concluded by stating that in the future attention would be given to deleting "as much as possible all profanity" from the Players' productions.[315]

When the Junior College closed, the Hershey Junior College Players established six, $50.00 scholarships with the funds which remained in their treasury. Lighting equipment was donated to the Harrisburg Area Community College.[316]

A Russian Culture Club was organized in 1959.[317] It was renamed the Foreign Culture Club in 1960 to reflect the broader range of topics discussed by the members.[318]

The Student Christian Association was organized during the 1955-1956 academic year.[319] Advised by Reverend Kermit Lloyd, the nondenominational group was dedicated to the promotion of "Christian fellowship and service."[320] The Association remained active throughout the history of the College.[321]

In 1959, a Newman Club of 25 students was organized. The members discussed "all aspects of Catholicism in relation to college life."[322]

The Hershey Junior College began participation in the Intercollegiate Conference On Government in 1947-1948.[323] Members devoted their attention to "government and practical politics." Delegates regularly attended the annual state convention held in the legislative chambers of the Capitol at Harrisburg. Women students participated in "I.C.G." activities in 1952-1953 for the first time.[324] Professor William Schmehl sponsored the nonpartisan organization which was active throughout the history of the College.[325]

Phi Theta Kappa, the National Junior College Honorary Scholastic Society, was chartered at the Junior College during the 1958-1959 academic year.[326]

---

[314]"Administrative Report," *loc. cit.*

[315]*Ibid.*

[316]"Hershey Junior College Players," *The Format,* Vol. XIX, No. 5, May, 1965.

[317]"Information Bulletin," Vol. XXI, No. 9, January 27, 1959.

[318]"Foreign Culture Club," *The Format,* Vol. XV, No. 2, November 3, 1960, p. 2.

[319]"Student Christian Association," *HEJUCO,* Vol. II, 1956, p. 27.

[320]"Student Christian Association," *HEJUCO,* Vol. IX, 1963, p. 30.

[321]The Reverend Kermit Lloyd, personal interview, February 23, 1970.

[322]"Newman Club Formed At College," *The Format,* Vol. XIII, No. 4, March 25, 1959, p. 1.

[323]"This Is I.C.G.," Hershey Junior College (I.C.G. files).

[324]"Women in I.C.G.," *The Format,* Vol. VII, No. 1, Fall Edition, n.d., p. 4.

[325]"Intercollegiate Conference On Government," *HEJUCO,* 1965, p. 62.

[326]"Scholastic Society For Junior College," *Hershey News,* Vol. VI, No. 4, January 23, 1958, p. 2.

The objects of the society were "to promote scholarship, to develop character, and to cultivate fellowship among the students of both sexes of the junior colleges of the United States of America. To be elected to membership, students had to rank in the upper 10 percent of the student body.[327]

Kappa Kappa, organized in 1957, was "an organization of male students interested in performing services for the College and the Community." New members had to be approved by all active members and then serve a period of "pledgeship" prior to initiation. The group completed one service project a month, often unannounced. The alumni of the organization still meet with Reverend Kermit Lloyd and the fraternity is now functioning at the Harrisburg Area Community College.[328]

Alpha Tau Delta, a girls' sorority with a purpose similar to that of Kappa Kappa, was organized in 1958. Members were selected by unanimous vote. Miss Pauline Copp was the first advisor to the group.[329]

Ahtletics

As was true during Dean Breidenstine's administration, basketball was the major Hershey Junior College sport during Dean Fenstermacher's tenure. The 1947–1948 schedule included 18 games with 10 opponents.[330] In 1957 and 1959 the Leopards placed third in Pennsylvania Junior College tournament play. The team enjoyed its best seasons from 1961–1962 through the closing of the College in 1965.[331] Under Coach Harry Harlacher, the Leopards won the 1962 Pennsylvania Junior College Athletic Association tournament held in Hershey.[332] It was the sixth tournament for which the Hershey Junior College team qualified.[333] The basketball team again won both the league and state championship the following year.[334] That year the Leopards also captured the Eastern Division Championship for the first time. In its last season of play the team took third place in the state tournament.[335]

Golf competition was interrupted between 1948 and 1954. Under Coach William Landis, the team was undefeated in 1954, maintaining an undefeated record throughout the history of golf competition by the College. The team went on to win first place in the Junior College Eastern Regional Tournament, although official honors could not be accepted because the College was not

---

[327]"Information Bulletin," Vol. XX, No. 9, January 7, 1958.

[328]The Reverend Kermit Lloyd, personal interview, February 23, 1970.

[329]"Society Formed At H.J.C.," *The Format,* Vol. XIII, No. 3, February 20, 1959.

[330]"Junior College Basketball Team Schedules 18 Contests," *Hotel Hershey High-Lights,* Vol. XV, No. 25, December 13, 1947, p. 4.

[331]"Basketball," *HEJUCO,* Vol. III, 1957, p. 30; *HEJUCO,* Vol. V, 1959, p. 72.

[332]"Basketball," *HEJUCO,* Vol. VIII, 1962, p. 37.

[333]"17th Annual Pennsylvania Junior College Basketball Tournament," Hershey High School Gymnasium, February 23-24, 1962, souvenir program.

[334]"H.J.C. Captures League, State Championship," *The Format,* Vol. XVII, No. 4, March, 1963, p. 1.

[335]Hershey Junior College Stages Final Athletic Awards Convocations," *Lebanon Daily News,* May 15, 1965, p. 11.

then a member of the Junior College Athletic Association.[336]   Available records show the team officially won the Eastern Junior College Tournament in 1955,[337] 1958,[338] and 1961.[339]   The last golf team in the history of the College, under Coach John Bushey, placed third in the state and fifth in the regional tournament.[340]

Tennis was resumed in 1955 as an intercollegiate sport after a lapse of several years.[341]   In 1958, Larry Strait was the National Singles Champion.[342]   The National Junior College Athletic Association regional team championship was captured in 1960.[343]   According to the yearbooks, the College did not participate in intercollegiate tennis after that year.

Swimming, as an intercollegiate sport, got under way for the first time during the 1962-1963 academic year.   The swimmers, coached by William Harrison, placed second in the Pennsylvania Junior College Athletic Association Swimming Meet in 1964-1965.[344]

The first student-organized, uncoached wrestling team competed in 1954 in a three-meet schedule.[345]   Officially, the first intercollegiate team took to the mats in 1963-1964 when it compiled a record of four wins and one loss and placed second in the regional tournament.[346]   Under the volunteer coaching of Samuel Harry and Allen Fasnacht, the 1964-1965 team compiled an amazing record.   The undefeated team won the state tournament and placed third in the regional tournament, gaining two individual regional championships. Mat Kline went on to become the Junior College's first National Wrestling Champion.   He was the only member of an Eastern school to perform the feat that season.[347]

Intramural athletics were offered throughout the history of the College. During the latter years the "Alfred E. Newman Bowl" served to build school spirit among the students and faculty.   The "Bowl" was a series of athletic contests between the freshmen and sophomores.[348]

Baccalaureate and Commencement

Because of the close association of the Hershey Junior College with the Hershey High School, as integral parts of the Derry Township Public School System, differences of opinion regarding Junior College baccalaureate and

[336] "Golf Team," *Pleasant Memories,* mimeographed yearbook by Class of 1954, n.p.

[337] "Golf," *HEJUCO,* Vol. II, 1956, p. 36.

[338] "Golf," *HEJUCO,* Vol. V, 1959, p. 76.

[339] "Golf," *HEJUCO,* Vol. VII, 1961, p. 38.

[340] "Golf," *HEJUCO,* 1965, p. 81.

[341] "Tennis," *HEJUCO,* Vol. IV, 1956, p. 37.

[342] "Tennis," *HEJUCO,* Vol. IV, 1958, p. 24.

[343] "Tennis," *HEJUCO,* Vol. VI, 1960, p. 67.

[344] "Swimming," *HEJUCO,* 1965, p. 80.

[345] "Wrestling Team," *Pleasant Memories, op. cit.,* n.p.

[346] "Wrestling," *HEJUCO,* 1964, p. 62.

[347] "Hershey Junior College Stages Final Athletic Awards Convocation," *loc. cit.*

[348] V. H. Fenstermacher, personal interview, February 23, 1967.

commencement ceremonies arose. It will be recalled that the two institutions held combined ceremonies in the Little Theatre of the Community Building during Dr. Breidenstine's tenure.

Hershey, Pennsylvania, celebrated its fiftieth anniversary in 1953.[349] In recognition of the event, a special combined commencement of the graduating classes of Hershey High School, Milton Hershey School, and Hershey Junior College was staged in the Hershey Arena.[350] Through a request by the Junior College faculty to the School Board, Dean Fenstermacher was granted permission to present the diplomas to the Class of 1953, but to that class only.[351] Apparently plans were changed because Dean Fenstermacher presented the 29 graduates of the Junior College and E. Morse Heisey, President, Board of School Directors, awarded the diplomas. Dr. Milton S. Eisenhower, then President of The Pennsylvania State College, was the commencement speaker.[352]

Students, alumni, faculty, and administration had long desired to hold a separate Hershey Junior College commencement. The request was approved for the graduation of the 42 members of the Class of 1954, on a trial basis.[353] Baccalaureate remained combined with the Hershey High School.[354] It was both considerate and significant that Dr. Breidenstine was invited to be the commencement speaker at the May 24 ceremony. He closed his speech, "An Idea Becomes Reality," with the following words:

> To the graduates of 1954, the first to have their own commencement, our heartiest congratulations and best wishes. Hold your heads high, you are a choice lot. Make your beloved Hershey Junior College proud of you and, even though you have many years ahead of you, never neglect your support of your alma mater.

> Milton S. Hershey had a great idea. Its reality is a thrilling fact. The early beginnings are now history; the first fruits of Hershey Junior College are still with us, only God knows what the maturity of Hershey Junior College will bring forth. Yours is indeed a great heritage; I salute you![355]

A year later, the Lebanon Valley College historian, Dr. Paul A. W. Wallace, delivered the commencement address, "Milton Hershey's Approach to Education."[356]

By 1960, there was discussion regarding a single ceremony in which the Junior College baccalaureate and commencement exercises would be com-

---

[349]"Hershey, Pennsylvania," 50th Anniversary of Chocolate Town, 1903-1953, personal files of V. H. Fenstermacher.

[350]Derry Township Public Schools, "Board Minutes," May 21, 1952; and "Dr. Eisenhower To Speak At Mass Commencement Exercise," The Format, Vol. VIII, No. 4, Commencement Edition, 1953, p. 1.

[351]Derry Township Public Schools, "Board Minutes," March 25, 1953.

[352]Commencement Exercises for the graduating classes of Hershey High School, Milton Hershey School, Hershey Junior College," May 25, 1953, program.

[353]Derry Township Public Schools, "Board Minutes," October 15, 1953.

[354]"Plan to Hold Graduation," Hershey News, Vol. II, No. 8, February 25, 1954.

[355]A. G. Breidenstine, "An Idea Becomes Reality," May 24, 1954.

[356]Paul A. W. Wallace, "Milton Hershey's Approach to Education," Hershey Junior College Commencement Speech, May 28, 1955.

bined.[357] Dr. Jacques, Superintendent of Schools, stated his preference for the combined services "as a show of strength of a single school district."[358] Dr. Fenstermacher argued for the separate service as follows:

> The faculty requests the single Baccalaureate-Commencement service after this year. Students have requested the Junior College single ceremony each year. The Alumni Association recommended the single ceremony at the annual meeting this year and the members of the Hershey Ministerium have indicated that they favor the proposal since it permits better allocation of their services. Parents, particularly those from a distance, annually suggest a single ceremony because of travel, conflicts in services scheduled elsewhere which they feel obligated to attend, and so on. This year the Junior College will have approximately 80 graduates and their families in attendance, which may be the beginning of a problem in seating and sharing of gowns for the Baccalaureate Services.
>
> Considering all factors there appears to be no benefits to the High School or the Junior College in the combined Baccalaureate Service or any loss to each institution while there are certain advantages to be gained by both by the separate ceremonies of each school.[359]

The following year the School Board, in a four to two vote, granted the Junior College permission to hold its own baccalaureate-commencement program.[360] The Reverend Kermit L. Lloyd delivered the baccalaureate sermon and Dr. A. C. Baugher, then President of Elizabethtown College, gave the commencement address.[361]

It is interesting to note the title of the 1963 commencement address was, "Alma Mater—What of the Morrow." The speech was delivered by Dr. Frederic K. Miller, then President of Lebanon Valley College,[362] to the 90 members of the graduating class.

During the latter years of the College, a number of awards were made to deserving students at the end-of-the-year ceremonies. Included among the awards were the following: Dean's, Faculty, Hershey Junior College Alumni, Milton Hershey School Alumni, Foreman's Club, Senate, Rotary Club, Lions Club, DAR, SICO Foundation, Business and Professional Women, Bausch and Lomb, Danforth Foundation, and Class of 1950.[363]

The "Report of the 1952 Visiting Committee" of the Commission on Institutions of Higher Education made the following comment on the extracurricular program of the College:

> The extracurricular activities are limited both in scope and in members participating. This is considered by the students to be compensated for by the unusual opportunities for college-age activities provided in the building in

---

357 "Information Bulletin," Vol. XXII, No. 6, January 14, 1960.

358 Discussion between Dr. Jacques and Dr. Fenstermacher, March 23, 1960, notes from V. H. Fenstermacher's personal files.

359 Memorandum from Dr. Fenstermacher to Dr. Jacques, February 29, 1961.

360 Derry Township Public Schools, "Board Minutes," January 9, 1961.

361 Hershey Junior College Baccalaureate-Commencement Program, May 29, 1961, personal files of V. H. Fenstermacher.

362 "Twenty-fourth Annual Commencement," Hershey Junior College, May 28, 1963.

363 "Information Bulletin," Vol. XXII, No. 12, April 26, 1960.

which the college is housed, and in the clubhouse for women across the street. A modest program of athletics is carried on. . . .

A large part of the student body, to judge by a sample interviewed by the committee, belongs to community clubs in which social and recreational experience are provided. However, the college has a unique responsibility here which it may not relinquish. Dean, faculty and students could with profit, explore the contributions which social and intellectual activities under college sponsorship may make toward realizing the objectives of this college.[364]

As noted earlier, the Committee recommended the College consider expanding the activities and student health programs.[365] The College apparently felt that any lack of social and cultural enrichment in the College program was compensated for through the opportunities available in the community as the following comment suggests:

It might be said that there is an emphasis on academic activities which overshadow the social or cultural segments of the educational program. This is probably true but, appears to be of little consequence to students exposed throughout the year to a variety of professional talent.[366]

The 1963 report of the Evaluation Committee contained few comments or recommendations regarding the Hershey Junior College extracurricular program. The Committee did note that, other than basketball and golf, intercollegiate athletics depended upon the availability of material. The nonathletic program was judged to be "well supported and under competent advisors." It was also observed that there was no nurse or infirmary available at the College. The Student Senate was commended for its efforts with respect to the establishment, supervision, and financial support of the "comprehensive extracurricular program."[367]

Enrollment and Student Achievement

Except for the 1950–1952 period, the enrollment pattern of the Junior College during Dean Fenstermacher's administration was characterized by relatively steady growth. The rate of growth of full-time students accelerated sharply between 1952 and 1955, largely the result of the broadened admissions policy which was passed in 1951. Conversely, the number of part-time students decreased rapidly during the 1952-1957 period. The largest increase in any one year during Fenstermacher's administration was in 1964-1965 when full-time enrollment jumped by 42 to an all-time high of 300 students; grand total enrollment also reached a record of 317. Increases in enrollment,

[364]"Report of the 1952 Visiting Committee," *op. cit.,* p. 5.

[365]*Ibid.,* p. 14.

[366]"The Institution," (Introduction to "Report of Self Evaluation"), Hershey Junior College, to the Commission on Institutions of Higher Education, Middle States Association of Colleges and Secondary Schools, January, 1963.

[367]"Report of Evaluation Committee," Commission on Institutions of Higher Education, Middle States Association of Colleges and Secondary Schools, February 24–27, 1963, p. 4.

during the last two years, were probably brought about by the fact that the College was going to close and students and parents were prompted to take advantage of the free education. The national admissions picture character-ized by increasing selectivity on the part of colleges, may also have had an in-fluence on students' decisions to attend the Hershey Junior College. It is interesting to note that although maximum enrollment had been set at 150 in 1951, it was permitted to double.

From 1947 through the 1964–1965 academic year, the total enrollment was 3,120 (2,795 full-time and 335 part-time). During the entire history of the College, total full-time enrollment was 3,581 and part-time enrollment was 851. Grand total enrollment reached 4,332. A total of 1,079 students graduated from the Junior College from 1948 through 1965. During the history of the institution, a grand total of 1,271 students were graduated.

In spite of the enrollment growth reviewed above, the overall growth, com-pared to national trends, was relatively slow. The report of the study of the Derry Township School District in 1951–1952 suggested the small enrollment did not permit the College to realize its potential. The 1952 Middle States Visiting Committee suggested enrollment should have been increased.

The Hershey Junior College celebrated its 25th anniversary in 1962. In an article on the College in September of that year, John D. Husband reflected on the lack of change and growth in the institution as follows:

Hershey Junior College has begun its 25th year of classes.

And if a middle-aged alumnus came back to visit his old alma mater, he probably would be surprised at how little the place has changed.

Though the school has doubled its faculty, enrollment and classroom space, it hasn't grown at anywhere near the rate a free junior college might be ex-pected to grow.

The coeducational school's enrollment has grown and decreased in spurts.
. . . .
Like most schools, Hershey was hit hard in enrollment during the war years. But, since the school charges virtually no tuition, it was not caught in the post-war college boom brought on by the GI bill.[368]

The proportion of Hershey High School graduates who enrolled at the Junior College remained relatively low for most of the history of the College. However, a significant increase was realized the last year. From 1947 through 1951, approximately 11 percent of all Hershey High School graduates enrolled at the Junior College.[369] The distribution of students attending the Junior College in 1952, by high school, was: Hershey High School, 19 percent; Milton Hershey School, 16 percent; Hummelstown, 14 percent; and Palmyra, 20 percent.[370] As of September, 1964, 60 percent of the total Junior College

---

[368] John D. Husband, "25th Year of Operation Opens at Hershey College," *The Even-ing News* [Harrisburg], September 21, 1962, p. 2.

[369] O. H. Aurand, *et al.,* A Study of the Schools of Derry Township, Dauphin County, Pennsylvania, 1951–1952, p. 132.

[370] Hershey Junior College "Administrative Report," August, 1952. (A large number of Hershey Chocolate Corporation employees lived in nearby Hummelstown and Palmyra whose dependents were eligible to attend the Junior College in 1952.)

enrollment had Hershey addresses, nine percent had Hummelstown addresses, and 12 percent had Palmyra addresses. A total of 18 different locations, by addresses, were represented in the 1964-1965 student body.[371] Of the 225 Hershey High School students who graduated in 1964, 45 percent enrolled in the Hershey Junior College, all but 10 percent of those who enrolled in any college or university that year.[372]

It is interesting to note, in comparison, that of those Hershey High School graduates of the classes of 1965 and 1966 who enrolled in college the following fall, approximately 40 percent of each class enrolled at the Harrisburg Area Community College.[373] Of the 190 freshmen who attended the Hershey Junior College in 1964-1965, 107 transferred to the Harrisburg Area Community College in 1965. Of that number, 63 were graduates of Derry Township schools.[374]

The number of Milton Hershey School students who attended the Junior College during the last ten years remained relatively constant. According to Rodney E. McLaughlin, currently Director of Student Personnel Services of the Milton Hershey School, the average enrollment was, approximately, 30-35 boys per year.[375]

The rate of student withdrawal from the College, as suggested above, was surprisingly low. Records show that for the year 1952-1953 through 1961-1962, the average yearly freshman withdrawal rate was, approximately, 12 percent. The sophomore rate of withdrawal for the same period was five percent. Total withdrawal, including freshmen, sophomores, and part-time students, averaged, approximately 10 percent over the 10-year period.[376]

The proportion of those Hershey Junior College graduates who continued their education in senior institutions remained high throughout the history of the institution. Of the 61 graduates of the Class of 1948, 42, or 69 percent, intended to enroll in 21 senior institutions.[377] An average of 69 percent of all graduates from 1948 through 1951 transferred to senior institutions; 12 percent of those who transferred in the Classes of 1948 and 1949 earned honors.[378] Of 190 students who graduated from the Junior College from 1947 through 1951, 126 or 66 percent transferred to 50 different institutions. Senior colleges receiving the largest number of transfers were Elizabethtown, Franklin and Marshall, Lebanon Valley, and Pennsylvania State College.

371 "Home Address Roster, 1964," Hershey Junior College files, Office of the Superintendent of Schools.

372 "Hershey Schools In Action," Derry Township School District, Hershey, Pennsylvania, Vol. VIII, No. 1, October 22, 1964, p. 1.

373 "Class of 1965" and "Class of 1966," statistics on file in the Hershey High School Guidance Office.

374 Letter from Fred A. Snyder, Dean of Students, Harrisburg Area Community College to writer, September 22, 1967.

375 Rodney McLaughlin, personal interview, February 23, 1970.

376 "Report Of Self Evaluation," 1963, op. cit., p. 72.

377 "42 Of 61 Graduates Of Hershey Junior College To Transfer To 21 Colleges And Universities," Hotel Hershey High-Lights, Vol. XVI, No. 3, July 10, 1948, p. 1.

378 "Data Presented For Consideration . . . ," 1952, op. cit., n.p.

Graduates of the same classes also enrolled in 18 graduate and professional schools.[379]   The 1952 Visiting Committee determined that, through a spot check of the Class of 1949, most of the students had done "above-average work" in College.[380]   The Committee felt the College had "excellent evidence of the subsequent performance" of graduates who had transferred.   The list of colleges to which Junior College students transferred was described as "fairly impressive."   Concerning the College's alumni follow-up procedures, the Committee was impressed.   It also determined that local businessmen were well satisfied with the semi-professional and vocational training Hershey Junior College students had received.   The Commission's report was concluded with the following:

> The committee was satisfied that the college itself is concerned to keep evaluating the outcomes of the work which it is doing, in terms of the achievement of its former students. Moreover, as far as the committee was able to discover, the results, (again, in human terms) reflect credit upon the institution.[381]

As a major recommendation with respect to outcomes of the academic program, the Commission recommended the College give serious thought "to the adoption of the Sophomore College Testing Program."[382]

The following table was submitted to the 1963 Commission on Institutions of Higher Education to show the employment and transfer pattern of the College's graduates over the five-year period.

TABLE 8

NUMBER AND PERCENT OF GRADUATES WHO WERE PLACED IN
EMPLOYMENT AND OTHER INSTITUTIONS
FROM THE CLASSES 1956 to 1960[a]

GRADUATES		TERMINAL		TRANSFER		BACHELOR'S DEGREE		HONORS		GRADUATE SCHOOL
YEAR	NO.	NO.	%	NO.	%	NO.	%	NO.	%	NO.
1956	59	14	24	45	76	42	71	12	20	10
1957	54	11	20	43	80	36	67	10	19	6
1958	59	8	14	51	86	39	66	18	31	10
1959	55	15	27	40	73	35	64	6	11	5
1960	80	7	9	73	91	49	61	14	18	12

[a]"Report of Self Evaluation," 1963, op. cit., p. 96.

A list of institutions to which Junior College graduates transferred from 1952 through 1962 was also presented to the Evaluation Committee.   It re-

[379] *Ibid.*
[380] "Report of the 1952 Visiting Committee," *op. cit.*, p. 12.
[381] *Ibid.*, pp. 12–13.
[382] *Ibid.*, p. 14.

vealed that 445 students transferred to 95 senior institutions. In addition to the previously mentioned colleges, Bloomsburg State College, Cornell University Hospital, University of Denver, Dickinson College, Lafayette College, Millersville State College, Shippensburg State College, and Tri-State College had become popular with Junior College graduates.[383] By 1963, Dean Fenstermacher reported that approximately 80 percent of Junior College graduates were attending graduate and professional schools.[384]

In 1962, the Dean of Instruction of Shippensburg State College wrote to Dean Fenstermacher praising the Junior College for the quality and success of its graduates who enrolled at the State College. It read:

> Again Shippensburg has reason to express its appreciation for the quality of students it receives by transfer from Hershey Junior College.
>
> A recent study by Mr. Gilmore Seavers of Hershey students admitted from September 1957 to March 1962 shows that all of these students either graduated or are currently attending the college with satisfactory academic standing. No other Junior College can match this remarkable record.[385]

The 1963 Middle States Evaluation Committee concluded its report with the following paragraph with respect to "outcomes" of the Hershey Junior College. It commended the institution highly.

> Since the proof of the pudding is in the eating, the material compiled on outcomes is of special interest to all who are in any way associated with the College. A large collection of material was made available to the team. It is very impressive. The percentage of graduates who transfer to four-year institutions is very high. The final product in terms of professional careers, leadership positions in business and industry, and success in relationship to a number of yardsticks, is admirable indeed. The faculty and administration of Hershey Junior College appear not only to provide sound education for two years, but also to trigger a high degree of motivation which stays with the students throughout their succeeding years of higher education.[386]

There are many individual interest and success stories of Hershey Junior College graduates but it is not the purpose of this study to report them. However, the reader may be interested to know that the College did not serve recent high school graduates only. Mrs. Laura Muth attended the College to take courses for her enjoyment. She was pictured in a 1955 edition of *The Pittsburgh Press* in a German class. The caption read, "Never too old to learn." She was 83 at the time.[387]

An example of a success story is that of John I. Grosnick. By attending evenings, he earned his Junior College diploma in 1946.[388] Upon graduation, he enrolled at Lebanon Valley College, from which he was graduated in 1953. In 1959, Grosnick received a Master of Education degree from Temple Uni-

[383] *Ibid.,* pp. 97–98.

[384] *Ibid.,* p. 95.

[385] Letter from Dean Paul Smay, Shippensburg State College to Dean Fenstermacher, August 14, 1962.

[386] "Report Of Evaluation Committee," 1963 *op. cit.,* pp. 10–11.

[387] "CO-ED AT 83," *The Pittsburgh Press,* Roto Magazine, November 27, 1955, p. 52.

[388] "Enrollment," *The Literary Artisan,"* Vol. XI, No. 1, May, 1950, p. 8.

versity. Later he was graduated from the Federal Bureau of Investigation National Academy.[389]

Grosnick was a member of the Pennsylvania State Police since 1937. On April 2, 1964, he was promoted from the rank of Captain to Lieutenant Colonel and to the new post of Chief of Staff of the Pennsylvania State Police.[390]

According to Dr. A. G. Breidenstine, there are many other similar examples of accomplishment on the part of Hershey Junior College graduates.[391]

The Hershey Junior College Closes

Several factors had a bearing, directly or indirectly, on the closing of the Hershey Junior College. The immediate reasons for its discontinuance are considered in this section. Included is a review of two pieces of state legislation and their influence on the fate of the Junior College.

The School District Reorganization Law

The School District Reorganization Law (P.L. 1283–Act 561) was passed by the 1961 Legislature of the Commonwealth of Pennsylvania and was signed into law on September 12, 1961. Briefly, the Reorganization Law provided for the establishment of larger school districts "based upon student population as reported for the 1960–1961 academic year." An average daily membership of 4,000 was specified although under certain conditions, districts with an average daily membership of 2,500 in 1960-1961 could have been approved. According to the timetable, each county board of school directors was required to have submitted "a plan of organization of administrative units conforming to the State Council's standards" by January 1, 1963. As of July 1, 1965, "all administrative units contained in county reorganization plans" were to have been established as school districts and belong to the class described in the law.[392] It was claimed that reorganization would result in a generally strengthened academic program and more efficient operation.[393]

On February 12, 1962, the Derry Township School Board went on record as being opposed to Act 561 and favoring its repeal.[394] The Board of School Directors opposed inclusion "in any plan of reorganization" because "the plans proposed by the Dauphin County Board threatened financial loss to Derry Township taxpayers...." A major concern was that the plans were

[389]"Police Staff Chief Named by Purdy," *The Patriot* [Harrisburg], April 1, 1964, p. 4.
[390]*Ibid.*
[391]A. G. Breidenstine, personal interview, July 27, 1967.
[392]P. L. 1283 (School District Reorganization) and the Derry Township School District, n.p.
[393]"The School District Reorganization Law," pamphlet, Office of Information and Publications, Department of Public Instruction, Harrisburg.
[394]P. L. 1283, *loc. cit.*

thought to jeopardize the continued receipt of the following private grants to the School District:

(1) Income of trust under the will of M. S. Hershey. The terms of the will specify this to be paid to "the School District of Derry Township, Dauphin County." The school district received $101,279.26 from this trust during the 1961–1962 school term, with this money being included in the General Fund.

(2) Grants from The M. S. Hershey Foundation. These grants have amounted to $25,000.00 annually, and are placed in the General Account.

(3) Entire financial support of the Hershey Junior College. (This budget is operated separately from the General Budget for Kindergarten–Grade 12.) The 1962–1963 Junior College budget totals $153,700.00, with 100% of the funds contributed by the Hershey Foundation. (The total of these three grants, $280,009.26, equals 21% of the *combined* General and Junior College Budgets.)

(4) The furnishing of building and equipment to the Hershey Junior College.

(5) All existing school buildings in the Derry Township Schools have been constructed and donated to the people, either by M. S. Hershey or by the Hershey Foundation. The effect of this is the absence of any large debt service costs in the budget.[395]

The School Board also objected to reorganization because other costs would be incurred.[396]

The following statement expressed the opinion of the School Board with respect to any advantages which might accrue to the Derry Township School Directors as a result of reorganization.

It is difficult to find any benefits or to determine any purposes to be served since our schools now meet, or exceed, the standards established for reorganized schools by the State Council of Education.[397]

The possible loss of Foundation financial support of the Junior College through reorganization was, then, a major concern. Discussion of the situation resulted in the first direct reference to the possible closing of the College.

In conjunction with the School Board's consideration of the various reorganization plans, a request was made to The M. S. Hershey Foundation Board of Managers for information concerning the effect the adoption of one of two County Board alternative plans might have "on the continuance of financial support to Derry Township schools by The M. S. Hershey Foundation and the trust established under the will of M. S. Hershey."[398] The reply of September 19, 1962 was made by Mr. Arthur Whiteman for the Hershey Trust Company, Trustee and the Managers of The M. S. Hershey Foundation. Mr. Whiteman reviewed the provisions of the trust which was established by Mr. Hershey's will. Concerning the beneficiary of the trust and the effect of

---

[395] *Ibid.*
[396] *Ibid.*
[397] *Ibid.*
[398] Letter from A. R. Whiteman, Hershey Trust Company and the Managers of The M. S. Hershey Foundation to Derry Township Board of School Directors, September 19, 1962.

reorganization, Mr. Whiteman wrote:

> ... Derry Township School District is the sole beneficiary of this trust, and the Trustee is required to pay the income to it. Should Derry Township School District cease to exist, and be superceded by a new and different school district, embracing additional areas, there would immediately arise a serious legal question whether the Trustee would have the legal power, under Mr. Hershey's will, to pay the income to the new school district, not only because the identity of the beneficiary would have changed but because the benefits would then be extended well beyond the residents of Derry Township, in whose interest alone the trust was established. It appears that only a court decision could settle this question. Conceivably, substantial litigation might be involved.[399]

The use to which the funds of the Foundation had been put, including the Junior College, were enumerated in the letter.

> The payment of all operating expenses of the Hershey Junior College. This currently involves an annual budget of approximately $155,000. In addition, classroom and other physical facilities are furnished free of charge at the Hershey Community Building.... It was created upon application of the Derry Township School District to the Department of Public Instruction and approved by the State Council of Education. It has at all times been administered by the school district as an integral part of the Derry Township School System. The funds contributed by the Foundation for support of the Junior College are paid to the school district and disbursed by it.[400]

With respect to the legality of the payment of the funds of the trust and the continuance of the Junior College, if reorganization occurred, Mr. Whiteman explained:

> ... The Managers of the Foundation are not required to make, or continue, any of these grants, and they are free to devote the Foundation's funds to other uses within the general purposes of the trust. However, the real concern of the Managers is whether they could lawfully continue to make such grants if Derry Township School District should cease to exist. The Foundation, as is the trust, is faced with a grave legal question whether grants to a school district which included other areas than Derry Township and were for the benefit of substantial numbers of people residing elsewhere could lawfully be made.

> With respect to the Junior College, there are problems in addition to the legal question. If the Junior College were continued as an activity of a larger school district, it would be expected that its facilities would be made available equally to all residents of the district and that enrollment inevitably would increase. The classroom and other facilities now provided without cost to the school district are being used at or very near the maximum capacity. Any appreciable increase in Junior College enrollment would, in all probability, require the construction of a separate building or buildings. The increased costs of operating a larger school and of providing new housing for it would very likely exceed the funds available from the Foundation, adding perhaps $50,000 to the annual budget. Whether a new school district would be willing to provide tax revenues to support such a project is hard to predict.

---

[399]*Ibid.* It is interesting to note that Dr. Fenstermacher contended that it was not the Derry Township School District that was the beneficiary of the trust, but, rather, the residents and employees who lived in Derry Township. Consequently, Fenstermacher felt the reorganization issue had no bearing on the continuance of the College.
[400]*Ibid.*

From this recitation, you can appreciate the dilemma which would face us if Derry Township School District were to be abolished and its functions absorbed by a new and larger district. The powers of the Trustee and of the Managers to continue support of the public schools would be seriously in question. Court litigation might well be the only means of resolving the issue, with the ultimate decision difficult to predict. Of course, the Managers of the Foundation could avoid the uncertainty and the litigation by diverting funds to uses other than support of the public schools, but this they have no desire to do. The Trustee, on the other hand, having no such discretion, probably would be obliged to have the court direct where the trust income now paid to Derry Township School District should go.

At this point, the Trustee under Mr. Hershey's will and the Managers of the Foundation have reached no decision as to whether, consistently with the trust terms, they can continue grants to the public schools as in the past or continue to support the Junior College, once Derry Township becomes a part of a larger school district. There is little doubt in our minds, however, that the Foundation, at best, will not be in a position to assume the increased cost of operating a junior college large enough to accept students from throughout either of the possible reorganized school districts, into which Derry Township would fall.

If there is to be no junior college, the last class which could be admitted with any assurance of graduating would be the one to enroll in September, 1963. With today's conditions, students and parents must begin planning for college far in advance. Often a year is not time enough in which to select a college and gain admission. Problems could be even more acute for parents whose planning has presupposed two years of tuition-free college work in Hershey, if they were confronted, even now, with the prospect of having to finance those two years of college elsewhere. This is not to lose sight of those students whose only hope of higher education may rest on the two years offered at Hershey Junior College. If that is not to be in prospect, their vocational futures might be best served by modifying, as early as possible, the high school curricula which they follow.

These considerations, it seems to us, make it absolutely imperative that no time be lost in exploring every aspect of the problems which reorganization of the school district promises to create, so that the people of Derry Township may know as soon as possible what the prospects for continuance of the Junior College are. If it cannot be carried foreward after school reorganization, that fact should be determined at the earliest possible time, in order to minimize the unhappy consequences of discontinuing the Junior College.

It is the unqualified desire of the Managers of The M. S. Hershey Foundation to see Hershey Junior College continue. We believe this desire is shared by the Derry Township School Board. However, the carrying out of the school reorganization program puts this beyond the power of these two bodies, by themselves, to assure. The Foundation offers its fullest cooperation in any effort your board sees fit to undertake in the interest of preserving the future of the Junior College.[401]

After review and discussion of Mr. Whiteman's letter, the School Board unanimously voted to go on record as wishing to have the Derry Township School District remain an independent unit.[402] At a subsequent meeting of the Derry Township and the Dauphin County School Boards, the Derry

---

[401] *Ibid.*

[402] Derry Township Public Schools, "Board Minutes," September 19, 1962.

Board requested that Derry Township be included in the County plan as an independent district. The Board's lengthy statement in justification of the District remaining independent included the following with respect to the Junior College.

> There is grave doubt that they [private grants from the trust created by M. S. Hershey] *can be paid to a district including areas other than Derry Township.* Even if this were possible, it is highly improbable that the Junior College could be maintained for a district adding the five additional districts or the entire county as proposed. We are proud of our Junior College which our people desperately want to preserve and which should be preserved as a prototype [*sic*] for community junior colleges throughout the state.[403]

The Community College Act of 1963

The Community College Act of 1963, Act 484 of 1963 effective August 24, 1963 (P.L. 1132), provided for:

> ... the creation, establishment and operation of community colleges, granting certain powers to the State Board of Education, the Council of Higher Education and the Department of Public Instruction, authorizing school districts, county boards of school directors and municipalities to sponsor community colleges; authorizing school districts and municipalities to levy certain taxes; ... [404]

The first public community college to be established in Pennsylvania under this Act was the Harrisburg Area Community College. It was officially approved by the State Board of Education on February 14, 1964.[405] The "Board Minutes" show that the Derry Township School Board was invited to participate in the sponsorship of the Harrisburg Area Community College. The invitation was extended by Mr. Bruce E. Cooper of the Harrisburg Community College Committee. At its meeting on January 16, 1964, the Derry Township School Board voted unanimously to "decline the invitation to participate in such a community college."[406] However, on April 3, 1964, a special meeting of the Derry Township Board of School Directors was called to order by the President, Mr. Harry B. Reese, Jr. to discuss "the merger of the Hershey Junior College with the Harrisburg Area Community College." Other members present were: Mr. Clever Ernst, Mr. E. Morse Heisey, Mr. Jefferson C. Barnhart, Mrs. Hope Emerich, Mr. John Meszaros, Mr. William Saye, Solicitor, Dr. L. Eugene Jacques, Superintendent of Schools, and Mr. William Black, Secretary. Six members of the Hershey Junior College faculty and a representative of the Hershey Education Association also

---

[403] Derry Township Public Schools, "Board Minutes," October 9, 1962. Eventually, the District was permitted to remain independent of the larger proposed County unit. The reorganization issue did not, directly, cause the Hershey Junior College to close.

[404] Commonwealth of Pennsylvania, Department of Education, Office of Higher Education, Bureau of Community Colleges, *Suggested Procedures For The Establishment of a Community College in Pennsylvania,* Appendix C, Revised January, 1970.

[405] Letter from Elwood A. Shoemaker, Bureau of Management Services, Department of Public Instruction, Commonwealth of Pennsylvania to writer, July 8, 1970.

[406] Derry Township Public Schools, "Board Minutes," January 16, 1964.

attended.[407]   Dr. Fenstermacher was not present at the meeting; he was attending an American Association of Junior Colleges meeting in Miami, Florida at the time.[408]   The minutes of the meeting are important in that they provide a review of the events which were reported to have led to the decision to merge the Hershey Junior College with the Harrisburg Area Community College and, thus, subsequently cause the Junior College to cease to exist. For this reason, the minutes are included here in their entirety.

> Mr. Reese opened the meeting stating that the Hershey Foundation explained to us that to continue the Hershey Junior College there would have to be a tuition charge of $300.00 for the year 1964–1965 and $500.00 for the year 1965–1966. At this meeting and subsequent ones the School Board with their Solicitor were informed by the Department of Public Instruction that it would be impossible to make a tuition charge to the residents of Derry Township. Continuing our conversations with the Foundation they informed us that it would be impossible to continue operating the Hershey Junior College due to increased costs each year, because the funds of the Foundation are limited to its income. Therefore, it was necessary for us to search for a solution to this problem. This led to various meetings and, finally, with people from the Harrisburg Area Community College. In our meeting with trustees of the Harrisburg Area Community College explaining our situation in Derry Township we asked to be accepted as a member of their organization. Our negotiations with them have developed the following tentative plans. They have assured us that our present staff will be retained for at least one year. The facilities currently being used by the Hershey Junior College will be continued for a minimum of two years. Concerning our students, the present freshmen, who will be sophomores next year, will have their tuition paid by the Foundation and all the incoming freshmen class will have their tuition paid. The necessary tuition will be paid by the Hershey Foundation who, in turn, will reimburse the School District for any charges for their share of the cost.
>
> Mr. Reese asked Mr. Saye to give a brief history of the merger of the Hershey Junior College with the Harrisburg Area Community College. He stated that in February the first meeting of the School Board, along with the Board of Managers, was held. At that time the School Board was informed that in order to continue the Junior College they would have to require a tuition charge of $300.00 for the next school year and a tuition charge of $400.00 for the following year. This amount of money would be necessary to make up the difference between the income from the Foundation and the actual cost of operation. Mr. Saye received this information and immediately met with Mr. John D. Killian, representing the Attorney General's office of the Department of Public Instruction. He informed Mr. Saye that no tuition charge could be made by law, since the Junior College is an intrical [sic] part of the Public School System. However, it could be possible to charge tuition to nonresident students based on the same facts and formula used by the School District to establish their tuition for nonresident students. At that time Mr. Killian suggested operating as a private school or as a community college under the new community college law and this way a tuition charge could be made. After his interview with Mr. Killian the Junior College Committee of

---

[407]Derry Township Public Schools, "Board Minutes," April 3, 1964.

[408] Derry Township Public Schools, Personal Expense Account of V. H. Fenstermacher for American Association of Junior Colleges meeting held in Miami, Florida, April 20, 1964.

the School Board met with the Junior College Committee of the Board of Managers to review the information Mr. Saye had obtained at his interview. At that time the Board of Managers said that they had no desire to operate as a private college and to operate as a community college would be too competitive with the one operated in Harrisburg.

After discussing many possibilities, two major problems developed.

1. Since no tax money is involved with the operation of the Junior College, would it be possible to obtain special permission to charge tuition or a student fee to cover the difference between Foundation funds and the money necessary for complete operation?
2. What would the status of the faculty be concerning the Public School Employees' Retirement if the school were operated as a private institution?

They decided to appoint a committee to investigate further with the Department of Public Instruction concerning these problems. The following committee was appointed: Mr. Jefferson C. Barnhart of the School Board, Mr. William Saye, Solicitor for the School Board and from the Foundation Dr. J. O. Hershey and Mr. Gilbert Nurick, legal representative for the Foundation. This committee is to meet with the Department of Public Instruction and Mr. Killian for an official opinion on these problems.

On March 25 a report of this committee meeting with the Department of Public Instruction was presented to the combined committees from the School Board and the Foundation. They were informed that no tuition charge would be permitted under any conditions under the Public School Code except for nonresident students. The staff would not be under Public School Employees' Retirement if operated as a community college since there is no provision in the law to permit it. They further stated that under no conditions would they permit a student fee or a tuition charge.

The following possible solutions were discussed to try and solve the situation and continue the operation of the Hershey Junior College. Much discussion was held on the possibility of changing the Hershey Junior College to our own community college and operate it on the same basis as the one being formed in Harrisburg. There was considerable doubt in the minds of the men that the Department of Public Instruction would approve a community college located within twelve miles of the one in Harrisburg. They also felt the competition for students and faculty would be too great. The other possibility, of course, would be to join with the Harrisburg Area Community College which would give the students a wider program of studies and greater opportunities for education.

The final decision of this meeting was to appoint the following committee to meet with representatives of the Harrisburg Area Community College: Mr. John Meszaros, Mr. Harry B. Reese, Jr., Mr. Jefferson C. Barnhart and Mr. William Saye all representing the School District; Dr. J. O. Hershey and Mr. Gilbert Nurick representing the Foundation. This meeting took place on March 27 making the offer to have the Junior College join with the Harrisburg Area Community College. The indication from the representatives of the Harrisburg unit were not very receptive to the idea. It was explained that this was an exploratory meeting and would be discussed further by our Board and the Board of Managers.

On March 30, 1964 the School Board met with representatives of the Foundation at the Community Inn. At this meeting it was decided that the best possible solution would be to offer the facilities of the Junior College to the Harrisburg Area Community College complete with faculty and facilities for a two-year period, giving them a good basis to start the operation of their

191

school. Again the same committees were appointed to meet and discuss further the details of this association.

On March 31, 1964 the committee consisting of Mr. Meszaros, Mr. Saye, Dr. Hershey and Mr. Nurick met with the following representatives of the Harrisburg Area Community College: Mr. Cooper, Mr. Whitmoyer and Dr. Berrier. After considerable discussion they felt it would be a very good idea to accept our offer on our conditions and in the afternoon they would present it to their Board of Trustees for a final decision. The trustees met at 1:30 p.m. and unanimously agreed to accept the offer and take the Junior College in with their operation next September and operate it as the Hershey Branch of the Harrisburg Area Community College.

Mrs. Hope Emerich gave a further explanation that the Foundation took the attitude they could offer no more assistance and they would have to refuse future expansion of the program.

Mr. Castelli, Mr. Vanderwall and Mr. Schmehl presented their personal views on this possible merger and indicated that the entire faculty was very much opposed to this move of joining with the Harrisburg Area Community College.

Following lengthy discussions between representatives of the faculty and the Board, the President requested the Board to take care of the business at hand. Mr. Meszaros made a motion, seconded by Mr. Heisey, to request a letter from the Foundation stating that they could no longer support the operation of the Junior College to its fullest extent and have the Secretary make this contact. All members voted the affirmative. Immediately following the vote on the above motion, Mr. Reese contacted Mr. James Bobb, Chairman of the Foundation, by telephone and he was assured that a letter would be in the mail the following day.

Mr. Curry made the following motion: I hereby move that the School District of the Township of Derry, Dauphin County, Pennsylvania make application to the Harrisburg Area Community College and to the State Board of Education for admission to membership as a local sponsor in the Harrisburg Area Community College. This was seconded by Mr. Ernst and all members voted the affirmative.

Following passage of the above motion, the Board held lengthy discussion and the decision was made that the motion be changed. Therefore, Mr. Meszaros made a motion, seconded by Mr. Heisey, to rescind the motion made by Mr. Curry and seconded by Mr. Ernst. The Board voted unanimously to pass this.

Mrs. Emerich made the following motion: I hereby move that the School District of the Township of Derry, Dauphin County, Pennsylvania, make application to the Harrisburg Area Community College and to the State Board of Education for admission to membership as a local sponsor in the Harrisburg Area Community College.

PROVIDED THAT, the academic school or entity known as the Hershey Junior College be preserved and continued as the Hershey Branch of the Harrisburg Area Community College for a period of at least two years in its present location and that the faculty and staff of the Hershey Junior College be retained for at least one year beginning July 1, 1964, and that the proper officers of the Board of School Directors of the School District of the Township of Derry, be authorized and empowered to do all things necessary to carry out the intents and purposes of this motion. And, further, that the Board of School Directors of the School District of the Township of Derry take action upon receipt of its acceptance as a local sponsor in the Harrisburg Area Community College to dissolve the present public school known as the Hershey

Junior College effective June 30, 1964, merging its function and facilities with the Harrisburg Area Community College effective as of July 1, 1964. This motion was seconded by Mr. Barnhart and passed unanimously.

Mr. Reese, President of the Board, requested a news release be issued by the Board concerning this action of joining with the Harrisburg Area Community College. The Publicity Committee, along with the Solicitor, prepared the following statement which all members gave their verbal consent to release.

The members of the School Board of the School District of Derry Township were recently advised by the Board of Managers of the M. S. Hershey Foundation that the income from the Foundation which for many years completely supported and operated the Hershey Junior College had become insufficient to cover the College's annually increasing budget, nor could it provide for the expansion of the library, nor provide for other needed improvements and facilities. Under the circumstances it appeared that beginning with the next school term, a tuition charge would have to be made on the students of the Junior College to make up the deficit. Further study indicated that inasmuch as the Junior College was part of the Derry Township Public School System, no tuition could legally be charged to those students who were residents of Derry Township.

The General Assembly of the Commonwealth provided legislation during its 1963 session for the establishment of community colleges. These colleges are authorized to make tuition charges the ultimate cost of which to be absorbed by the State, the sponsoring school district and the student.

After studying various alternatives, the Board of School Directors of the School District of Derry Township concluded that the interests of the students of Derry Township could be best served by the Hershey Junior College becoming a part of the Harrisburg Area Community College. In addition to financial help from the Commonwealth and the student, merger with the Harrisburg Area Community College would avoid competition for faculty members, would permit the use of extensive federal funds for the erection of buildings and facilities, and would provide State reimbursements to the School District. In addition, the Area Community College provides for a much broader curriculum program than does the Hershey Junior College, especially in technical fields. A merger now would permit joining the present Hershey Junior College faculty with the Harrisburg Area Community College faculty insofar as this is practicable and workable.

The present Board of School Directors of the School District of Derry Township is vitally concerned with providing the best education opportunities for its pupils and to these ends has carefully considered the advantages to be gained by membership in the Harrisburg Area Community College and in the Area Technical High School, the latter now in the formative stages.

With the best interests of its students in mind, the School Board of the School District of Derry Township has arranged with the Board of Trustees of the Harrisburg Area Community College for the Hershey Junior College to become a part of the new Area Community College. The conditions of the consolidation include the continuation of all of the professional staff who desire to become affiliates with the new program and the continued registration of all of the current Freshman class, plus the enrollment of all applicants of the new Freshman class scheduled by the Hershey Junior College for enrollment this September. The M. S. Hershey Foundation has agreed to make the present Junior College facilities in the Community Center building available for a two year period while the Harrisburg Area Community College is establishing itself in adequate quarters in the Harrisburg area.

The Derry Township School District costs to the Harrisburg Area Community College for the next two years will be borne entirely by the M. S. Hershey Foundation. In addition, the personal tuition for the current Freshmen will be paid next year by the Foundation and the Foundation will cover the tuition for two years for those applicants whom the Hershey Junior College enrolls in the new Freshman class scheduled for this September.

The members of the School Board regret that the Hershey Junior College as a separate body will cease to exist. It has been a vital part of the public school system of Derry Township since 1938. It has educated hundreds of young people; it is nationally accredited; it possesses an excellent faculty; it has been a prime example of the generosity, farsightedness and the concern and devotion of the late Milton S. Hershey to the cause of higher education. However, the budget requirements having apparently outgrown the income from the trust, it becomes our concern and duty to continue the fine educational opportunities which have existed for our young people over the past twenty-five years and to provide, if possible, even greater opportunities. We believe these opportunities can be best provided, in the light of present circumstances, by joining with the Harrisburg Area Community College in the launching of a larger public institution with a wider scope of educational offerings and supported in such a manner as to assure the continuing of higher education at a low cost to the student. Our Board of School Directors is grateful for the twenty-six years our Junior College has served the educational needs of many in our community. The Board appreciates the generosity of Milton S. Hershey and we feel sure that the present Board of Managers as well as future ones of the M. S. Hershey Foundation will continue to use the income from the Foundation to support the public schools of Derry Township, to continue to improve their standards of education and to provide for the vocational, cultural or professional education of Township residents as expressly intended by Mr. Hershey.

> BOARD OF SCHOOL DIRECTORS OF THE
> SCHOOL DISTRICT OF THE TOWNSHIP
> OF DERRY
>
> by—William H. Saye, Esq.,
> Solicitor[409]

Public Reaction

Public announcement of the decision, two days later, shocked the residents of Hershey. The bold headline of the front page of the *Sunday Patriot News* [Harrisburg] read: "Hershey Junior College Joins Harrisburg Educational Setup." Subheadlines stated: "Facilities Made Available For Two Years" and "Faculty Put At Disposal of Merger." Pictured conferring about the merger were the following men: Attorney, Bruce Cooper, chairman of the Board of Trustees, Harrisburg Area Community College; James E. Bobb, chairman of the Board of Managers, The M. S. Hershey Foundation; William H. Saye, attorney for Derry Township School District, and Harry Reese, president, Derry Township School Board. On the other hand, the announcement that the Junior College would operate as a division of the Community College delighted many residents of Harrisburg, particularly those associated with the

---

[409] Derry Township Public Schools, "Board Minutes," April 3, 1964.

founding of the Community College. *The Patriot* [Harrisburg] article reflected the pleasure with the decision.

> Higher education in the Harrisburg area took a giant step forward last night with the announcement that Hershey Junior College will become a part of the Harrisburg Area Community College.[410]

Bruce E. Cooper, chairman of the Community College's Board of Trustees, stated in the same article:

> It is well known that the Hershey Junior College is an accredited institution. This should give further assurance to our students that high quality education is not a future goal, but is a present reality.

> Through the amalgamation of the Hershey Junior College into our program, the Harrisburg Area Community College now has at its disposal a highly trained faculty and an excellent administrative staff.[411]

Much of the remainder of the article was devoted to the explanation of the circumstances which led to the forced discontinuance of the Hershey Junior College. The report corresponded with the statement that was agreed upon at the April 3 School Board meeting. The article closed with a statement by Mr. Gilbert Nurick, attorney for The M. S. Hershey Foundation and Mr. Harry Reese, Jr., president of the Derry Township School Board. Mr. Nurick said of the merger, "It is a source of deep and genuine gratification to note that the wonderful spirit of Milton S. Hershey lives on."[412]

The statement by James E. Bobb, chairman of the Board of Managers of the Foundation, was included in a sub-article in the same newspaper. Mr. Bobb explained:

> We, who are charged with the responsibility of administering the various trusts and enterprises of Milton S. Hershey, make a conscientious effort to base our actions on what he would have done under the circumstances if he were still living.

> He always believed that everyone should have the opportunity to acquire an adequate education. It was on the basis of this principle that the Hershey Junior College was established by the Derry Township School District and was wholly subsidized by the M. S. Hershey Foundation during and since his lifetime.
> . . . .
> We understand, moreover, that the school district has been advised that it has no authority to charge tuition under existing law.

> Recent developments on both the federal and state levels encouraging the establishment of community colleges indicate that the government has adopted Mr. Hershey's basic philosophy of availability of advanced and technical education without burdensome costs to students.

> The Harrisburg Area Community College, which has been established with the overwhelming support of the constituent school districts, will offer a broad

---

[410] Bill Campbell, "Faculty Put At Disposal of Merger," *Sunday Patriot News* [Harrisburg], April 5, 1964, pp. 1, 13.

[411] *Ibid.* All but two members of the Hershey Junior College faculty assumed positions at the Harrisburg Area Community College. Clyde E. Blocker, President, Harrisburg Area Community College, personal interview, June 30, 1970.

[412] *Ibid.*

scope of instruction and curricula, and we endorse the decision of the Derry Township School District to affiliate with it.[413]

The statement went on to explain the financial arrangements that had been made to subsidize the costs of Junior College students who would be attending the Harrisburg Area Community College. The use of the Hershey Community Building by the new Community College during the transition period was also explained by Mr. Bobb. He ended his statement with the following words:

> We are gratified that through these gestures we will have the opportunity to demonstrate again the generous and public-spirited deeds which exemplified the life of Milton S. Hershey.[414]

On April 7, an editorial, "Community College Gets A Big Boost From Hershey," appeared in *The Patriot* [Harrisburg]. The commentary must have sounded strangely familiar to the older residents of Hershey:

> The joining of the Hershey Junior College with the Harrisburg Area Community College is one of the best pieces of higher education news the Tri-County Area has had in a long time.
> ·
> There will be growing pains for the Tri-County Area's new college. Perhaps some of the growing pains will be severe. But for this college—the first of its type in Pennsylvania—many things have been accomplished already.
> The joining of Hershey Junior College can be nothing else but a welcome addition to the Community College.[415]

The Hershey community reacted to the announcement of the closing of the Hershey Junior College immediately and vociferously. Many residents were angered and offended with what they considered to be not only an unwise decision but one in which they were entitled to have a voice.

The most dramatic protest of the announcement of the merger and the closing of the College was the staging of a "funeral parade" on a drizzly April 7. An estimated 250 students and alumni participated in the mock funeral.[416] The "funeral cortege," which consisted of approximately 60 cars, was led by a hearse which bore a sign reading, "His deeds are his monuments—Is this why they are abolishing H. J. C.?" The hearse carried other signs: "Money is the root of all evil," "First the trustees killed our college. Now we have the sad task of burying Hershey Junior College," and "Good colleges never die; they're just given away." The students planned a service, with eulogies, at the tomb of Milton S. Hershey but the faculty members dissuaded them from staging that part of the demonstration.[417]

413"Foundation Head's Statement,"*Sunday Patriot-News* [Harrisburg], April 5, 1964, p. 13.
414*Ibid.*
415"Community College Gets A Big Boost From Hershey," *The Patriot* [Harrisburg] (editorial), April 7, 1964, p. 18.
416"Hershey College Students Stage 'Funeral' Parade," *Lebanon Daily News,* April 8, 1964, p. 1.
417"Hershey Class Protests 'Give-Away' To Area Community College Project," *The Evening News* [Harrisburg], April 8, 1964, p. 49.

Efforts on the part of students and Hershey residents were launched to try to save the Hershey Junior College. A "Student Committee for the Preservation of Hershey Junior College" was organized and literature appropriate to the cause was printed and distributed.[418] A "citizens committee" was also established in an effort to fight the merger and the end of the free College. The two groups combined their efforts.[419] A fund was even established for the preservation of the college and an account of $500 was opened in the Hummelstown Bank.[420] Eventually, 2,000 persons signed a petition to keep the College open.[421]

Many interesting opinions regarding the decision to merge were expressed by Hershey residents. It has been suggested that the Junior College faculty and Hershey residents never accepted the reasons offered for the closing. The following "letter to the editor," by John Zimmerman, probably expressed the true feelings of most "Hersheyites."

> There is no joy in Mudville, mighty Casey has struck out. This week, Mudville can be spelled H-E-R-S-H-E-Y.
>
> Over 6,000 residents of Derry Township have been enthusiastic one-man (or one-woman) chambers of commerce, ready at the drop of a hat to extoll the virtues and benefits of residence in "their town." Very few of their neighbors have been spared the ordeal of learning about the wonderful Community Center, the Theatre, Sports Plaza, the school system, etc. Very few could have missed the particular note of pride and gratitude that always accompanied the phrase "and two years of college, highly accredited, with no tuition charge." No particularly gifted insight was needed to discern that the schools and the Junior College were the real source of confidence in their decision to raise their children in Derry Township. The response in the fall of 1962 to the threat of an unnecessary and poorly planned county reorganization was a testimonial to their deep concern over these institutions.
>
> That confidence has been replaced with a mixture of shock, bewilderment and, to a large segment of the residents, a feeling of having been betrayed. The *Sunday Patriot-News* front page story on April 5th was the first single indication given that the Hershey Junior College was destitute and that, suddenly, the planned education for their children might never materialize. They were shocked with a "fait-accompli"—a surrendering of their proudest possession without having been told it was vulnerable, without an opportunity to work to save it, with no chance to fight for their interests. The very rallying point in the earlier reorganization fight had become a hollow illusion.
>
> It is not the intent of this letter to argue the wisdom of the decision. This would be impossible without access to the facts. It is not the intent to comment on the shallow tone of the news release with its repetitive platitudes and exaggerated emphasis on the value of this "crutch" for the Harrisburg Area Community College.

---

[418] "The Student Committee for the Preservation of Hershey Junior College," pamphlet.

[419] "Hershey Citizens Organize To Battle College Merger," *The Evening News* [Harrisburg], April 10, 1964, p. 8

[420] "Efforts Proceed on 2 Fronts To Preserve Junior College," *The Evening News* [Harrisburg], April 17, 1964, p. 13.

[421] "2000 Sign Form to Keep College Free," *The Patriot* [Harrisburg], May 1, 1964, p. 10.

I would rather reflect on the future of a community. How many years must pass before this paternalistic decision is forgotten? How long before even one of these 6,000 chambers of commerce will dare to be proud of their trusted leaders who had so little faith in them? Perhaps the "dis-trust" fund established so easily will out-live the multi-million-dollar trust fund that can create Medical Centers and a national image. I wonder if mutual respect and consideration is really necessary in modern industry and modern living. I suspect that the brillance of hindsight will show that Mighty Casey did, indeed, strike out.[422]

Another letter to the editor by Frederick R. Houser, an alumnus of the Junior College and, then, Registrar of George Washington University, expressed his disbelief that means to finance the Junior College could not be found. For Mr. Houser, as well as many alumni and Hershey residents, this was incomprehensible, particularly after $50,000,000 had been transferred from the Milton Hershey School trust to establish The Milton S. Hershey Medical Center of The Pennsylvania State University about a year earlier. Houser's letter, in part, stated:

The news that Hershey Junior College is to be "merged" with the Harrisburg Area Community College came as quite a shock to one who is a graduate of the Hershey Junior College. Since I am working in Washington, D.C., my information concerning this matter has been in the form of newspaper clippings. Based upon these articles, it is my feeling that there has been a "murder" rather than a "merger."

... It is my understanding, that the Board of Managers of the M. S. Hershey Foundation contends that lack of funds has forced this action upon them. This is difficult to understand in light of the announcement last summer that $50,000,000 from another trust fund established by Mr. Hershey, was given to Penn State for a medical school. I am sure that the Hershey interests could find additional money from other sources under their control, to increase the trust funds for the Junior College, if they so desired. I personally cannot accept the lack of funds statement as the real reason for this unfortunate and retrogressing decision.

It is also contended in an editorial in a Harrisburg newspaper of April 7, 1964 that "By law the Junior College was prohibited from charging tuition because of its public-school-operated status." I contend that this is incorrect or the law has been changed since 1946–47. I attended the HJC during that period and my tuition was paid by the Veterans Administration to the HJC as it was for hundreds of other veterans. If tuition was charged then, why can't it be charged now?
. . . .

Mr. Hershey was far ahead of his time in his educational philosophy. Unfortunately, it would appear that those who have been given the responsibility of administering this trust are not only behind the times but are purposely going in the opposite direction. They have betrayed the very trust they are to guard.
. . . .

I have no quarrel with the desire of the Harrisburg area in its efforts to establish a Community College. I do quarrel with the "Murder" of Hershey Junior College. It was established by a man of great imagination and foresight. It

---

[422] "Hershey Decision Came as a Shock," *The Sunday Patriot-News* [Harrisburg], April 12, 1964, p. 23.

became a reality and produced hundreds, if not thousands, of fine students during its 26-year history who are now solid citizens making outstanding contributions to our state and nation in a great variety of fields of endeavor. The Board of Managers of the M. S. Hershey Foundation has taken a negative action. It is my hope that they will reverse their decision and accept the responsibilities of the trust they hold.[423]

At about the same time, Dr. A. G. Breidenstine, then Dean of Academic Affairs at Millersville State College, wrote the following letter to Dr. Fenstermacher about the closing of the College.

April 17, 1964

Dr. Varnum Fenstermacher
Hershey Junior College
Hershey, Pennsylvania

Dear Varnum:

During the last week a great number of persons have spoken to me about the closing of Hershey Junior College. All, every one, spoke regretfully. I have not been asked to do anything, nor to lend a voice of protest. However, even my bones cry out for the institution about which many important memories remain. These memories compel me to speak out.

1. What has changed the basic purpose as forged out with Mr. Hershey to provide for the Hershey Community a two-year college of merit?

2. What now about the promise given during the initial accreditation that the College would continue even though not included within the tax structure of Derry Township? (On this point I have given my word after due consultation with Mr. Hershey.)

3. What has happened, or is to happen, to the charter; to the document of formal approval by the DPI?

4. Lastly, what of the promises, actual and implied, which have brought many people into the Hershey Community? Are all of us in the position of not having kept our word?

Beyond these considerations, however, is the very serious one of blotting out an institution; not just a business institution, but one with an enviable record of distinction in preparing young men and women for useful citizenship. It would be simple to close a business by comparison. But HJC can be closed. All of us know this bald fact. To do so, however, will engender regret, ill will, distrust, and deep-seated anger for a period of time beyond the life-span of those responsible for the decisions. Only a bold new venture can possibly heal the wounds already opened.

What could be done? This is now a difficult and complicated question; it would have been simple prior to the recent precipitous action. For example – Why couldn't HJC have been the nucleus of a Commonwealth College in the Hershey Area bearing its present name of distinction? Even the status of a small, private JC of high quality would have been an honorable decision. Also, a private junior college of HJC's reputation would be a welcome feeder for the renowned universities and accredited senior colleges.

---

[423] "College Merger: Alumnus Hits Hershey Step,"; "Merger or Murder?" *The Patriot* [Harrisburg], (letter to the editor), April 18, 1964, p. 12.

These are but rambling thoughts, written in haste, by one who has had a part in giving HJC its birth. You are at liberty to use this letter as you see best. I didn't know to whom else to direct it.

Sincerely yours,

A. G. Breidenstine
Dean of Academic Affairs[424]

Two weeks after the public announcement of the merger and closing of the College, a Harrisburg resident wrote of the necessity for the residents of Hershey to accept the fact that things that are given free may also be taken away:

The two letters in last week's "Sunday Patriot-News" on the Hershey College affair represented a good contrast on the feelings of the Hershey Community — the student's outraged whine and the thoughtful reflection of the parent.

While I must stand with the parent in his belief that the community should have been given a chance to try and take over the responsibilities of the college, I feel that there is really no basic complaint to be made. In truth, all of the extra things that Hershey has, as compared with most any town of similar size, have been gifts, not earned and not paid for by those receiving the benefits. As the parent rightly senses, the decision was "paternalistic," but no more so than the existence of the school or town itself.

I would venture a guess that no great hue and cry will be raised and no strong community counter-attack will be launched, because people who are in the habit of getting something for nothing are always afraid of what will happen to the remaining "gravy" if they up and stop the train. Perhaps a few citizens will see the light and set up a new political organization free of control of the Estate and determined to pay their own way, even though it means frightening the goose.

It may come as a surprise to Hersheyites, but their story is an old one, having been told for years in mill towns of the South where the benefits, though less sophisticated, are even greater in extent and kind. But there, as here, one usually finds out, along with Dr. Faustus, that sooner or later the conversation gets around to the "price."

—John R. Hopkins, Harrisburg[425]

The Hershey Education Association was strongly opposed to the decision to discontinue the College and to the manner in which it was made. The Association's letter to the Board of Managers is reproduced below:

Hershey Education Association
Derry Township Schools
Hershey, Pennsylvania
April 22, 1964

Trustees
M. S. Hershey Foundation
Hershey, Pennsylvania

Gentlemen:

The Hershey Education Association of Derry Township at its last meeting voiced its disapproval of your recent decision to discontinue the active support

[424]Letter from A. G. Breidenstine to V. H. Fenstermacher, April 17, 1964, personal files V. H. Fenstermacher.
[425]"Hershey Dilemma Is An Old Story," *Sunday Patriot-News* [Harrisburg], (letter to the editor), April 19, 1964, p. 27.

to the Hershey Junior College. We are primarily disturbed by the method in which the Foundation announced the lack of funds available in the trust and your determination not to subsidize the Hershey Junior College beyond the annual income of the trust.

From the beginning, we should like to clarify that the Hershey Education Association well realizes the financial implications relative to the support of the Hershey Junior College; but this does not justify the action of secretive planning with the Derry Township School Directors initiated at your request. By doing so, the prerogatives of the citizenry were violated, thus jeopardizing the rapport between them and the school directors.

Realizing that this is a private trust, we recognize your obligation to guard your trust and your right to discretion in its administration. However, you are ethically bound to divulge to the legacees periodic information relative to its solvency and jeopardy. Precluding exigencies limit the initiative of the legacees, but they are still entitled to referundum and the opportunity to formulate alternative solutions; e.g., amusement tax, wage tax, increase of property tax, re-evaluation of the tax structure, or merger with the Harrisburg Area Community College.

Further, your uncommunicative attitude toward the Hershey Junior College faculty concerning the resolving of this dilemma cannot be sanctioned by those of us who are professional educators.

Finally, we cannot condone your decision or accept unquestionably that this action is in the interest of the terms of the trust as established by Milton S. Hershey.

Sincerely,
Hershey Education Association[426]

Numerous meetings were held with representatives of The M. S. Hershey Foundation, the Derry Township Board of School Directors, and the Harrisburg Area Community College Board in an attempt to reverse the decision and have the Junior College continue operation. Various proposals, as suggested in the Hershey Education Association letter, were made. However, none of the suggestions proved feasible. The "Board Minutes" of May 11, 1964 reflected the futility of the situation. The Secretary of the Board, Mr. William D. H. Black, a member of the first class to graduate from Hershey Junior College, entered the following words after the Junior College Committee Report to the Board: "Dead duck."[427] Their meaning was obvious.

On June 8, 1964, the School Board voted, unanimously, to pay the organization cost of the Harrisburg Area Community College.[428] An Administrative Board, which was to be responsible for the administration of the Hershey Junior College as a merged institution with the Harrisburg Area Community College, was appointed on June 22. The Administrative Board, which served for one year, consisted of the eight members of the Derry Township School Board.[429] At this same meeting, the Citizens Committee requested the

[426]Letter from Hershey Education Association to M. S. Hershey Foundation, April 22, 1964.

[427]Derry Township Public Schools, "Board Minutes," May 11, 1964.

[428]Derry Township Public Schools, "Board Minutes," June 8, 1964.

[429]Derry Township Public Schools, "Board Minutes," June 22, 1964.

Board to reconsider its decision to participate in the Harrisburg Area Community College and to give the Committee an opportunity to submit possible plans to continue the operation of the Junior College as an "independent institution." The School Board agreed to hear any possible solutions the Committee could offer.[430]

As late as August 10, the Citizens Committee was still attempting to reverse the decision. On that date the Committee met with the Board and several suggestions to finance the College were made, including a one percent assessment on wages, the levying of a $600.00 "student fee," increasing real estate taxes, and charging tuition for nonresident students. It was also suggested that a 20-room building be constructed at the same time the new high school was being constructed and that it be financed through the local building authority. The Board indicated it would give consideration to the Committee's proposals.[431] At the same meeting the report of the Hershey Junior College Committee indicated that four Harrisburg Area Community College students were granted permission to attend the Junior College as sophomores. This was done "as a favor to them with the provision that Harrisburg collect tuition and all necessary fees." It was also reported that the Junior College would operate "the same as in past years with no changes in admissions."

According to the newspaper account of the August 10 Board Meeting, the Citizens Committee had little reason to be encouraged. It was reported that 200 residents appeared at the meeting with the Committee. The opening paragraph of the article stated:

> Chances of pulling the Hershey Junior College out of its merger with the Harrisburg Area Community College seemed slimmer than ever last night as the Derry Township School Board met with the Citizens Committee for the preservation of that institution.[432]

The continuing efforts by the Citizens Committee proved to be unproductive.

The 1964–65 academic year opened with a record enrollment of more than 300 students.[433] There was little hope that the College could be saved. Several faculty members resigned during the year, and, as reported previously, Dean Fenstermacher was granted a leave of absence for the spring semester. A January 24, 1965 newspaper article, "Hershey JC Nears End of the Trail," suggests the hopelessness of the situation. The article opened with the first verse of the College's alma mater and continued:

> When Richard Seiverling, Class of 1940, Hershey Junior College, wrote the words for his school's alma mater, he had no reason to doubt that the proud red and white would wave on forever.

---

[430]*Ibid.*

[431] Derry Township Public Schools, "Board Minutes," August 10, 1964.

[432]"3 Proposals Made to Keep Junior College in Hershey," *The Patriot* [Harrisburg], August 11, 1964, p. 5.

[433]"Student Enrollment and Staff Members—September 30, Annually," personal files of V. H. Fenstermacher.

Today, Seiverling and countless other Hershey JC alumni are waiting for the death of their once proud school.[434]

In describing the 26-year old College, the writer stated:

Housed in the Hershey Community Center, the college is a unique institution. It's the kind of place where you can leave your hat and coat on a chair in the lobby and know they'll be there when you return.

It's the kind of place where a student can take a problem to Dean Varnum H. Fenstermacher and know he'll get sincere guidance.

It's the kind of place where everybody knows everybody. It's the kind of school which has taken borderline students and molded them into future doctors, lawyers and engineers.[435]

By April 10, the Junior College Committee had made plans for the handling and storage of all Junior College records upon the closing of the institution. It was determined that they would be transferred to the High School storage vault. Also the secretary of the Junior College was to be retained for at least two years to handle necessary correspondence and requests for transcripts. Likewise, physical properties were to be transferred to the High School. Trophies and flags were to be displayed in the new High School building.[436] Later it was agreed that all records of the members of the Hershey Junior College Class of 1965 would be transferred to the Harrisburg Area Community College.[437]

"Hershey Junior College Era to End" was the title of a May 20 article which appeared in *The Patriot*. It reported starkly:

It has been a time of hopeful and ambitious beginnings for higher education in Central Pennsylvania.

It is also a time for endings.

It is such a time for Hershey Junior College as it prepares for its 25th Commencement, scheduled June 1 at 8 p.m. at the Hershey Community Theatre.

Almost everything Harrisburg Area Community College had done—and is doing—comprises "firsts."

Concurrently, almost everything Hershey Junior College has been doing comprises "lasts."

It recently held its gala spring formal at the West Shore Country Club. It was its last.

The Format, student newspaper, recently made its deadline. It was its last.

Dr. A. G. Breidenstine, first dean of Hershey Junior College, will deliver the Commencement address June 1.

He will speak on "The Eternal Enterprise." But this will be the college's last such address.

---

[434]"Hershey JC Nears End of Trail," *Sunday Patriot-News* [Harrisburg], January 24, 1965, p. 40.

[435]*Ibid.*

[436]Junior College Committee Report, April 10, 1965, files of V. H. Fenstermacher. It was reported to the writer that some Junior College records were lost in the move from the Community Building to the Hershey High School.

[437]Derry Township Public Schools, "Board Minutes," September 28, 1965.

More than 100 graduates will move in academic procession into Hershey Community Theatre to receive associate in arts degrees.

They will be the last—bringing to more than 1,250 the number of students who have been graduated from Hershey Junior College since it was founded in 1938.[438]

In a letter to Mr. W. Allen Hammond, Acting Dean of the College, Richard F. Seiverling expressed his reaction to the above article. As reported earlier, Mr. Seiverling wrote the words of the Junior College alma mater. His letter follows, in part:

I read with interest and nostalgic memories the article in today's Harrisburg "Patriot" entitled "Hershey Junior College Era to End."

As a member of the first graduating class - 1940 - it seems like only yesterday that some of us, then in the M.H.S.'s Class of 1938, were fortunate enough to enjoy the opportunity of pursuing a higher education program via a two-year start at H.J.C.

With the comforting knowledge that "records of the college will go into a vault at the Hershey Junior High School," I assume the H.J.C.'s Alma Mater also will be placed with such documents, and take its proper place, among the archieves.[439]

The final ceremonies of the 1964–65 academic year symbolized the end of the existence of the Hershey Junior College.[440] On May 27, 1965, the last "All College Dinner" was held at Hotel Hershey.[441] Four days later, on June 1, 1965, the twenty-sixth and the last Baccalaureate-Commencement program was held in the Hershey Community Theatre.[442] An estimated one thousand people witnessed the graduation[443] of 98 members of the Class of 1965.[444] (See Appendix B for a list of the members of the Class of 1965.) Mr. Harry Harlacher, Class Adviser, Mr. W. Allen Hammond, Faculty Representative, and Dr. Varnum H. Fenstermacher, Dean of the College, conferred the Associate of Arts Degree to the members of the Class. Dean Fenstermacher also presented the awards. Alic Thair, president of the Sophomore Class, was awarded the final diploma to be conferred by the College.[445]

---

[438]"Hershey Junior College Era to End," *The Patriot* [Harrisburg], May 20, 1965, p. 29.

[439]Letter from Richard F. Seiverling, Director of Publications, Department of Public Instruction to W. A. Hammond, Acting Dean, Hershey Junior College, May 20, 1965, from V. H. Fenstermacher's personal file.

[440]Technically, the Hershey Junior College passed out of existence on July 1, 1965, when it legally merged with the Harrisburg Area Community College.

[441]"All College Dinner," May 27, 1965, program, personal files of V. H. Fenstermacher.

[442]The Twenty-Sixth Annual Commencement Program, Hershey Junior College, June 1, 1965.

[443]"Final Baccalaureate-Commencement of Hershey Junior College is Held," *Lebanon Daily News,* June 2, 1965, p. 2.

[444]The Twenty-Sixth Annual Commencement Program, *loc. cit.*

[445]John D. Husband, "Last Class Graduated at Hershey," *The Evening News* [Harrisburg], June 2, 1965, p. 29; and personal commencement program notes of V. H. Fenstermacher, p. 10.

The Venerable Kermit L. Lloyd, Chaplin of the College, gave the final Baccalaureate sermon.[446] Father Lloyd indicated that closing the College "was a mistake and an error for the community." He also said, "People are in a fog" and "the eternal message of wisdom has been bypassed."[447]

Significantly, the last Hershey Junior College Commencement Address was presented by Dr. Aaron G. Breidenstine, then Dean of Millersville State College. Dr. Fenstermacher introduced Dr. Breidenstine as the first Dean of the Hershey Junior College and stated that Dr. Breidenstine "nurtured the fledging institution from 1938, through accreditation in 1953, to recognized professional status by senior colleges and educational organizations."[448] On his having been asked to present the last Commencement Address, Breidenstine remarked, "This gives me a deep feeling tonight. The college is coming to the end of a brilliant career but lives on in the minds of those who have graduated."[449] Dr. Breidenstine told his audience, "I have the feeling here tonight of being both a father and an undertaker."[450] "But," he added, "this is not a time for mourning—the college will continue as an 'Essential Enterprise' in our day."[451] Breidenstine challenged the graduating class "to enhance a culture which is theirs and to share their skills among all people." Dr. Breidenstine concluded his remarks with the admonition: "You must learn that no man is an island. We must live in the image of God himself."[452]

It was reported that Dr. Fenstermacher made no mention of the closing of the College until he had extended his traditional congratulations to the graduating class. Then he referred to the somber ceremony as "the last commencement program." Dr. Fenstermacher described the College as "a good, solid little school that has served the community well."[453] The singing of the alma mater and the recessional marked the end of the 26th commencement program and the Hershey Junior College.[454]

---

[446]The Twenty-Sixth Annual Commencement Program, *loc. cit.*

[447]"Final Baccalaureate-Commencement of Hershey Junior College is Held," *loc. cit.*

[448]V. H. Fenstermacher's personal commencement program notes, p. 3.

[449]"Final Baccalaureate-Commencement of Hershey Junior College is Held," *loc. cit.*

[450]John D. Husband, "Last Class Graduated at Hershey," *loc. cit.*

[451]John D. Husband, *loc. cit.;* and "Final Baccalaureate-Commencement of Hershey Junior College is Held," *loc. cit.*

[452]"Final Baccalaureate-Commencement of Hershey Junior College is Held," *loc. cit.*

[453]John D. Husband, *loc. cit.*

[454]The Twenty-Sixth Annual Commencement Program, *loc. cit.*

CHAPTER VI

SUMMARY, CONCLUSIONS, RECOMMENDATIONS, AND RECOMMENDATIONS FOR FURTHER STUDY

Summary

The purpose of this historical-descriptive. study was to examine and record the particular history of the growth and development of the Hershey Junior College, Hershey, Pennsylvania, from its founding in 1938 to its closing in 1965. Permission to undertake the study was granted by the Derry Township Board of School Directors.

Available data were collected with primary sources utilized whenever possible. The personal files of the two deans of the Hershey Junior College as well as information obtained through personal interviews with other individuals associated with the institution were of inestimable value. Some data could not be obtained because they were lost at the time of the closing of the College. Financial records of The M. S. Hershey Foundation which pertained to the Junior College were not made available to the writer. The topical-chronological arrangement of data was employed to direct attention to major topics and problems and to make the study more interesting and readable.

This study revealed that the Hershey Junior College was founded by the industrialist and philanthropist, Milton Snavely Hershey, who amassed a fortune through the highly successful chocolate manufacturing enterprise which he established in Hershey, Pennsylvania, in 1905. Mr. Hershey provided numerous services and facilities for the residents of Derry Township and the employees of the Chocolate Corporation and related enterprises. Hershey's own education did not extend beyond the fourth grade and he had no heirs. It is theorized that these facts prompted him to found The Hershey Industrial School, now the Milton Hershey School, for orphan boys in 1909. Mr. Hershey also financially supported public education in Derry Township, kindergarten through high school.

The depression of the early 1930's caused idleness among the youth of Hershey and Derry Township. In his quest for a means by which recent high school graduates might become profitably occupied, Hershey was advised of the purpose and function of a junior college. Mr. Hershey recognized the two-fold purpose a junior college could serve in Hershey. Through foresight and for benevolent as well as practical reasons, Hershey, in 1935, created and endowed with 5,000 shares of Hershey Chocolate Corporation common stock, in perpetuity, The M. S. Hershey Foundation for educational purposes. It was under the provisions of this trust that, after several years of preliminary planning, the Hershey Junior College was founded.

This study disclosed that the Hershey Junior College was unique in the history of higher education in so far as it was founded as a publically controlled, privately financed institution which offered two years of post high school education without tuition charge. Free education was made available to residents of Derry Township and, later, to employees and dependents of employees who were employed by the Hershey Chocolate Corporation and any other bona fide business in Derry Township.

Throughout its existence the Junior College utilized the facilities of the Hershey Community Center Building, one of the many work projects which were financed by M. S. Hershey during the depression. The Center was intended, primarily, for the use and enjoyment of the residents of Hershey. Located in the Community Building was the Hershey Public Library which also served as the Hershey Junior College Library.

The lounge, theatre, and other facilities of the Community Center were also used by both the Junior College and the general public. In addition, the Junior College used some of the facilities of the Hershey High School and the High School shared certain facilities of the Community Building with the Junior College.

The Board of Directors of the Derry Township School District administered the Junior College although no public funds were used to finance it. The institution was personally financed by M. S. Hershey and through the endowment which was created by the establishment of The M. S. Hershey Foundation *Agreement of Trust*. The trust was managed by a Board of Managers which was comprised of employees of the Hershey Chocolate Corporation or associated enterprises. The chief administrative officer of the Junior College was the Dean who reported to the Board of School Directors through the Superintendent of Schools until 1962 when the Dean reported directly to the School Board.

The Junior College faculty was composed of full-time, part-time, and adjunct members. Most of the latter two groups also worked in the public secondary school system or the Hershey Community Center and they were included on those payrolls.

Faculty members were capable and genuinely interested in the welfare of their students, facts which contributed to the effectiveness of the program. The two Deans of the Junior College made significant contributions in accordance with the unique abilities of each. Dr. A. G. Breidenstine served from 1938 through 1947; Dr. V. H. Fenstermacher served from 1947 through the closing of the institution in 1965. Both were genuinely dedicated to and interested in the welfare of the College, in general, and its students, in particular. They worked tirelessly to improve all phases of the College program. The Deans and the faculty had considerable autonomy for planning and implementing the curriculum within the basic purposes of the institution and the financial and physical resources available to the Junior College.

Terminal and transfer programs were offered by the College throughout its history. The original purposes of the institution, as envisaged by Mr. Hershey, placed emphasis on terminal education. In general, terminal rather than transfer programs were stressed, and the demand for them was greatest during Dr. Breidenstine's tenure. Changing socio-economic conditions during Dr. Fenstermacher's administration resulted in a decreasing demand for terminal programs with an accompanying greater emphasis on transfer programs.

Admission requirements with respect to residence eligibility and maximum enrollment quotas were established by the Board of Managers of The M. S. Hershey Foundation. Academic and personal qualifications of applicants were judged by a committee of the School Board established for this purpose. Yearly enrollment fluctuated during the 27-year history of the College although the grand total enrollment increased from 131 in 1938-1939 to 317 in 1964–1965. The greatest increase in growth took place during the last five years of the College.

The Hershey community and Junior College students were well served by the College throughout its history. Consistent with M. S. Hershey's intent, one or two years of post-secondary education was made available to many students who might otherwise not have had the opportunity to attend any college. This was made possible because no tuition was charged and, except for restrictions of residence, the College maintained a policy of what today would approximate an "open-door" or nonselective admission policy. A significant number of students was able to obtain employment of the type for which their Junior College programs prepared them. Also, a high proportion of those students who were enrolled in transfer programs did, in fact, transfer to senior institutions and an exceptionally high percentage of them satisfactorily completed their bachelor's degree programs. Many continued their studies at the graduate and professional level. Employers expressed general satisfaction with Junior College graduates. Many of the alumni have indicated they both appreciated and profited by the education they received.

The College received considerable recognition of which it was justly proud. The quality of instruction was cited as one of the College's major strengths by the Commission on Institutions of Higher Education of the Middle States Association of Colleges and Secondary Schools which initially accredited the College in 1943 and reaccredited it for the last time in 1963.

This study indicated that there were several reasons for the closing of the Hershey Junior College. The primary reason, according to the Board of Managers of The M. S. Hershey Foundation, was that the income which was produced from the trust (which was established to finance the College) was no longer sufficient to meet the increasing costs of operation. Coincident with the realization that the financial problem had become a serious one, the School Reorganization Act of 1961 and the Community College Act of 1963 were enacted by the Commonwealth of Pennsylvania. The Community College Act provided for the establishment and operation of public community colleges. The Harrisburg Area Community College was the first to be approved under the Act. After a series of discussions between representatives of the Derry Township School Board and the Foundation Board of Managers with representatives of the Harrisburg Area Community College Committee, it was decided to merge the Junior College with the new Community College. The cost to continue the Hershey Junior College was more than could be justified in light of newly available educational facilities and programs. The Hershey Junior College functioned as a branch of the Harrisburg Area Community College during the 1964–1965 academic year and it legally ceased to exist as an institution of higher education as of July 1, 1965.

Conclusions

The conclusions of this study were derived from a careful review and analysis of the data presented in previous chapters. They relate to the founding, the growth and development, and the closing of the Hershey Junior College.

1. The story of the Hershey enterprise epitomizes the typical American tale of success against odds. It is also illustrative of the pervasive philanthropy of one person heading a financially highly successful basic industry in a one-industry town—a "company town"—but one run by a benevolent and paternalistic entrepreneur. Milton Snavely Hershey is best known for the chocolate "Hershey Bar," which he so successfully produced and marketed, and for the fortune which he amassed and gave to the orphan boys of the United States. But, Mr. Hershey was not content having established the Milton Hershey School for boys. He aided the elementary and secondary schools of Hershey and Derry Township to enable them to offer high quality education.

Later, the depression created the conditions which prompted M. S. Hershey to see the need for and value in post-secondary vocational education. The Hershey Junior College, which he founded, served a far more valuable purpose than getting young people off the streets. It offered strong, comprehensive programs of up to two years of post-secondary, terminal and college transfer work. The institution made it possible for many young people to obtain, at practically no cost, a high quality education which provided an opportunity for them to live a more productive and satisfying life.

2. The function of the Hershey Junior College, like most institutions, underwent some changes during the 27 years of its existence. These internal modifications, primarily brought about by changing external socio-economic conditions, were made in harmony with the underlying purpose of the institution. Essentially, the changes reflected students' increased need for and interest in transfer programs.

The residence eligibility requirements also underwent some revision. This was prompted by the need to expand enrollment to enable the Junior College to offer a broader program and by changing residence patterns and increasing mobility of Hershey employees. Consequently, it was appropriate to broaden the residence eligibility rules.

3. The major problems with which the students, faculty, and administration had to contend were concerned with facilities, sharing of personnel, and the administrative organization of the College, all of which related to finances. The overlapping use of the Community Building, Women's Club, and the Hershey High School created space and scheduling problems. The use of the Library as both a public library and a college library was probably the most serious single deficiency of the College. Similarly, the need to share personnel of the secondary school and the Community Building caused administrative problems that, at times, had detrimental effects on the academic and nonacademic programs of the Junior College.

The overall administration of the College was complicated by a highly complex organizational system whereby decisions with respect to financing the College were made by the Board of Managers of The M. S. Hershey Foundation. On the other hand, the College was administered by the Board of Directors of the Derry Township School Board but whose primary function was that of governance of the public elementary and secondary schools. The influence of the School Board was probably not as great as a separate Junior College Board of Directors would have been. As a consequence of this organizational arrangement, the administrative function of the Dean was sometimes made difficult. He was often required to meet with several committees of either or both boards and to obtain agreement from the Board of Managers and the School Board. This organizational plan also caused the Dean to be insulated from the Board of Managers throughout the history of the College. Furthermore, until 1962, the Dean reported to the School Board through the Superintendent which resulted in further insulation and lack of communication. The close association of the Junior College student body with the students of the high schools of the Township, as well as the interrelatedness of the faculties, administrations, and governing boards, both physically and philosophically, did not permit the Junior College to grow and develop as it might otherwise have done. The College, through its administrative organization and its use of the Community Center Building, was probably too closely associated with the Hershey Chocolate Corporation, the Hershey Estates, and the Milton Hershey School. The lack of adequate facilities and the complicated administrative organization were major obstacles to the smooth operation of the Junior College.

4. Both Deans of the Junior College had a definite influence on the institution. Dr. A. G. Breidenstine was successful in establishing the College in 1938. He registered a sufficient number of students to justify opening the institution, hired an able, dedicated faculty, and organized the curricula of the three divisions of the College. Under Breidenstine's dynamic leadership, the College was accredited by the State Council on Education, the Middle States Association of Colleges and Secondary Schools, and it was recognized

by other state and national agencies and organizations. Dean Breidenstine worked untiringly to improve the Junior College generally.

As an administrator, Dr. Breidenstine probably enjoyed Milton S. Hershey's interest in and support of the Junior College until Hershey's death in 1945. Breidenstine resigned as Dean two years later. With the loss of Hershey's direct influence, Dr. Fenstermacher was required to work with and rely upon a larger number of individuals. Consequently, a greater range of alternatives with respect to the governance of the College was presented. Ultimately, the decision was made to close the institution.

Breidenstine and Fenstermacher knew their students well and spent much time in counseling enrolled students and in doing follow-up studies and keeping in contact with graduates. Both deans were dedicated to the students and the College. They were both greatly disappointed in learning that the decision had been made to close the institution.

5. The Hershey Junior College has an enviable record of accomplishment. The overall strength and effectiveness of its faculty and program were attested to through reports of Middle States Association of Colleges and Secondary Schools evaluating committees, The Pennsylvania State College survey team, and those of administrators of Elizabethtown College, Lebanon Valley College, The Pennsylvania State College, and Shippensburg State College.

The influence of the faculty on the academic program and, especially on the students, was significant. Teaching was the primary interest and strength of the faculty and they were cognizant of the fact that a substantial proportion of the student body was admitted on "marginal" credentials. Patience and extra time were required to help motivate these students. The deans and full-time faculty members served faithfully as advisers to students. Many of the full-time faculty also served as advisers of extracurricular activities which provided the opportunity for professors and students to get to know each other well. This close, friendly relationship between faculty and students was a major factor in building a spirit of unanimity among the student body and faculty. In turn, both faculty and students developed an unusual sense of loyalty to the Hershey Junior College.

Through the efforts of a highly dedicated faculty, an unusually high proportion of Junior College students (many with moderate ability) were able to complete successfully their programs of study. Further, a significant proportion of graduates continued their education in senior, graduate, and professional institutions and are now making valuable contributions to society. Graduates and nongraduates of the institution appreciated the education they received.

In view of this record of accomplishment the Hershey Junior College did serve and still can serve as a prototype for other institutions, particularly new ones. It can serve as a model of the integration of teaching and guidance, and of an institution which provided to the residents of the community the opportunity of receiving two years of post-secondary education at little or no cost.

6. Having given due consideration to the situation that existed during the last few years of the College and to the external changes that were taking place in higher education, the writer has concluded that it was a logical decision to merge the Junior College with the Harrisburg Area Community College and, subsequently, have the College cease to exist. To do otherwise would have required major administrative and financial policy changes.

The Hershey Junior College may have suffered from public inertia which resulted in its demise. The Junior College, in effect, was founded by one man—Milton S. Hershey. His paternalistic philanthropy may have had the effect of creating in its beneficiaries an attitude of lethargy and disinterest—a "take it for granted" attitude—of which they were not fully aware.

The Library and other physical facilities as well as the faculty and administration were being strained the last few years the College was in operation. Provincialism among the students and, probably, the faculty, was setting in. This provincialism was reinforced by a restricted curriculum and a geographically if not culturally delimited student body. The Junior College had probably reached its maximum potential. Only a new, modern, enlarged plant and campus would have permitted the enrollment and, in turn, the total program to grow and develop according to contemporary conceptualizations and standards. However, the income from The M. S. Hershey Foundation trust was apparently insufficient to support the College fully during the last few years, much less finance a new plant and an expanded program for a larger student body from which no tuition was received. (It was maintained that the School District could not legally charge tuition.)

On August 23, 1963, a far-reaching decision was made which may well have resulted in a further decline of interest in the Junior College as well as a reduction in support by those responsible for its governance and financing. On that date the President Judge of the Orphans' Court of Dauphin County signed a decree which permitted the transfer of $50 million from the Milton Hershey School trust to The M. S. Hershey Foundation for the creation of the College of Medicine and The Milton S. Hershey Medical Center of The Pennsylvania State University. With the transfer of the money the Hershey Junior College in effect, lost its vitality.

Coincident with the announcement of the grant for the establishment of the Medical Center was the enactment of The Community College Act of 1963 which provided for the establishment of public community colleges in Pennsylvania. The Harrisburg Area Community College, the first one to be approved and opened, offered an expanded academic program in adequate facilities. In addition, a broad financial base was established and, although student tuition was charged, it was relatively low. The modern highway system between Hershey and the Community College made access easy. Furthermore, Derry Township students had the advantage of profiting from association with students from other districts who also attended the Community College.

The closing of the College was an immediate and a real loss to Derry Township residents and employees. Moreover, the announcement of the decision to close the Junior College was a profound shock to the residents of Derry Township. (History shows that social institutions rarely die although their purposes and functions may change.) On the other hand, its merger with the Harrisburg Area Community College will probably prove to be an advantage to the Community College and to the larger community through an expanded curriculum, larger enrollment, improved facilities and student services, and other advantages.

Recommendations

The conclusions of this study suggest the following recommendations may be worthy of consideration by individuals who have responsibilities in institutions of higher education.

1. Every institution should be legally chartered and provisions relating to the establishment, operation, and continuance of the institution should be clearly enunciated.

2. Institutions should recognize that their immediate function may be required to undergo modification, particularly as changes occur in socioeconomic conditions and in the constituencies of governing bodies, administrations, faculties, and student bodies. However, the original basic purposes of the institution should be observed.

3. The administrative organization of educational institutions should not be allowed to become so complex that decision-making becomes seriously impeded, if not impossible. Provisions should be made for easy and effective communication among all segments of the institution. The chief executive officer should report directly to the governing board.

4. Institutions should make adequate plans to effect a smooth change of administration.

5. Governing boards of colleges and universities should be composed of individuals who are genuinely interested in higher education, in general, and the purposes of the institution they serve, in particular.

6. Junior and community colleges should not be directly associated with secondary schools with respect to governance, physical location, or the use of physical plant and personnel.

7. Educational institutions should give serious consideration to recommendations offered by professional agencies, such as regional associations of colleges and secondary schools and state education departments.

8. To maintain public interest and to remain a viable institution, the general public in which it is located and which it serves must participate and become involved in the various activities of the institution. This is particularly true of a public community college.

9. Every institution should designate someone to serve as an historian. Also, provisions for the storage of institutional records and memorabilia should be clearly established.

10. All institutional reports and other communications should be clearly dated, titled, and the writer should be identified. Copies should be filed.

Recommendations for Further Study

This study revealed a need for further study. The following suggestions are made.

1. A follow-up study of the academic and nonacademic accomplishments of Hershey Junior College alumni should be undertaken. The study could show the correlation between academic accomplishment in the Junior College with further academic as well as career and other accomplishments in adult life.

2. A comparative study of the college-going pattern of Hershey High School and Milton Hershey School graduates, before and after the closing of the Hershey Junior College, should be undertaken.

3. A controlled study should be undertaken to determine whether differences exist in attitude toward education and in academic accomplishment on the part of students who receive a free (or very low cost) education as compared to those who pay standard tuition and other costs.

4. A study should be conducted among institutions of higher education which have ceased to exist to determine whether there is a common factor or set of factors which contributes to the decision to close.

SELECTED BIBLIOGRAPHY

A. Manuscript Sources

"Administrative Report," Hershey Junior College, 1950-1962.

"Board Minutes," Derry Township Public Schools, 1936-1966.

Breidenstine, A. G. "A Partial Analysis of the Hershey Junior College Dean's Position."

——. "An Idea Becomes A Reality." Commencement Address, Hershey Junior College, May 24, 1954.

——. "Annual Report of the Hershey Junior College to Superintendent Raymond H. Koch." July, 1945.

——. "In The Life of a College." Speech, January 6, 1939.

——. "Offerings of Hershey Junior College." Speech at Opening Program, September 14, 1938.

——. "Our First Year Achievement Results, Hershey Junior College."

——. Personal Data Sheet. March 15, 1970.

——. "Report On Hershey Junior College." Fall, 1944.

"Brief Submitted in Support of Application to State Council." October 12, 1939.

"Class of 1965" and "Class of 1966." Hershey High School Guidance Office.

"Data Presented for Consideration of the Commission on Institutions of Higher Education, Middle States Association of Colleges and Secondary Schools." January, 1952.

"Data Presented for Consideration of the Commission on Institutions of Higher Education for Re-evaluation After 3-year Period." Prepared for Middle States Association of Colleges and Secondary Schools, November 22, 1946.

"Data Submitted for Consideration of the Commission on Institutions of Higher Education of the Middle States Association of Colleges and Secondary Schools." March 25, 1943.

"Day Student Body of the Hershey Junior College: Report to Dr. J. I. Baugher." November, 1939.

Farrell, Harry C. Jr. "Temple Junior College: Its Founding, Growth, and Development, 1926-64." Unpublished Doctoral thesis, Colorado State College, 1964.

Fenstermacher, Varnum Hayes, Personal Summary.

Hershey Junior College Baccalaureate-Commencement Program. May 29, 1961.

"Hershey Junior College Faculty Roster." 1938-1965.

Hershey Junior College. "Information Bulletin." Vol. XIV, No. 8, February 26, 1952– Vol. XXVII, No. 6, March 11, 1965.

Hershey Junior College. Twenty-Fourth Annual Commencement Program. May 28, 1963.

Hershey Junior College. Twenty-Sixth Annual Commencement Program. June 1, 1965.

"Historic Old Derry: Historical Sketch of Derry Presbyterian Church, Hershey, Pennsylvania." Read by the pastor, Reverend R. H. Taylor at the 205th Anniversary, June 20, 1929.

Klotz, Richard R. "A Historical Study of the Development and Changing Function of Bucknell University, 1842-1963." Unpublished term paper. The Pennsylvania State University, July, 1963.

Laughlin, Maud P. "Hershey, A Model Community." Hershey Junior College, 1945.

Letters. Items of correspondence that were used in the foregoing study included the following letters, listed in the order in which they were cited.

L. Eugene Jacques to the writer, May 17, 1966.

Rodney McLaughlin to the writer, July 21, 1969.

Cooperative Test Service of the American Council on Education to A. G. Breidenstine, September 20, 1939.
Richard F. Seiverling to W. Allen Hammond, May 20, 1965.
C. E. Ackley to J. I. Baugher, May 17, 1940.
C. E. Ackley to J. I. Baugher, June 25, 1940.
A. G. Breidenstine to Ralph D. Owen, April 2, 1947.
A. G. Breidenstine to the writer, June 9, 1970.
Jack Gernhart to the writer, December 11, 1969.
Henry Klonower to A. G. Breidenstine, September 21, 1942.
Frank H. Bowles to A. G. Breidenstine, October 11, 1940.
Charles Tillinghast to A. G. Breidenstine, April 30, 1943.
J. Hollis Miller to A. G. Breidenstine, November 19, 1944.
Raymond H. Koch to V. H. Fenstermacher, October 9, 1952.
J. E. Bobb to Paul Curry, July 14, 1961.
L. Eugene Jacques to James E. Bobb, September 7, 1961.
J. E. Bobb to L. Eugene Jacques, September 20, 1961.
V. H. Fenstermacher to John Zerbe, September 22, 1964.
L. Eugene Jacques to James E. Bobb, January 18, 1962.
J. E. Bobb and S. F. Hinkle to Carl Foreman, July 21, 1954.
L. Eugene Jacques to James E. Bobb, September 7, 1961.
James E. Bobb to L. Eugene Jacques, September 20, 1961.
Paul D. Shafer to V. H. Fenstermacher, February 28, 1963.
E. K. Smiley to V. H. Fenstermacher, May 1, 1952.
V. H. Fenstermacher to E. K. Smiley, November 12, 1952.
E. Morse Heisey to V. H. Fenstermacher, January 19, 1954.
Mrs. V. H. Fenstermacher to the writer, July 9, 1970.
J. E. Bobb to L. Eugene Jacques, June 30, 1955.
Norman Vanderwall to V. H. Fenstermacher, May 29, 1962.
Jefferson Barnhart to Norman Vanderwall, June 18, 1962.
V. H. Fenstermacher to Carl E. Seifert, July 7, 1955.
Carl E. Seifert to V. H. Fenstermacher, September 19, 1955.
Raymond H. Koch to V. H. Fenstermacher, December 14, 1950.
Albert E. Meder, Jr. to V. H. Fenstermacher, June 28, 1963.
Norman Vanderwall to the writer, August 20, 1970.
Fred A. Snyder to the writer, September 22, 1967.
Paul Smay to V. H. Fenstermacher, August 14, 1962.
A. R. Whiteman to Derry Township Board of School Directors, September 19, 1962.
Elwood A. Shoemaker to the writer, July 8, 1970.
A. G. Breidenstine to V. H. Fenstermacher, April 17, 1964.
Higher Education Association to The M. S. Hershey Foundation, April 22, 1964.
"Milton Hershey School." 1968. (Mimeographed.)
Murrie, Richard Wallace. "The Story Behind A Hershey Bar." Unpublished thesis, Princeton University, Princeton, New Jersey, 1939.
Opening Program, Hershey Junior College, September 14, 1938.
Personal files of A. G. Breidenstine. The files contained newsclippings, notes, programs, notices, posters, reports, enrollment records, speeches, correspondence, and memorabilia pertaining to the Hershey Junior College.
Personal files of V. H. Fenstermacher. The files contained newsclippings, notes, programs, notices, posters, reports, enrollment records, speeches, correspondence, and memorabilia pertaining to the Hershey Junior College.
Program from The First Combined Commencement. Hershey Community Theatre, May 29, 1940.
Program of The First Annual Institute on State and Local Government. Hershey, Pennsylvania, 1939–40.

216

"Report of Evaluation Committee." Commission on Institutions of Higher Education, Middle States Association of Colleges and Secondary Schools, February 24–27, 1963.

"Report of Self Evaluation." Submitted to the Commission on Institutions of Higher Education, Middle States Association of Colleges and Secondary Schools, January 24, 1963.

"Report of the 1952 Visiting Committee." Commission on Institutions of Higher Education of the Middle States Association of Colleges and Secondary Schools, April 15, 1952.

Rudisill, Richard H. "Hershey Junior College." Unpublished term paper, University of Pennsylvania, Philadelphia, Pennsylvania, January, 1961.

Second Annual Senior Day Program. Hershey Junior College, February 12, 1940.

Senior Day Program. Hershey Junior College, February 15, 1939.

"Statement of Understanding, Hershey Community Center and Hershey Junior College (Agreed upon by both the Center and College–November, 1962)."

"Student Body of the Hershey Junior College: Report to Dr. J. I. Baugher." November, 1938.

"Student Committee for the Preservation of Hershey Junior College." (Mimeographed.)

"Student Enrollment and Staff Members–September 30, Annually." 1938–1965.

"Student Evaluation of Teaching Techniques."

"Student Survey of Teaching Techniques."

"Summary Conclusions In High School and Junior College Achievement." Classes of 1940, 1941, and 1942.

Tillinghast, Charles C. "Report on Inspection of Hershey Junior College." Middle States Association of Colleges and Secondary Schools, April 27, 1943.

Wallace, Paul A. W. "Milton Hershey's Approach to Education." Commencement Speech, Hershey Junior College, May 28, 1955.

———. *Milton S. Hershey*. Hershey: Milton Hershey School, 1956. (Mimeographed.)

Wisor, Harold C. "A History of Teacher Education at Lock Haven State College, Lock Haven, Pennsylvania, 1870–1969." Unpublished Doctoral dissertation, The Pennsylvania State University, 1966.

B. Printed Sources

Academy for Educational Development, Inc. *Elements Of A Master Plan For Higher Education in Pennsylvania.* A Report to the State Board of Education of the Commonwealth of Pennsylvania, December 31, 1965.

Agreement of Trust. The M. S. Hershey Foundation, Hershey, Pennsylvania, December 5, 1935.

Annual Report, 1968, 1969. Hershey Foods Corporation, Hershey, Pennsylvania.

Aurand, O. H., et al. *A Study of the Schools of Derry Township, Dauphin County, Pennsylvania, 1951–1952.*

Bogert, George Gleason. *Handbook of the Law Of Trusts.* St. Paul, Minnesota: West Publishing Company, 1952.

"Chocolate Town U.S.A., Progress Through Vision." Official Statement, $2,150,000 Derry Township School Building Authority, School Revenue Bond–Series of 1970.

College of Medicine, The Milton S. Hershey Medical Center. College of Medicine, The Pennsylvania State University, Vol. III, No. 1, August, 1968.

Commonwealth of Pennsylvania. Department of Education, Office of Higher Education, Bureau of Community Colleges, *Suggested Procedures for the Establishment of a Community College in Pennsylvania.* Appendix C, Revised January, 1970.

Commonwealth of Pennsylvania. Department of Public Instruction, *Biennial Report of the Superintendent of Public Instruction for the Two-Year Period Ending May 31, 1940.*

Commonwealth of Pennsylvania. Department of Public Instruction, *Guidelines for the Establishment of Public Community Colleges in Pennsylvania*. April, 1965.

Commonwealth of Pennsylvania. Department of Public Instruction, Office of Information and Publications, "The School District Re-organization Law."

Commonwealth of Pennsylvania. State Board of Education, *A Master Plan for Higher Education in Pennsylvania*. January, 1967.

"Derry Township School News," Vol. 4, No. 3, February 6, 1953.

Fields, Ralph R. and Associates. "Community Colleges in Pennsylvania." A Report to the State Board of Education, June 30, 1965.

Handbook of Data and Definitions in Higher Education. Committee on Data and Definitions in Higher Education, American Association of Collegiate Registrars and Admissions Officers, 1962.

HEJUCO, 1954 to 1965. This was the annual Hershey Junior College yearbook. The first yearbook, "Pleasant Memories," was mimeographed.

Hershey Junior College Bulletin, 1938-1939 to 1964-1966.

Hershey Junior College Evening School Bulletin, 1949-50.

Hershey's Annual Report, December 31, 1966.

"Hershey, Pennsylvania." 50th Anniversary of Chocolate Town, 1903-1953.

"Hershey Schools In Action." Derry Township School District, Hershey, Pennsylvania, Vol. 8, No. 1, October 22, 1964.

"Interim Report." Hershey Foods Corporation, September 30, 1969.

Items of Business, Journals of Meetings and Annual Report of the State Council of Education, Secretary, July 1, 1937 to June 30, 1938.

Joint Committee on Junior and Senior Colleges. *Guidelines for Improving Articulation Between Junior and Senior Colleges*. Washington, D.C.: American Council on Education, July, 1966.

Junior College Directory, 1939; 1965. Washington, D.C.: American Association of Junior Colleges.

Leopard, The. Student Handbook, Hershey Junior College, 1958, 1961.

"Last Will and Testament of Milton S. Hershey." September 29, 1944.

Milton Hershey School. "Deed of Trust." November 15, 1909.

Olena, Benjamin F., and John O. Hershey. "Milton Hershey School Graduates in Hershey Junior College, 1938-1952."

"Selected Hershey Chronology, 1724-1967.". Milton Hershey School, 1967.

The Pennsylvania State University Bulletin, The Capitol Campus, 1968-1969.

C. Books

Barzun, Jacques, and Henry F. Graff. *The Modern Researcher*. New York: Harcourt, Brace, & World, Inc., 1957.

Bishop, Morris. *A History of Cornell*. Ithaca, New York: Cornell University Press, 1962.

Blocker, Clyde E., Robert H. Plummer, and Richard C. Richardson. *The Two-year College: A Social Synthesis*. Englewood Cliffs, New Jersey: Prentice-Hall, Inc., 1965.

Bogue, Jessie P. *The Development of Junior Colleges*. Washington: American Association of Junior Colleges, 1957.

Brickman, William H. *Guide to Research in Educational History*. New York: New York University Bookstore, 1949.

Brubacher, John S., and Willis Rudy. *Higher Education in Transition*. New York: Harper & Row, Publishers, Inc., 1968.

Campbell, Doak S. *A Critical Study of the Stated Purposes of the Junior College*. Contribution to Education, #70, George Peabody College for Teachers, Nashville, Tennessee, 1930.

Campbell, William Giles. *Form and Style in Thesis Writing*. Boston: Houghton Mifflin Company, 1954.

Clark, Burton R. *The Open Door College: A Case Study*. New York: McGraw-Hill Book Company, Inc., 1960.

Corson, John J. *Governance of Colleges and Universities*. New York: McGraw-Hill Book Company, Inc., 1960.

Dunaway, Wayland F. *A History of Pennsylvania*. New York: Prentice Hall, Inc., 1948.

Fields, Ralph R. *The Community College Movement*. New York: McGraw-Hill Book Company, Inc., 1962.

Gleazer, Edmund J. Jr. (ed.). *American Junior Colleges*. 6th ed. American Council on Education. Menasha, Wisconsin: George Banta Company, Inc., April, 1966.

Good, Carter V. *Introduction to Educational Research*. New York: Appleton-Century Crofts, Inc., 1963.

Gottschalk, Louis. *Understanding History*. New York: Alfred A. Knopf, 1967.

Gray, Wood. *Historian's Handbook*. Boston: Houghton Mifflin Company, 1964.

Griffiths, Daniel. *Administrative Theory*. New York: Appleton-Century Crofts, Inc., 1959.

Hammond, Allen W. *A Man and His Boys*. Manheim, Pennsylvania: Stiegel Printing Company, 1969.

Harris, Chester W. (ed.). *Encyclopedia of Educational Research*. New York: The Macmillan Company, 1955.

Henry, Nelson B. (ed.). *The Public Junior College*. The Fifty-fifth Yearbook of the National Society for the Study of Education, Part I. Chicago, Illinois: University of Chicago Press, 1956.

Hubley, John E. *Fountainhead of Good Teachers: A History of the First Ninety Years of Shippensburg State College*. Shippensburg, Pennsylvania: News-Chronicle Publishing Company, 1964.

Jones, Barbara. *Bennington College: The Development of an Educational Idea*. New York: Harper & Brothers Publishers, 1946.

Knight, Edgar W. "History of Education." *Encyclopedia of Educational Research*. Walter S. Monroe (ed.). New York: Macmillan Company, 1941.

Lewis, Norman (ed.). *The New Roget's Thesaurus*. New York: G. P. Putnam's Sons, 1964.

Manual of Style, A. 12th Edition, revised. Chicago: The University of Chicago Press, 1969.

McConnell, T. R. "Needed Research in College and University Organization and Administration." *The Study of Academic Administration*. Terry F. Lunsford (ed.). Boulder, Colorado: Western Interstate Commission on Higher Education, 1963.

Medsker, Leland L. *The Junior College: Progress and Prospect*. New York: McGraw-Hill Book Company, 1960.

Millett, John D. *The Academic Community: An Essay on Organization*. New York: McGraw-Hill Book Company, Inc., 1962.

Monroe, Walter S. (ed.). *A Cyclopedia of Education*. New York: The Macmillan Company, 1913.

———. *Encyclopedia of Educational Research*. New York: The Macmillan Company, 1940.

Plum, Dorothy A., and George B. Dowell. *The Magnificant Enterprise: A Chronicle of Vassar College*. Princeton, New Jersey: Princeton University Press, 1961.

Reynolds, James W. "Needed Changes in Purposes and Programs of Community Colleges." *Universal Higher Education*. Earl J. McGrath (ed.). New York: McGraw-Hill Book Company, 1966.

Rothe, Anna (ed.). *Current Biography: Who's News and Why*. New York: The H. W. Wilson Company, 1945.

Sack, Saul. *History of Higher Education in Pennsylvania*. Vol. II. Harrisburg: Commonwealth of Pennsylvania, The Pennsylvania Historical and Museum Commission, 1963.

Sanford, Nevitt. *The American College*. New York: John Wiley & Sons, Inc., 1962.

Shippen, Katherine B., and Paul A. W. Wallace. *Milton S. Hershey*. New York: Random House, 1959.

Snavely, J. R. *A Chat With Mr. Hershey*. Hershey: J. R. Snavely, 1932.

_____. *An Intimate Story of Milton S. Hershey*. Hershey: J. R. Snavely, 1957.

_____. *Meet Mr. Hershey*. Hershey: J. R. Snavely, 1940.

_____. *Milton S. Hershey—Builder*. Hershey: J. R. Snavely, 1935.

_____. *M. S. Hershey Lives On*. Hershey: J. R. Snavely, 1947.

_____. *The Hershey Story*. Hershey: J. R. Snavely, 1950.

_____. *The Story of Hershey: The Chocolate Town*. Hershey: J. R. Snavely, 1953.

Stein, Jess (ed.). *The Random House Dictionary of the English Language*. New York: Random House, 1967.

Thornton, James W. *The Community Junior College*. New York: John Wiley & Sons, 1966.

Turabian, Kate L. *A Manual For Writers of Term Papers and Dissertations*. Chicago: The University of Chicago Press, 1956.

Walsh, Louise G., and Matthew J. Walsh. *History and Organization of Education in Pennsylvania*. Indiana, Pennsylvania: R. S. Grosse Print Shop, 1930.

Wickersham, James P. *A History of Education in Pennsylvania*. Lancaster, Pennsylvania: Inquirer Publishing Company, 1886.

D. Newspapers, Periodicals, & Articles From Periodicals

Blocker, Clyde E. "Pennsylvania's New Progeny: The Community College," *Pennsylvania School Journal*, Vol. 113, No. 8, April, 1965.

"Co-ed At 83," *The Pittsburgh Press*, Roto Magazine, November 27, 1955.

Evening News [Harrisburg], September 21, 1962; August 23, 1963; April 8, 1964 to June 2, 1965.

Format, The, Vol. I, No. 1, March, 1947 to Vol. XIX, No. 5, May, 1965. It was the Hershey Junior College student newspaper.

Gallico, Paul. "$80,000,000 Worth of Orphans," *The American Weekly*, December 23, 1945.

"Hershey Enjoys Unsurpassed Education Opportunities," *Pennsylvania Labor Record*, August, 1951.

"Hershey Junior College, The," *School and Society*, 47:822-3, June 25, 1938.

"Hershey's Sweet Tooth Starts Aching," *Business Week*, February 7, 1970.

"Hershey's Troubles: Big Chocolate Maker, Beset by Profit Slide, Gets More Aggressive," *The Wall Street Journal*, February 18, 1970.

"Honor Roll of American Public Schools," *Look*, October 1, 1945.

Hotel Hershey High-Lights, Vol. V, No. 11, September 18, 1937 to Vol. XVII, No. 33, February 4, 1950. It was a weekly magazine published by Hotel Hershey.

Johnson, Leighton H. "Education Needs Historical Studies," *Phi Delta Kappan*, 36: 157, 159, January, 1955.

Lebanon Daily News, April 8, 1964; June 2, 1965; April 29, 1967; July 28, 1967.

Literary Artisan, The, January, 1939 to May, 1958. It was a literary magazine written and designed by students enrolled in Writing Arts. Students, faculty members, and others contributed to the publication.

Logan, Harlan. "The Hope of American Education," *Look*, October 1, 1946.

"M. S. Hershey Dead; Chocolate King, 88," *New York Times*, October 14, 1945.

McKenna, Ken. "Milton Hershey's Dream Shattered By Violence in Labor Dispute in '37," *New York Herald Tribune*, March 7, 1961.

"Model Town, The," *The School Industrialist*, Vol. XIII, No. 2, November, 1945.

"Mr. Hershey Gives Away His Fortune," *Fortune*, Vol. IX, No. 1, January, 1943.

Patrick, Robert B. "The Community College for Pennsylvania," *Pennsylvania School Journal*, 104: 310-11+, April, 1956.
Patriot, The [Harrisburg], April 1, 1964 to May 20, 1965.
Perham, John C. "Chocolate Kingdom," *Barron's*, April 30, 1965.
"Plan to Hold Graduation," *Hershey News*, Vol. II, No. 8, February 25, 1954.
"Real Dutch Treat For Ike," *Hershey News*, Vol. I, No. 1, October 1, 1953.
Sack, Saul. "The First Junior College," *Junior College Journal*, 30: 13, 15, September, 1959.
"Scholastic Society For Junior College," *Hershey News*, Vol. VI, No. 4, January 23, 1958.
School Executive, The, Vol. 64, No. 9, May, 1945.
Sears, Jesse B. "Philanthropy in the History of American Higher Education," Bulletin, No. 26, Washington, D.C.: U.S. Bureau of Education, 1922.
Stanley, James W. "The Oldest Junior College?" *Junior College Journal*, 36: 37-8, November, 1965.
Sunday Patriot News [Harrisburg], August 25, 1963; April 5, 1964 to June 24, 1965.
"The Town That Chocolate Built," *The Review*, Vol. 3, No. 9, Annville, Pennsylvania: Lebanon Valley College, September, 1969.
"Two Capitals and a Kingdom," *The Saturday Evening Post,* May 16, 1964.
Young, James C. "Hershey, Unique Philanthropist," *New York Times,* November 18, 1923.

E. Other Sources

Burnett, Collins W. *The Community Junior College: An Annotated Bibliography.* College of Education: The Ohio State University, 1968.
Interviews. Sources of information obtained through personal interviews by the writer are listed in the order in which they were cited.
Rodney McLaughlin, February 23, 1970.
Joseph S. Gumpher, July 28, 1967.
A. G. Breidenstine, July 19, 1967.
A. G. Breidenstine, February 8, 1967.
H. H. Hostetter, July 18, 1967.
A. G. Breidenstine, August 27, 1967.
Frederick D. Miller, July 26, 1967.
Mr. and Mrs. John Lanz, July 27, 1967.
V. H. Fenstermacher, February 23, 1967.
Kermit Lloyd, February 23, 1970.
Clyde E. Blocker, June 30, 1970.
Morrison, D. G., Ken August Brunner, and S. V. Martorana. *The 2-Year Community College: An Annotated List of Unpublished Studies and Surveys, 1957-61.* Office of Education. Washington: United States Government Printing Office, 1963.

APPENDIX A

THE HERSHEY JUNIOR COLLEGE FACULTY 1938-1965
BY TITLE AND/OR DEPARTMENT
AND YEAR OF APPOINTMENT

Name	Title and/or Department	Year
Charles R. Atherton	Professor of Mathematics	1938
Sterling Banta	Coach of Athletics	1946
William A. Batchelor	Art	1950
Jacob I. Baugher	Superintendent of Schools	1938
Albert L. Bell	Professor of Business Administration	1942
William D. H. Black	Business Manager	1964
Lorna M. Bode	Assistant in Commercial Science	1938
Harry F. Bolich	Professor of English	1946
Aaron G. Breidenstine	Dean Professor of Psychology Director of Guidance	1938
Alpheus O. Brittain	Director of Physical Education and Health Science	1938
Carl T. Britton	Director of Hershey Community Building	1938
John I. Bushey	Psychology	1963
W. Paul Campbell	Supervisor of Music	1947
Dennis M. Castelli	Social Science	1961
Robert V. Clery	Mathematics and Science	1962
William H. Connor	Professor of Social Studies	1942
Pauline E. Copp	Registrar-Secretary	1953
Herbert S. Curry	Director of Music Education	1944
Charles A. DeHaven	Professor of Business Administration	1946
Robert E. Devine	Psychology and Philosophy	1962
Janette Dickson	Dean of Women Professor of English and Social Studies	1947
Irene C. Dietrich	Librarian	1946
Viola R. Dietrich	English Literature	1958
Angus H. Douple	Supervisor of Art	1938
Beatrice E. Downin	Director of Women's Recreation Education	1945
Raymond F. Evans	Director, Vocational Education	1952
Orpha M. Fausnacht	Secretary of Dean	1938
Varnum H. Fenstermacher	Dean Professor of Psychology Director of Personnel Service	1947

222

Name	Title and/or Department	Year
Paul G. Fisher	Supervisor of Music	1957
C. Elizabeth Foutz	Secretary to the Dean	1942
Peter C. Foltz	Mathematics and Science	1964
Ruth Freyberger	Supervisor of Art	1946
Iris Fridy	Director of Women's Recreational Education	1938
Hiram J. Frysinger	Assistant in Physics	1942
Henry Glade	Modern Language	1950
Marion K. Goodman	Secretary	1962
Vincent H. Haag	Professor of Mathematics	1942
Elwood S. Hackman	Professor of Secretarial Science	1946
W. Allen Hammond	English Literature	1960
John K. Hanshue	Coach of Athletics	1949
Harry Harlacker	Coach	1955
James H. Hartzell	Social Science	1964
Betsy M. Hazen	Supervisor of Art	1944
Mark O. Henry	Coach of Basketball	1947
Eugene B. Herr	Assistant in Chemistry	1942
Grace Hershberger	Instructor of Home Economics	1945
W. Lyndon Hess	College Hall Master	1956
Ralph Hoar	Home Economics	1951
Kathryn E. Hoerner	Registrar-Secretary	1946
Louise E. Hoffman	Assistant Librarian	1938
Paul E. Hoffman	Biological Science	1955
H. H. Hostetter	College Physician	1939
Robert Jacoby	Director of Vocational Education	1945
Richard C. Johnson	College Hall	1957
William M. Kishpaugh	Professor of Business Administration	1938
Germaine Klaus	Professor of Foreign Language Dean of Women	1946
Raymond H. Koch	Superintendent of Schools	1942
Alexander N. Konrad	Modern Languages	1958
O. Robert Koth	Instructor of Drafting	1945
Edward S. Kraus	English and Literature	1962
William E. Landis	Professor of Business Administration Professor of Secretarial Science Coach of Golf	1947
Harry K. Lane	Professor of Science	1938
John C. Lanz	Mathematics	1949
Maud Peet Laughlin	Professor of Social Studies	1942
Rosalinde Lepke	Modern Language	1962
Kathleen A. Lewis	Physical Education	1953
Kermit L. Lloyd	Chaplain	1958
Ralph Lowet	Modern Language	1953
Marion H. Lowright	Secretary	1964
Grace M. McCorkel	Assistant Librarian	1954
Regis A. McKnight	Coach of Athletics	1942
Harriette E. Macfadden	Librarian	1942
Maud Briel Maines	Librarian	1943

Name	Title and/or Department	Year
August F. Meyer	Director of Men's Recreational Education	1938
Frederick D. Miller	Coach of Athletics	1938
William B. Miller	Assistant Professor of Technical Education	1938
Jennie D. Moyer	Assistant Librarian	1942
Emma C. Musselman	Director of Women's Recreational Education	1943
Richard G. Neubert	Director of Music Education	1938
Anna K. O'Toole	School Psychologist Director of Music Education	1942
Robert B. Patrick	Professor of Social Science	1939
Elias H. Phillips	Professor of Languages	1938
Gilbert A. Phillips	Professor of English	1942
Dorothea E. Ruth	Supervisor of Home Arts	1942
Frederick E. Sanders	English and Speech	1964
Clifford Sarver	Assistant in Chemistry	1939
William L. F. Schmehl	Professor of Social Studies	1947
A. Mary Scott	Assistant in Secretarial Science	1939
Marion Sheaffer	Physical Education	1963
Lillian Shenk	Assistant Librarian	1939
Donald Smith	Physical Education	1952
Wayne D. Stettler	College Physician	1950
Clyde S. Stine	Assistant Professor of History	1938
Robert T. Stoner	Director of Vocational Education	1938
Elizabeth L. Taylor	Psychology and Education Dean of Women	1956
Daniel N. Tippin	Professor of Secretarial Science	1938
Curtis Tracy	Assistant in Technical Drawing	1939
Rudolf Sturm	Modern Language	1956
Luella M. Umberger	Professor of Foreign Language Dean of Women	1939
Norman Vanderwall	Professor of English and Literature	1947
Robert W. Warrington	Mathematics Science	1958
Kathryn Weltmer	Assistant Librarian	1945
Marion E. Wenger	Librarian	1939
Wolff von Wernsdorff	Professor of Modern Language	1947
George H. Weydling	Modern Language	1960
Ralph D. Widdowson	Instructor in Engineering Drawing	1942
Aimee F. Witmer	Librarian	1940
Helen E. Wright	Instructor of Secretarial Science	1942
Richard Yingling	Assistant Director of Men's Recreational Education	1938
J. Atlee Young	Supervisor of Music	1964
Marko Zuzic	Modern Language	1963

APPENDIX B

CLASS OF 1965
THE LAST CLASS TO BE GRADUATED FROM
THE HERSHEY JUNIOR COLLEGE

Adela R. Balaster
James G. Balmer
Donald C. Beck
Janis Bomgardner
David R. Bordlemay
Mary E. Brown
Carol A. Brubaker
Jay H. Brubaker
Marilyn K. Buck
Barbara A. Bushey
Carol A. Cave
Nancy L. DeAngelis
Janet L. DeHart
Audrey S. Demuth
William G. Eckert
Carole A. Edgar
Ralph H. Espenshade, Jr.
Terry L. Esworthy
Neill J. Flaherty
Ellen J. Focht
Carol L. Frazier
Judith A. Gabriel
James E. Gahagan
Linda K. Gantz
Barbara L. Gasper
Barry L. Gingrich
George E. Gish
Ann F. Goldsworthy
James R. Gould
Russell W. Grubb
James J. Harrington
Steven C. Harris

Wayne E. Heller
Jacqueline R. Henry
Terry D. Henry
Carl F. Hetrick
Sandra K. Hiler
Dianne L. Hite
Mary I. Hoerner
Betty J. Huffman
Grant W. Hummer
John J. Jennings
Robert L. Keck
Bruce D. Keener
Dale F. Keyser
Richard Krause
Daniel P. Kriston
George W. Kunkle, Jr.
David T. Kupp
Gregory Kutz
Leslie L. Lauzon
Gale A. Light
Effie M. Masimer
Richard A. Mattis
Constance H. McMullen
David D. Meashey
Howard R. Messick
Rodney S. Miller
Gary L. Mostoller
Paul F. Mott
Franklin E. Neiswender
Michael J. Ney
Robert D. Noble
Karen O'Boyle
Donna M. Parks

Neal C. Parks, Jr.
Albert E. Pera
Frances E. Perez
Lawrence C. Pierce, Jr.
Thomas C. Pierce
Paul V. Radavsky
Allan J. Ream
Terry L. Rinesmith
Susan M. Rissmiller
Ernest E. Roush
Lorna B. Rudisill
Michael B. Russell
Ronald E. Saint Sing
Richard A. Schafebook
Gary N. Shenk
Gwen N. Skinner
Howard J. Smith
Harry A. Snell
Richard W. Stamm
Michael J. Stauffer
James A. Stover
Alic Tahir
David L. Tarbell
William A. Trimbur, Jr.
George E. Trump
Susan E. Twohig
Michael Urbanavage
Larry Wanger
Sandra M. Walters
Allan K. Warren
Richard B. Wood
Loretta J. Yasson

Vita

Richard Russell Klotz, born on September 2, 1934, in Sheridan, Lebanon County, Pennsylvania, graduated from Manheim Township High School, Neffsville, Pennsylvania, in 1953.

He was awarded both the Bachelor of Arts degree (Social Science) in 1956 and the Master of Arts degree (Guidance and Administration) in 1959 by Bucknell University. The degree of Doctor of Education (Higher Education) was awarded by The Pennsylvania State University in 1970.

Dr. Klotz taught social studies in the Northern Joint High School, Dillsburg, Pennsylvania, from 1956 to 1959; he taught and served as guidance counselor in the James Buchanan Joint Schools, Mercersburg, Pennsylvania, during 1959–1960. From 1960 to 1962 he was a guidance counselor in the Manheim Township Schools.

Between 1962 and 1964 he was assistant director of admissions at Bucknell University. At The Pennsylvania State University, 1964–1967, he served as assistant to the dean of admissions, assistant director of admissions, and admissions director of the Capitol Campus of the University in Middletown. In 1967 he was appointed the first director of admissions of Eisenhower College, Seneca Falls, New York, a position which he held for nearly six years.

His articles include: "The School Year," *Pennsylvania State Education Journal;* "Recruiting or Informing the College-Bound," *The Journal of the Association of College Admissions Counselors;* "Getting Into College," *Penn State Alumni News;* and "Curbing the Chaos In College Admissions," *Proceedings*, 4th Annual Space Congress, Cocoa Beach, Florida.

Dr. Klotz is an active member of various honorary and state and national professional associations including the American Personnel and Guidance Association, American Association for Higher Education, American Association of Collegiate Registrars and Admissions Officers, National Association of College Admissions Counselors, Kappa Phi Kappa, and Phi Delta Kappa.